Volume 31, Number 3

d i f f e r e n c e s

Narratives of Debt

*E*ditor's Note. The contributions gathered in this issue of *dif-ference*s were, for the most part, presented at the Narratives of Debt conference that Emmanuel Bouju and I organized at Brown University on April 5 and 6, 2019. The conference was the inaugural event of the Economies of Aesthetics initiative that I currently direct at the Cogut Institute for the Humanities at Brown.

In the program for these two days, we announced our intention to examine "the various ways of narrating—witnessing—the condition of being indebted and the historical rise of indebtedness as a mode of governance (each narrative entailing decisions about justice, ethics, politics)." Debt, then, was to be the explicit topic or theme of the narratives we would auscultate (they range from literary genres like "finance fiction" to legal practice, from philosophy and theory to insurance in the context of the Atlantic slave trade). But beyond this obverse side, there was another question, the reverse (the "tails") side of the same coin: "Debt itself will also be considered as a narrative, that is, a performative fiction that organizes time by linking past, present, and future in a diegetic chain. Money, if we define it with Deleuze

Volume 31, Number 3   DOI 10.1215/10407391-8744413

and Guattari as 'the means for rendering the debt infinite,' constitutes the backdrop of this economic narratology." Our discussions during these two days revolved in various ways around the node where debt and narrative are intertwined (as they perhaps always are).

To the revised versions of the talks presented at the conference, this issue adds two unexpected and most welcome punctuations. French novelist Vincent Message wrote and contributed an original short story, "And Suddenly I Owed Nothing," translated by Cole Swensen. From among Silvia Federici's papers deposited in the Pembroke Center's archives, Arlen Austin chose and presented some unpublished fragments on debt that she wrote in Nigeria during the 1980s in the midst of what was often called at the time "the third world debt crisis."

To all the contributors to this issue of *differences*, I would like to express my deepest gratitude.

—P.Sz.

Infinance, or Narration and Solvency

*T*he one says: "What a wonderful story is this!"

And the other replies: "The remainder of it [. . .] is more surprising [. . .]."

The lines of this dialogue, or some variation on them, take place every night, before daybreak, in what one could consider as the emblem of storytelling in general: *Les mille et une nuits* (*A Thousand and One Nights*), introduced in Europe by the French orientalist Antoine Galland, who translated this collection of stories and started publishing them in 1704 based on manuscripts from the fourteenth or fifteenth century purchased in Aleppo (and now kept at the Bibliothèque nationale in Paris, annotated in the margins by Galland, who, for example, numbered the nights). Galland added to the manuscripts some other stories, like "Aladdin or the Wonderful Lamp" and "Ali Baba and the Forty Thieves," that were supposedly told to him by an oral source, a Syrian Maronite Christian named Hanna Diab.

This composite French text was almost immediately translated into English (in 1706) by an unknown translator and published under the title of *Arabian Nights Entertainments.* With its anonymous and compilatory

Volume 31, Number 3   DOI 10.1215/10407391-8744427
© 2020 by Brown University and **d i f f e r e n c e s :** A Journal of Feminist Cultural Studies

character, this first English version, usually referred to as the "Grub Street" edition (Grub Street in London being where many impoverished writers and aspiring poets lived), evokes what Walter Benjamin, in his essay "The Storyteller," imagined as a "web [*Netz*] which all stories together form in the end," a network or a texture of texts in which all the possible narratives would be interwoven: "One ties on to the next, as the great storytellers, particularly the Oriental ones, have always readily shown. In each of them there is a Scheherazade who thinks of a fresh story whenever her tale comes to a stop" (98).

Strikingly, when he mentions again the *Thousand and One Nights* later in his essay, Benjamin emphasizes "the by no means insignificant share which traders [*Handeltreibenden*: those who deal in commerce] had in the art of storytelling," not so much in the content of the stories told than by "refin[ing] the tricks with which the attention of the listener was captured" (101). "Storytelling," Benjamin adds, plays a crucial role "in the household of humanity," *im Haushalt der Menschheit.* The word *Haushalt*, in German, clearly belongs to an economic or financial paradigm: it means not only "household," but also "budget"; and *haushalten*, the verb that corresponds to the noun, means "to manage," "to economize." In sum, storytelling, Benjamin suggests, is closely tied to what in Greek was called *oikonomia*, the management of the house or home. Indeed, narration might well have an intrinsically economic dimension.

■

With an eye to this economic fabric or texture of narration, let us reread the end—the interruption—of the first of the thousand and one nights, of which we have read already two lines; the storyteller has hardly begun her story (the story of "The Merchant and the Genie") when dawn approaches and threatens to break:

> *As Scheherazade had spoke those words, perceiving it was day, and knowing that the sultan rose betimes in the morning to say his prayers, and hold his council, Scheherazade held her peace. Lord, sister, says Dinarzade, what a wonderful story is this! The remainder of it, says Scheherazade, is more surprising; and you will be of my mind, if the sultan will let me live this day, and permit me to tell it out next night. Schahriar, who had listened to Scheherazade with pleasure, says to himself, I will stay till to-morrow, for I can at any time put her to death, when she has made an end of her story. (18–19)*

Contrary to what is generally believed, Scheherazade doesn't tell her stories to the sultan, her husband. She tells them to her sister Dinarzade, whom Scheherazade actually asked to request that Scheherazade tell them so that the sultan could hear them. The addressee of the narratives is thus double: they are narrated to be not only heard but also overheard, or heard twice at the same time.[1]

Within this oblique or triangulated narrative structure, it doesn't take long before we hear about *debt*: the word occurs in the story of "The Merchant and the Genie," when it is continued during the second night, after Shahriar has decided to let Scheherazade live for one more day, out of narratological curiosity. This story strikingly mirrors the story that frames it, that is, Scheherazade's own story: "When the merchant saw that the genie was going to cut off his head, he cried out aloud, and said, For heaven's sake, hold your hand! allow me one word, be so good as to grant me some respite" (19). Once he is granted this respite of one year, the merchant goes home to his wife and children: "Next morning, the merchant applied himself to put his affairs in order; and, first of all, to pay his debts" (20).

This first thematic or diegetic mention of debt (there will be many others) occurs within a narrative that, in its turn, soon includes another narrative. After his one-year respite is over, the merchant goes back to where the genie expects him in order to kill him and there he meets three old men. The first old man asks that the genie "suspend [his] anger" for the time of a story, a story in the story that will elicit forgiveness: "you will pardon the poor unfortunate man [that is, the merchant] the third of his crime" (22).

The story told by the old man within the story of the merchant and the genie told by Scheherazade thus introduces the idea that a story can bring about forgiveness, that is, absolution, but not a complete absolution at once; rather, an absolution that happens step by step, piece by piece.

> *When the first old man, Sir, continued the sultaness, had finished his story, the second [. . .] addressed himself to the genie, and says to him: I am going to tell you what happened to me [. . .] and I am certain you will say that my story is yet more surprising than that which you have just now heard, but when I have told it you, I hope you will be pleased to pardon the merchant the second third of his crime. (25–26)*

Absolution occurs by *installments*, so to speak. After this second old man—who happens to be also a merchant—it is the third old man's turn to tell his story to the genie: we anticipate that when its narration will be completed, the genie will forgive the three thirds of the merchant's guilt. But its completion, deferred by the interruption brought about by daybreak, is surprisingly elliptical; when Scheherazade resumes her narrative during the eighth night, she confesses for the first time that she is unable to tell the expected story:

> *Sir, replies the sultaness, the third old man told his story to the genie; I cannot tell it you, because it is not come to my knowledge, but I know that it did so much exceed the two former stories, in the variety of wonderful adventures, that the genie was astonished at it; and no sooner heard the end of it, but he said to the third old man, I remit the other third part of the merchant's crime upon the account of your story. (30)*

The narrative completion that allows for complete forgiveness thus appears as unfulfilling, and it has to be compensated by another story, "The Story of the Fisherman," that occupies the remaining time of the missing but complete story told by the third old man: "Dinarzade, perceiving that the sultan demurred, says to her, Sister, since there is still some time remaining, pray tell us the story of the Fisherman, if the sultan is willing. Schahriar agreed to it, and Scheherazade, resuming her discourse, pursued it in this manner" (30).

Other days and other nights pass: Scheherazade narrates how in his turn the fisherman tells another story to another genie ("The Story of the Grecian King and the Physician Douban"); and when she interrupts her narration after the eleventh night, her sister Dinarzade addresses her with a new variant of the formula we have by then already heard so many times: "The twelfth night was far advanced, when Dinarzade called, and says, Sister, you owe us the continuation of the agreeable history of the Grecian king and the physician Douban. I am very willing to pay my debt, replies Scheherazade, and resumed the story, as follows [. . .]" (37). The anonymous translator of the Grub Street English edition of *Arabian Nights* has supplemented here Galland's French text. The English rewriter or reteller interpolates the word *debt* into a passage that doesn't include it,[2] with the effect of introducing indebtedness on the metadiegetic level too: not only does Scheherazade tell stories (that tell stories that tell stories . . .) about debt, but she is indebted in her very storytelling. In other words, her narration itself has the structure of debt.

■

As arbitrary as it seems, the Grub Street translator's interpolation is nonetheless dictated by a rigorous necessity. For what he translates are not only Galland's words but the whole underlying logic of a narrative (made of and about narratives) that constantly interweaves narrating and absolving. "To absolve," according to the *Oxford English Dictionary*, is not only "to acquit or set free from blame, guilt," but also "to accomplish, complete, bring to completion," "to discharge or acquit oneself of (a task, etc.)." In book 7 of Milton's *Paradise Lost*, verses 93–94 read: "and the work begun, how soon / Absolved."

How could Scheherazade be absolved, and for what? Of what could she absolve herself?

In the frame story of *A Thousand and One Nights*, Scheherazade's predicament is that she can't pay off her debt: her guilt, in the sultan's eyes, is simply to be what she is, that is, a woman and a wife; as such she deserves to die. This structural and hence irredeemable debt drives her to indebt herself infinitely, to open more and more narrative accounts without closing or absolving them, precisely in order to stay solvent. Her narratological solvency can only be exhausted when, at the very end, the sultan decides to "forgive her" (*lui faire grace*, writes Galland), thereby absolving her narrative and at the same time absolving her from the obligation to narrate.

But the frame story of Scheherazade's indebtedness and absolution (a story that includes many other stories about debt and forgiveness, like the story of the merchant, the genie, and the three old men) might itself be part of a larger frame story. Her narrative of debt and as debt might itself belong to a broader narrative, a narrative about what Benjamin, in "The Storyteller," called the "household of humanity," inasmuch as this household or management pertains to an economy of ending as well as to the end (or ends) of economy.

In order to try and catch a glimpse of this overarching narrative that encompasses Scheherazade's narration, in order to tell at least a part of this frame story for the frame story of Scheherazade's storytelling, we should fittingly begin by the end, by what has for a long time been the very word for end or ending, that is, *finance*.

The first two senses listed by the *Oxford English Dictionary* for *finance* are the following (both marked with a cross, indicating that the meaning in question is dead, has ended, has reached its end): "†1. Ending, an end. *Obsolete. rare.* [. . .] †2a. Settlement with a creditor; payment of a debt; compensation or composition paid or exacted." One of the occurrences of the word given as an example of the first sense ("ending, an end") is to be found in John Bullokar's dictionary published in London in 1616, *An English Expositor: Teaching the Interpretation of the Hardest Words Used in Our Language*.[3] There, one reads this laconic definition that, to our contemporary ears, almost sounds like a sentence without a verb: "**Finance*, An end." The reason for the asterisk that precedes the word is explained in the brief "Introduction to the Reader": "Remember also that every word marked with this mark * is an old word, onely used of some ancient Writers, and now grown out of use." Like the cross in the *Oxford English Dictionary* entry, the asterisk here re-marks the meaning or folds it onto itself: *finance* as ending has ended. In sum, before the word "finance" *ended up* acquiring its modern sense (that is, "the management of money," listed as the last one in the *Oxford English Dictionary*), it meant "ending" or "end." Do we have to infer that it has later developed a meaning contrary to its meaning? Has finance become infinite?

While these questions resonate and wait, let us continue our attempt at telling the frame story for the frame story of Scheherazade's narratological indebtedness; let us pursue our etymological inquiry into the history of finance.

The etymology of *finance* leads back to the French word *finance*, itself derived from the verb *finer*. The *Littré* dictionary (1881) gives the following brief indication: "Finance. The old French had *finer*, from the Latin *finis*, meaning properly to end, hence to pay a sum of money or guarantee a debt. The present participle was *finant*, hence *finance*, as *croyant* from *croyance*, or *extravagant* from *extravagance*, etc."[4] *Finance*, then, seems to have been formed as the present participle of *finer*: it was the ending in progress, so to speak, the very process of ending.

More exhaustively than the *Littré*, the *Dictionnaire du moyen français* lists a number of meanings for the verb *finer* and classifies them as related, on the one hand, to "the idea of a term, of a completion" (*idée de terme, d'achèvement*), with a transitive use (*finer quelque chose* meant "to finish, to conclude something" [*achever, terminer quelque chose*]) as well as an intransitive use (*finer* meaning "to die" [*mourir*]); then, on the other hand, as related to payment: *finer une somme* meant "to pay, to spend" a sum of money (*payer, dépenser*), and *finer de quelque chose* meant "to acquit a debt" (*s'acquitter de quelque chose*) or "to pay off, to settle something" (*payer, régler quelque chose*).

As for the noun *finance*, the *Dictionnaire du moyen français* gives an interesting example taken from a late medieval narrative in verse by an anonymous merchant (a grocer, it seems) between 1319 and 1322 (when he wrote a first version) and 1328 and 1342 (when he wrote a revised version). It is titled *Le roman de Renart le contrefait*, since the merchant "forged" (*contrefesait*) the famous anthropomorphic character of Reynard the Fox in order to express opinions under the mask of his model. In the seventh part, the author says about Judas:

> *Judas, quant il ot Dieu traÿ,*
> *Repentance monlt l'envaÿ;*
> *Quant il vit la desconvenue,*
> *N'ot qui lui fesist nulle ayeue,*
> *Car Esperance point ne print,*
> *Pour ce, a lui pendre se tint;*
> *Ne sceut en lui aultre finance* (135).[5]

My tentative translation: "Judas, after he had betrayed God, was filled with repentance; when he saw the misfortune, he had nobody to help him, for Hope didn't hold, therefore he hung himself; he knew no other ending." It is tempting to read into this occurrence of the word *finance* the rejection of one of its senses ("money") for the sake of another ("ending"), especially if we recall that the passage draws on Matthew 27:3–5, where it is said (I quote the New International Version of the Bible): "[3] When Judas, who had betrayed him, saw that Jesus was condemned, he was seized with remorse and returned the thirty pieces of silver to the chief priests and the elders. [4] 'I have sinned,' he said, 'for I have betrayed innocent blood.' 'What is that to us?' they replied. 'That's your responsibility.' [5] So Judas threw the money into the temple and left. Then he went away and hanged himself." When *finance* as money has to be gotten rid of, *finance* as ending substitutes for it.

∎

Though the etymology of *finance* has led us to Middle French, we should also recall the history of the word in English, which is very close. Thus, according to the *Oxford English Dictionary*, *to fine*, a verb that means "to punish (a person) for an illegal or illicit act by requiring him or her to pay a sum of money," has long had the now obsolete sense of "to bring to an end; to complete, conclude," both senses deriving from the Middle French *finer*. And the noun, *fine*, also has these two meanings: the sense of "ending" is still alive in Shakespeare's *All's Well That Ends Well*, when Helena declares, at the end of act 4, scene 4: "'All's well that ends well,' still the fine's the crown; Whate'er the course, the end is the renown" (81). The crown, that is, the power, the ultimate and sovereign authority, Shakespeare suggests, lies in the ending that will be remembered. It resides in what could still be called, according to the lexicons of the time (think of the *English Expositor*), the "finance" of a storyline.

The question that awaits us, now that finance as ending has come to an end or has exhausted its former meaning, is the following: Isn't finance, on the contrary, becoming synonymous with infinitude? And if it is, what made that possible? When would finance have come to mean the unfinishable or infinite, the *infinance*? And hence, since when would finance have become impossible to narrate?

There are many stories to be told that would constitute as many tentative or inchoate answers to these questions. Like Scheherazade, I will lend my voice to one of them—postponing the others, deferring them until another night or day—though I am not sure that I subscribe without reservations (neither does Scheherazade, I guess) to what I am about to tell.

Benjamin's essay titled "The Storyteller" famously opens by diagnosing the "end" of storytelling: "the art of storytelling," he writes, "is coming to an end" (*zu Ende geht*) (83); in other, more ancient words, storytelling, Benjamin suggests, is reaching its *finance*: "Less and less frequently do we encounter people with the ability to tell a tale properly. More and more often there is embarrassment all around when the wish to hear a story is expressed. It is as if something that seemed inalienable [*unveräusserlich*] to us, the securest among our possessions, were taken from us: the ability to exchange experiences [*Erfahrungen auszutauschen*]."

Storytelling as trading in experiences, as swapping, borrowing, or lending one's life stories, storytelling as an economic practice, in sum, has long been inalienable, says Benjamin, that is, unforfeitable or untransferable, precisely as the condition of all experiential transfers; but it has recently become preempted, so to speak, it has been seized, confiscated. The reason Benjamin offers for this dispossession, as one reason among others, is puzzling, though. "One reason for this phenomenon is obvious," he writes: "experience has fallen in value" (*die Erfahrung ist im Kurse gefallen*: its exchange rate, its stock market quotation has fallen). Why would the devaluation of experience lead to the deprivation of the precious ability to share it? One would think, on the contrary, that the less valuable experience supposedly becomes, the more common its sharing would be (visit a Facebook page).

In any case, having long been the "securest among the secure," as Benjamin literally writes (*das Gesichertste unter dem Sicheren*), having long been the safest guarantee—like an absolute security or collateral—in experiential economics, the ability to tell stories seems to have had the reliability of death (of *finance*, we could say in Middle French). It is not surprising, then, that Benjamin, later in the essay, considers death as the source of authority in storytelling; and death, he writes, is being devalued too, losing its status as the gold standard against which stories can be weighed, evaluated:

> *[T]he thought of death has declined [*Einbusse leidet*: it has suffered losses, again a financial expression, slightly outdated] in omnipresence and vividness. [. . .] Dying was once a public process in the life of the individual and a most exemplary one [. . .]. Today people live in rooms that have never been touched by death, dry dwellers of eternity, and when their end approaches they are stowed away in sanatoria or hospitals by their heirs. It is, however, characteristic that not only a man's knowledge or wisdom, but above all his real life [*sein gelebtes Leben*: his life as he lived it]—and this is the stuff that stories are made of—first assumes transmissible form at the moment of his death. Just as a sequence of images is set in motion inside a man as his life comes to an end [. . .], suddenly in his expressions and looks the unforgettable emerges and imparts to everything that concerned him that authority which even the poorest wretch in dying possesses for the living around him. This authority is at the very source of the story. (93–94)*

We could seek the confirmation of the devaluation of death in the fascinating scene toward the end of Goethe's second *Faust*, soon after Faust's last lines.[6] Mephistopheles has just pronounced Faust dead (*es ist vollbracht*, he says, "it is finished," borrowing Christ's last words in John, 19:30); and the Lemures (the spirits or shadows of the departed in Roman mythology) echo him by declaring: "it is over!" (*es ist vorbei!*) (292–93). Mephisto briefly argues with them about this "stupid word" ("Why over?" he exclaims; "What's over, and mere nothing, are the same"), as if he were questioning the possibility that Faust's life is finally *absolved*, that is, complete. And indeed, in the very moment when the redeeming of Faust's debt coincides with the ending of his life (Faust's soul, as we know, has to go to Mephisto as a way of paying him back), in this very instant, death seems to lose the punctuality, and hence the trustworthiness, that allowed it to function as a reliable asset. The passage is masterfully prepared by the insistence of the Lemures on the economics of existence ("All items were on short-term loan" [*es war auf kurze Zeit geborgt*], they say while burying Faust in his grave, "and creditors are many" [*die Gläubiger sind so viele*]). Here is the passage:

> *Established usages and ancient rights—*
> *there's nothing we can count on any more [*man kann auf gar
> nichts mehr vertrauen*]!*
> *The soul used to emerge when someone breathed his last;*
> *I'd lie in wait and, like the nimblest mouse,*
> *snap! it was clenched within my claws.*
> *But now it hesitates to leave that dreary place,*
> *its noisome home inside a worthless corpse.*
> *[. . .] old Death has lost his former mettle [*der alte Tod verlor
> die rasche Kraft*: has lost its expediting power],*
> *[. . .] I've often coveted some limbs in* rigor mortis—
> *illusion only! They stirred and began to move again.*

The ending becomes dubious, Mephisto complains, as does the paying-off of the debt of existence. Death is diluted, it is losing its contours, and the lender is afraid he won't get his investment back. Faust's *finance* can hardly be trusted. Perhaps it is already on the way to what we could call, in the light of the fascinating history of this word, its *infinite infinance.*

PETER SZENDY is David Herlihy Professor of Humanities and Comparative Literature at Brown University and musicological advisor for the concert programs at the Paris Philharmony. His recent publications include *The Supermarket of the Visible: Toward a General Economy of Images* (Fordham University Press, 2019); *Of Stigmatology: Punctuation as Experience* (Fordham University Press, 2018); *All Ears: The Aesthetics of Espionage* (Fordham University Press, 2016); and *Kant in the Land of Extraterrestrials: Cosmopolitical Philosofictions* (Fordham University Press, 2013). He curated *The Supermarket of Images* at the Jeu de Paume museum in Paris, an exhibition that opened in February 2020.

Notes

1   See, for example, *Arabian Nights Entertainment* 16. This, Adriana Cavarero argues, is "a detail of the greatest importance that usually gets overlooked in the analyses of *The Arabian Nights*": "Scheherazade does not tell her first story [nor the following ones, I would add] to the sultan, but to her sister," so that the sultan is "only a listener" (123). On this triangulation of listening, see Szendy, *Listen* 142 and *Of Stigmatology* 41–43.

2   Galland's version reads: "Je le veux bien, répondit Scheherazade. En même tems elle en reprit le fil de cette sorte: [. . .]" (163).

3   I quote the "Newly Revised, Corrected" edition of 1656, printed by the same publisher (John Legatt).

4   My translation. The original French reads: "Finance. L'ancienne langue employait *finer* qui provenait du latin *finis*

et signifiait proprement terminer, d'où le sens de payer une somme d'argent et de fournir. Le participe était *finant*, d'où *finance*, comme de *croyant, croyance*, d'*extravagant, extravagance*, etc."

5 Transcribed into modern French, the passage would read as follows: *Judas, quand il eut Dieu trahi, Repentance moult l'envahit; Quand il vit la déconvenue,*

N'eut qui lui fit nulle aide, Car Espérance point ne prit, Pour ce, à lui pendre se tint; Ne sut en lui autre finance. (For the translation of *ayeue* as *aide*, see the *Vocabulaire* included in Deschamps 12).

6 These lines are quoted by Benjamin in his 1933 essay "Experience and Poverty" 734 (written three years before "The Storyteller").

Works Cited

"to absolve." *Oxford English Dictionary.* 3rd ed. Sept. 2009. www.oed.com.

Arabian Nights Entertainment. Ed. Robert L. Mack. Oxford: Oxford UP, 1995.

Benjamin, Walter. "Experience and Poverty." Trans. Rodney Livingstone. *Selected Writings.* Vol. 2, part 2. Cambridge, MA: Harvard UP, 1999. 731–36.

——————. "The Storyteller." *Illuminations.* Trans. Harry Zohn. New York: Schocken, 1969. 83–109.

Bullokar, John. *An English Expositor: Teaching the Interpretation of the Hardest Words Used in Our Language.* London: John Legatt, 1656.

Cavarero, Adriana. *Relating Narratives: Storytelling and Selfhood.* Trans. Paul A. Kottman. London: Routledge, 2000.

Deschamps, Eustache. *Oeuvres complètes d'Eustache Deschamps publiées d'après le manuscrit de la Bibliothèque nationale par Gaston Raynaud.* Vol. 10. Paris: Firmin Didot et Cie, 1901.

Dictionnaire du moyen français. 2015. www.atilf.fr/dmf.

"finance." *Oxford English Dictionary.* 3rd ed. Sept. 2009. www.oed.com.

Goethe, Johann Wolfgang von. *Faust 1 and 2.* Trans. Stuart Atkins. Princeton: Princeton UP, 2014.

Le roman de Renart le contrefait. Ed. Gaston Raynaud and Henri Lemaitre. Vol. 2. Paris: Honoré Champion, 1914.

Les mille et une nuits. Contes arabes. Trans. Antoine Galland. Vol. 1. Paris: Veuve de Claude Barbin, 1704.

Littré, Émile. *Dictionnaire de la langue française.* Vol. 2 (D–H). Paris: Hachette, 1881.

Milton, John. *Paradise Lost.* Oxford: Oxford UP, 2005.

New International Version (NIV) Zondervan Study Bible. Grand Rapids: Zondervan, 2015.

Shakespeare, William. *All's Well That Ends Well.* Cambridge: Cambridge UP, 2009.

Szendy, Peter. *Listen: A History of Our Ears.* Trans. Charlotte Mandell. New York: Fordham UP, 2008.

—— ————. *Of Stigmatology: Punctuation as Experience.* Trans. Jan Plug. New York: Fordham UP, 2018.

Earning to Give

I intend to confront Peter Singer's vision of the gift with Jacques Derrida's. Such a confrontation is risky, to say the least, as the two thinkers obviously have nothing in common and may even appear as radically alien to each other. I will then proceed to a *mise en abyme* of this philosophical extraneity, using Derrida's and Singer's mutual incompatibility as a way to approach the central issue they both address, which is the impossibility of mutualism itself. Exploring the reasons both thinkers provide in order to sustain this impossibility will lead me to address their respective visions of exchange and debt and determine what theoretical benefit we can draw from such a confrontation.

For Derrida, mutualism is impossible because he thinks that there is no such thing as a "pure gift." For Singer, mutualism is impossible because he thinks that something like a pure gift exists. The impossibility of mutualism signals the impossibility of the gift: Derrida. The impossibility of mutualism signals the effectivity of the gift: Singer.

Let me start with a few words on *effectivity*. I am using this term because Singer is a representative—the most prominent one—of "effective

Volume 31, Number 3   DOI 10.1215/10407391-8744441

altruism," a specific branch of utilitarianism. "Effective altruism," Singer writes, "is based on a very simple idea: we should do the most good we can" (*Most* vii). Effective altruism is "the project of using evidence and reason to figure out how to benefit others as much as possible, and taking action on that basis" (MacAskill 2). Taking action is giving.

In order to proceed to the Derrida/Singer confrontation, I will focus on the notion of the *circle*, an image to which they both refer when it comes to characterizing the logic of economic exchange. In *Given Time*, Derrida writes—and this has become a famous declaration:

> *Now the gift,* if there is any, *would no doubt be related to economy. One cannot treat the gift, this goes without saying, without this relation to economy, even to the money economy. But is not the gift, if there is any, also that which interrupts economy? That which, in suspending economic calculation, no longer gives rise to exchange? That which opens the circle so as to defy reciprocity or symmetry, the common measure, and so as to turn aside the return in view of the no-return? (7)*

Mutualism, understood here as reciprocity, engages the gift in the circle of exchange, that is, the circle of countergift and debt, so that giving for the sake of giving is impossible. Breaking the circle of "mutuality" (the word occurs in *Given Time* when Derrida analyzes Marcel Mauss's notion of *circulation*) therefore implies showing how the deadlock of reciprocity is exceeded, even if only problematically, by the unlimited space of what Derrida calls *aneconomy*. Aneconomy would then be what opens the circle.

As for Singer, he argues that the outside can only be reached from within, which does not mean that the mercantile exchange circle cannot be interrupted, but that it can only be interrupted by the inscription of another circle within the circle. Altruism can only be effective if it takes place in the very same place, or within the very same structure as what it opposes. Singer explains this in *The Expanding Circle: Ethics, Evolution, and Human Progress*: the circle is expanding, it can be expanded, but once again only from within an economy.

For Singer, mutualism pertains to altruism. In 1902, in *On Mutual Aid: A Factor of Evolution*, the anarchist thinker Peter Kropotkin affirmed that altruism is a biological fact. Species in nature do not only compete, they also collaborate. Mutual aid among living beings is primordial for survival and is even more important than natural selection in this respect. Such a view does not contradict Darwin, who already acknowledged this tendency in *The Descent of Man*; rather, it contradicts social Darwinism, grounded, according to Kropotkin, in a Hobbesian vision of society, that is, a state of permanent war and competition. Against such a vision, Kropotkin argues in favor of an immanent social rationality orienting humanity toward solidarity and cooperation. An altruistic behavior may be defined as a "behavior which benefits others at some cost to oneself" (Singer, *Expanding* 5).

Kropotkin's vision has opened an immense debate among philosophers, biologists, and economists. A vast majority of them have argued, against Kropotkin, that altruistic behaviors in reality proceed from a hidden egoism. There is no pure altruistic behavior to the extent that self-interest is always primordial. This would be true from a biological evolutionary perspective but also from the perspective of morals. In a certain sense, we find here the same conclusion as Derrida's: pure gift, that is pure sacrifice of oneself for others, pure generosity without any return or expectation of return, is impossible. Some biologists have shown that the only form of altruistic behavior in nature, for example, in monkeys, is always reciprocal (I do this for you if you do this for me), or limited to the individual's family members (I sacrifice myself for my children). In both cases, we find once again the impossibility of pure gift, altruism being linked with the debt contracted toward kinship or the group.

In *The Expanding Circle*, Singer argues that reason is what expands the circle of biological altruism—limited to kin, group, and reciprocal altruism as we just saw—and opens it to effective altruism. And effective altruism means nonreciprocal altruism:

> *[A]ltruistic impulses once limited to one's kin and one's own group might be extended to a wider circle by reasoning creatures who can see that they and their kin are one group among others, and from an impartial point of view no more important than others. Biological theories of the evolution of altruism through kin selection, reciprocity, and group selection can be made compatible with the existence of non-reciprocal altruism toward strangers if they can accept this kind of expansion of the circle of altruism. (134–35)*

Since reasoning here means foreseeing consequences of one's actions, effective altruism is a consequentialism that allows one to contradict the restriction of the circle of exchange to reciprocal relationships, a restriction that most capitalist economists share with biologists. To say that one always gives in order to be given to in return amounts, once again, to fostering the logic of debt.

Remember Singer's idea of effective altruism that I quoted above: "we should do the most good we can"—which means that we should give, and give to strangers who suffer. "I begin with the assumption that suffering and death from lack of food, shelter, and medical care are bad," Singer writes ("Famine" 231). "Good," then, characterizes everything that can prevent suffering and death. And preventing, here, implies giving, or more exactly, earning to give: "Earning to give is a distinctive way of doing good" (*Most* 55). The principle is apparently simple: people from affluent countries should give to people from poor countries without expecting anything in return to the extent that the givers and the receivers are anonymous.

Singer lists the fundamental elements linked with the injunction to give:

> *Effective altruists do things like the following:*
>
> - *Living modestly and donating a large part of their income—often much more than the traditional tenth, or tithe—to the most effective charities;*
> - *Researching and discussing with others which charities are the most effective or drawing on research done by other independent evaluators;*
> - *Choosing the career in which they can earn most, not in order to be able to live affluently but so they can do more good;*
> - *Talking to others, in person or online, about giving, so that the idea of effective altruism will spread;*
> - *Giving part of their body—blood, bone marrow, or even a kidney—to a stranger. (4)*

The effective altruist asks "how he can make the biggest possible reduction in the suffering in that larger universe of suffering" (94).

Singer's important article "Famine, Affluence, and Morality" was written in regard to the famine situation in East Bengal in 1971:

> *[P]eople are dying [. . .] from lack of food, shelter, and medical care. [. . .] The decisions and actions [of] human beings can prevent this kind of suffering. Unfortunately, human beings have not made the necessary decisions. At the individual level, people have, with very few exceptions, not responded to the situation in any significant way. [. . .] At the government level, no government has given the sort of massive aid that would enable the refugees to survive for more than a few days. (229)*

Instead of concluding that this is proof against altruism, Singer goes on affirming, to the contrary, that this proceeds from a lack of reasoning. It is reasoning that teaches us that help is indifferent to proximity or distance:

> *It makes no moral difference whether the person I can help is a neighbor's child ten yards from me or a Bengali whose name I shall never know, ten thousand miles away. [. . .] I do not think I need to say much in defense of the refusal to take proximity and distance into account. The fact that a person is physically near to us, so that we have personal contact with him, may make it more likely that we* shall *assist him, but this does not show that we* ought *to help him rather than another who happens to be further away. (231–32)*

In *The Most Good We Can Do*, Singer writes that effective altruists are "able to detach themselves from personal considerations that otherwise dominate the way in which we live" (85). He continues:

> *Here are some commonly expressed dispositions and affections that effective altruists would consider misguided grounds for giving:*
>
> • *I give to breast cancer research because my wife died of breast cancer.*
> • *I always wanted to be an artist but never had the opportunity, so now I direct my charitable contributions to organizations that provide opportunities for promising artists to develop their creative talents. (86)*

So, once again, it is a matter of giving to no one for nothing.

As we have seen, opening the circle, for Derrida, also means getting out of the circle of reciprocity, but by moving to the space of "aneconomy" that lies beyond economy and calculation. By contrast, in Singer, expanding the circle is precisely made possible by calculation: nonreciprocal altruism implies a constant calculation, and expanding the circle is possible thanks to economic calculation. It is a way of disrupting economy by using economy. It never breaks with quantification. Here are some additional examples:

1. Effective altruism is about *maximizing* happiness, or pleasure, and *minimizing* suffering, or pain, as evidenced in Singer's title, *The Most Good You Can Do*.

2.   Maximizing also means maximizing the effects of the gift by calculating how many people it will benefit and choosing each time the largest number:

Toby Ord [an Australian philosopher, founder of the effective altruism organization Giving What We Can] has given another example of the cost differences between helping people in affluent countries and helping people elsewhere. You may have received appeals for donations from charities in affluent countries providing blind people with guide dogs. That sounds like a case worthy of support—until you consider the costs and the alternative to which you could donate. It costs about $40,000 to supply one person in the United States with a guide dog; most of the expense is incurred in training the dog and the recipient. But the cost of preventing someone from going blind because of trachoma, the most common and preventable blindness, is in the range of $20–$100. If you do the math, you will see the choice we face is to provide one person with a guide dog or prevent anywhere between four hundred and two thousand cases of blindness in developing countries. (Singer, Most 110–11)

3.   Effective altruism entails determining and calculating how much you can give. In the chapter titled "Living Modestly to Give More," before asking "How Much Is Enough?," Singer thus describes what for effective altruist Julia is a "realistic breakdown of expenses":

· *$900 on rent and $100 on utilities each month (enough for a small apartment shared with friends in the Boston area)*
· *$150 a month on groceries [. . .]*
· *$300 a month for health insurance and other medical costs*
· *$70 for a public transit pass*
· *$250 a month for personal spending (phone, clothes, entertainment, etc.)*
· *Saving 10 per cent of income*
· *Donating 10 per cent of income. (Singer, Most 25)*

4.   Effective altruism requires the setting of limits to the circle's expansion: "[W]e ought to give until we reach the level of marginal utility—that is, the level at which, by giving more, I would

cause as much suffering to myself or my dependents as I would relieve by my gift" ("Famine" 241). There are calculable limits, then, beyond which giving would become counterproductive.[1]

Another important point regarding debt is that effective altruism does not proceed from guilt, nor even from empathy: "Effective altruists don't see a lot of point in feeling guilty. They prefer to focus on the good they are doing," Singer says (*Most* viii); or again: "[E]ffective altruism does not require the kind of strong emotional empathy that people feel for identifiable individuals" (78).[2] Once again, reason alone is at work here. In "Famine, Affluence, and Morality," Singer writes that "the imperatives of duty, which tell us what we must do [. . .], function so as to prohibit behavior that is intolerable if men are to live together in society" (236), such as killing, stealing, and so on. Poverty, illness, or homelessness, on the other hand, are not considered intolerable for the life of the community, and giving is not required. Charity, then, becomes what substitutes for such an absence of law against social exclusion: "The issue here is: Where should we draw the line between conduct that is required and conduct that is good although not required, so as to get the best possible result?" (237). Reasonable charity is a categorical imperative in the absence of a categorical imperative.

Finally, effective altruism presents itself as a way to dismantle the sovereignty of personal identity. In that sense, its dynamic is that of a desubjectivation. By giving to people I do not know, I also become anonymous to myself and disobey the government of the self. The other, in Singer, is only defined as a "life," and I myself am a "life." Singer never tries to define what he means by this term, but we can easily see that life has to be understood as the unity of symbolic life and biological life, that is, of life as a way of life, a form of life, and life as an empirical, material fact—a unity that both continental philosophers and biologists have failed to conceptualize, as they always tend to privilege one over the other. Is not the affirmation of such a unity a way to define life as having no proper sense? That is, no proper essence either? And no self-ownership? This could mark the end of the traditional altruism/egoism debate within which the problematic of mutual help has remained enclosed for decades.

Effective altruism is not restricted to the domain of morals but has crucial political aspects as well. It is a tentative remedy to the inertia of governments. "I do not want to dispute the contention that governments of affluent nations should be giving many times the amount of genuine, no-strings-attached aid that they are giving now," Singer writes in "Famine,

Affluence, and Morality" (240); and in *The Most Good You Can Do*, he expresses the hope that "effective altruists can become numerous enough to influence the giving culture of affluent nations" (9), that is, to create a genuine political and social sense (like the one that has emerged around vegetarianism, for example).

I find Singer's position highly interesting for at least three reasons: First, because the autonomous self-calculation of the good that it advocates for opens, within the circle of capitalist economy, the other circle of an anarchistic mode of distribution. There are no guides, no masters, no supreme authorities commanding the act of giving from above. Calculation is horizontal. The second reason is that the "strangers" to whom we should give include animals and "plants, or perhaps even mountains, rocks, and streams" (*Expanding* 121). It paves the way for a philosophy of ecology and antispeciesism that is perhaps a point of compatibility with Derrida's thinking. The third reason is that it forces the Derridean argument to respond to this notion of "effectivity." To state that pure gift is impossible can always be just a pretext for not giving.

Derrida would no doubt have argued that affirming that there are ways of escaping guilt and debt is irresponsible and impossible. Consequentialism obeys a logic of interest; it has in mind the survival of life on earth, and in that sense, it is a logic of gain, so that it does not expand the circle. This is another way to say that we cannot give anything but counterfeit money. When we give to strangers, we might just perpetuate the logic of poverty and dependency instead of coping with it.

Whether effective altruism proceeds from a critique or a defense of capitalism is not clear in Singer, and there is certainly a strong ambiguity in his project. Let me quote a last passage from *The Most Good You Can Do*:

> [E]ffective altruists typically value equality not for its own sake but only because of its consequences. It isn't clear that making the rich richer without making the poor poorer has bad consequences, overall. It increases the ability of the rich to help the poor, and some of the world's richest people, including Bill Gates and Warren Buffet, have done precisely that, becoming, in terms of the amount of money given, the greatest effective altruists in human history. [. . .] It would not be easy to demonstrate that capitalism has driven more people into extreme poverty than it has lifted out of it; indeed there are good grounds for thinking that the opposite is the case. (50)

Isn't this a way of blurring the lines between charity and neoliberalism?

Nevertheless, there are numerous debates on this question, and effective altruism deserves to be taken seriously as it orients the logic of the impossibility of mutualism toward the possibility of solidarity. Nonreciprocity may become the new form of cooperation.

CATHERINE MALABOU is a professor of philosophy at the Centre for Research in Modern European Philosophy at Kingston University in the United Kingdom and at the University of California, Irvine, where she regularly teaches in the spring. Her most recent books include *Before Tomorrow: Epigenesis and Rationality* (Polity, 2016) and *Morphing Intelligence: From IQ Measurement to Artificial Brains* (Columbia University Press, 2018). She is currently working on a new book project on anarchism and philosophy.

Notes

1 On calculation, see also Singer, *Most Good*:

> It is telling that effective altruists talk more about the number of people they are able to help than about helping particular individuals. [. . .] Consistent with the points just made, many of the most prominent effective altruists have backgrounds in or are particularly strong in areas that require abstract reasoning, like mathematics and computing. [. . .] My favourite example of the combination of effective altruism and numeracy is the website Counting Animals, which has the subtitle "A place for people who love animals and numbers." (89)

2 See also *Most Good*: "Altruism is contrasted with egoism, which is concern only for oneself, but we should not think of effective altruism as requiring self-sacrifice, in the sense of something necessarily contrary to one's own interests. If doing the most you can for others means that you are also flourishing, then that is the best possible outcome for everyone" (5).

Works Cited

Derrida, Jacques. *Given Time: 1. Counterfeit Money.* Trans. Peggy Kamuf. Chicago: U of Chicago P, 1992.

Kropotkin, Peter. *Mutual Aid: A Factor of Evolution.* New York: McClure Phillips, 1902.

MacAskill, William. "Effective Altruism: Introduction." *Effective Altruisim.* Spec. issue of *Essays in Philosophy* 18.1 (2017): 1–5.

Singer, Peter. *The Expanding Circle: Ethics, Evolution, and Moral Progress.* Princeton: Princeton UP, 2011.

——————. "Famine, Affluence, and Morality." *Philosophy and Public Affairs* 1.3 (1972): 229–43.

——————. *The Most Good You Can Do: How Effective Altruism Is Changing Ideas about Living Ethically.* New Haven: Yale UP, 2015.

Life after Debt

*F*or more than four decades, I have pondered the writings of Max Weber on the economy, and I continue to find much wisdom in his ideas, especially about the melancholic productivity of the Calvinist man of business. My thoughts about debt today owe much to Weber, both to his writings and to his ghost.

The main idea that Weber offered to readers in his own times and since then is to be found in his famous essay, *The Protestant Ethic and the Spirit of Capitalism.* It was the argument that the most this-worldly ethic of money making in the West, the methodical pursuit of capitalist profit, was a unique development whose main source was the uncertainty of bourgeois Calvinists about their own salvational status. The surest way to feel confident that you were on the right side of an already made divine decision was to display the virtues of methodical discipline in the form of sober profit making. The elected Calvinist soul was a practitioner of profitable double entry bookkeeping. I do not plan to address the numerous revisions, applications, and implications of this line of Weberian thinking today. I take it as an argument to think with, whatever its empirical weaknesses,

Volume 31, Number 3   DOI 10.1215/10407391-8744455
© 2020 by Brown University and d i f f e r e n c e s : A Journal of Feminist Cultural Studies

and would like to show that the horizon of salvation, of redemption, and of the mysterious workings of grace remain today an essential part of the apparatus of finance. To make this argument requires two steps: the first is a general characterization of the ethos of contemporary finance; the second is a discussion of the soteriology of debt.

The Dreamwork of Speculative Capitalism

Capitalism, normally considered the zenith of scientism, techno-rationality, and calculative reason, can fruitfully be seen as just the opposite of these things. It can be considered the dreamwork of industrial modernity, its magical, spiritual, and utopian horizon, in which all that is solid melts into money. Speculation is the motor of this dreamwork, and in this section I draw my inspiration from such thinkers as Ernst Bloch, Walter Benjamin, and Fredric Jameson, all of whom have seen in capitalism the makings of a new eschatology and a new magical imaginary.

Capitalism transforms the meaning of speculation, which has always been a part of mercantile behavior, even in pre- and noncapitalist economic orders. It does so in several ways. To begin with, it does so because, as Marx famously pointed out in his M-C-M formula, and in his brilliant discussion of the difference between the miser and the capitalist, the capitalist, in his never ceasing pursuit of exchange value, never allows money to terminate in the purchase of commodities but always throws money back into circulation in order to create increased (or surplus) value (254–55). In this very act of throwing money back into circulation (without cease) and by refusing to hoard money at any stage of its life in the circulation of commodities, the capitalist is first and last a speculator, that is, a person who is always making a wager on the positive risk of throwing money into circulation, in spite of the uncertainty of such a move.

The entrepreneur, who was not clearly distinguished from the capitalist producer by Marx but only later by Joseph Schumpeter, relies on the speculation of the capitalist investor, who seeks returns on his investment without ever getting rid of uncertainty. Insofar as investors never succeed in reducing all uncertainty to calculable risk, they are always and everywhere speculators, explorers of the uncertain and the unknown.

In addition, given the compulsion toward growth (in production capacity, in market share, in profits, and thus generally in scale) in industrial capitalism, there is always a pursuit of the periphery of the known market, in terms of new technologies, new consumers, new labor forces, and new geographies for raw materials. The dynamism of capital thus lives at its periphery. Put another way, the economy (at least in a certain neoclassical perspective) might seek equilibrium, but the capitalist always seeks disruption. Speculation about new markets, new products, new technologies, and new efficiencies is the principal source of such disruption. This sort of disruption, now a central mantra of business journals and corporate propaganda, is the normalized expression of Schumpeter's dynamic of "creative destruction." In this sense too, speculation is at the driving heart of capitalism, and not its magical other.

Speculation thrives in the zone where the visible and the invisible come together. Though capitalism depends on the production of both absolute and relative surplus value through the commoditization and exploitation of wage labor, it rests its legitimacy on disguising, obscuring, and denying the true source of surplus value, so that it can be harvested by the capitalist rather than by the laboring classes. On the other hand, the urge toward expanding its scale and scope drives all capitalist ventures (and the system as a whole) closer to the zone of the invisible, the most profound location of which is the future. Capitalist calculation is an endless effort to make the (invisible) future visible in the numerical symptoms of the present (charts, figures, estimates, trends, patterns, probabilities). This effort inevitably falls short of its aims to make the future entirely visible and is the primary site of competition between firms, managers and investors as they choose where to put their money back into play (in Marx's sense) in the endless circulation implied by M-C-M. In other words, the key to success in the endless battle between competitors in capitalist economies is to seek competitive advantages in the realm of the invisible rather than in the all too visible and calculable present. Since the future is always bigger than the numerical tools that are used to predict it, there is not only a space but also a compulsion to enter the zone of speculation and divination in order to grow, and growth in capitalism is the condition of survival. It is this zone of speculation and divination—the sine qua non and not the other of capitalist formations and mentalities—that invites the trope of dreamwork.

The idea of dreamwork brings together (in its two key elements) the space of fantasy, speculation, and unbridled imagination (key semantic associations with the notion of dreaming) and the space of productivity, discipline, and instrumentality (essential elements of the modern conception of work). Dreamwork, however, is neither an oxymoron nor a contradiction in relation to capitalism. Capitalism is fundamentally about disciplined dreaming, about playful calculation, and about speculative productivity.

In its visions of growth without limit, of innovation as habit, and of risk as something to be exploited and not only to be hedged against, capitalism is always a dream about future value, a stage for negotiations between the visible and the invisible, a procedure for the disruption of routine, and a set of rules for the always expanding realm of the unruly and the unruled.

Speculation, divination, fantasy, and dreamwork, even apart from the core practices of financial players in the Euro-American world, are to be found everywhere in the space in which information technology, social media, and "big data" come together, a space that can safely be seen as the next frontier in which the standard operating procedures of capitalism seek to reinvent themselves. Some key words of this new economy are *mine*, *cloud*, *meme*, *interface*, *code*, *algorithm*, and *pattern*. It does not require much thought to see that this is the vocabulary not of "normal capitalism" but of its current divinatory edge, which seeks to plumb, analyze, and then monetize the trillions of bits of information that are being produced every day, thus driving the need for machinic powers of truly Promethean proportions to profit from the study of them. Blurring the lines between human and nonhuman agencies, between users and makers, between "selves" and "selfies," between crowds and hordes, masses and classes, the world of big data can best be seen as the newest scene of what Marx called "primitive accumulation" at the very heart of contemporary capitalism in the West. Indeed, to "mine" data and to make all forms of human interaction and sociality (or at least those available to capture by machines) available for monetization, the heart of the strategy of Facebook, Google, Yahoo, and a hundred smaller imitators of these giants is the newest form of primitive accumulation.

What I have said so far might account for the viewpoint of the makers and shakers, the heroes and villains of global capitalism. But what about the rest of us, the consumers, the users, the borrowers, the debtors, the bottomless financial proletariat? To understand the subjectivity of the ordinary financial citizen, we need to look at what I have dubbed "life after debt."

Life after Debt

Everyday life is linked to capital today not so much by the mechanism of the surplus value of labor but through making us all risk bearers, whose aggregate risk can be endlessly combined and recombined to provide new forms of risk taking and profit making by the financial industries. Ordinary debtors remain believers in the debt-credit machinery even when it fails them repeatedly. We are all laborers now, regardless of what we do, insofar as our primary reason for being is to enter into debt and thus be forced to monetize the risks of health, security, education, housing, and much else in our lives. This labor of debt production is inconceivable without the normalization of failure, and that, too, at several levels. First, we have to assume and absorb our regular failure to live within our means and thus to view debt as a natural fact. Second, we have to accept that some of us will go bankrupt and that this is an acceptable outcome in the bigger scheme of things. Third, in the order of things, we learn to accept that some banks, hedge funds, and financial schemes will also fail and with them the dreams and hopes of those who invested in them. And finally, we learn to accept that the risk and the lived experience of failure constitute the price of entry into an inevitably deferred state of wealth, security, and happiness.

Today's financial capitalism, which Marx could not have entirely foreseen in his day, does not primarily work through the making of profit in the commodity sphere, though a certain part of the capitalist economy still operates in this sphere. By far the larger portion works by making profit on the monetization of risk, and risk is made available to the financial markets through debt in its myriad forms. All of us who live in a financialized economy generate debt in many forms: consumer debt, housing debt, health debt, and others related to these. Capitalist forms also operate through debt (since borrowing on the capital markets has become much more important for large corporations than issuing stock or "equity").

The notion that the big banks responsible for the mortgage collapse of 2007–8 were too big to fail also raises the question of temporality and of the staging of emergency in the dominant financial discourses of our times. The big banks are often argued to be in need of being broken up or reorganized, by voices both within and outside the financial industries, but *not yet, not now*. This is a particularly painful paradox because it is in the moment of crisis that banks reveal their greed for profit, their willingness to take risks with other people's money, their indifference to regulation, and their bottomless belief in the importance of what they do for capitalism as a whole. And yet this is the very moment in which they are able to argue that they cannot be reformed, restricted, or regulated because that would lead us over the edge, into an apocalypse from which there is no possible return.

Thus, the "now" of regulation and reform is deferred into a perpetual "later," and the later never comes because the habitual cycle of debt, interest, risk, profit, and failed promises reestablishes itself, after a little bloodletting of weak banks and some mild punishment of the greediest corporate actors. Indeed, the promise machine of the derivative-centered market has been more or less fully restored since 2008, and a decade later the biggest banks, hedge funds, and mega investors are making more obscene profits than ever.

The household debt in the world (consumer debt, household loans of every type, mortgages, insurance, and so on) appears to be about 12 percent of the world's total debt. But this number is a bit misleading, since governments, business corporations, and financial institutions also depend on investments and payments from the general public (as taxpayers, shareholders, bond holders, and investors, small and large). In this sense, all debt is consumer debt. But let us concede that 12 percent of the world's debt is directly produced by consumer borrowing and the rest by indirect extraction from consumers of every degree of wealth.

"Too big to fail" can be better translated into the proposition that no one is too small to fail, as debtors will likely see their personal economies crash (unpayable consumer loans, burdensome student loans, unaffordable insurance policies, ballooning second mortgages, bankrupted pension funds) so that the major financial players, in banks, pension funds, and other hugely leveraged financial institutions, can remain too big to fail. Thus, in the financial markets, the ordinary citizen, the quotidian producer of debt value, is systemically doomed to be exploited by the tiny financial elite. This is a *guaranteed failure*, whose continued reproduction is routinely represented as the main condition of the success of the global financial market.

How is this normalization of debt production accomplished? It is accomplished by a complex apparatus of financial news, expert reports by central bankers and policy makers, promotional texts from banks, financial analysts, and marketeers, and by the incessant chatter of social media in which the pleasures of debt-driven consumption and new product hysteria are maintained at a high pitch. All this news and information is a vast machine for the reimagining of debt as a salvational technology.

Debt is about the ever-receding tomorrow, which has a complex temporal architecture. In the near term, time becomes the discipline of periodic payments, of accumulating interest, of juggling creditors and credit cards, of borrowing from Peter to pay Paul. We all now live in this purgatory of plastic. In the medium term, this is a temporality of consumer pleasure, of tools, toys, experiences, and services purchased and enjoyed by the incurring of debt. This is the temporality of debt-induced gluttony, in which consumption offers a plateau of thingly pleasures. But these pleasures are always short-lived, as objects become obsolescent, fashions change, attention shifts, and new promotional additions are advertised and marketed. This process, in which debt goes quickly from pleasure to boredom to pain, requires a larger eschatology, a longer horizon of redemption and salvation in which the production of quotidian debt is secured against the pain of endless payments. This is where life after debt needs to be imagined and installed in popular consciousness.

There are three key elements to the architecture of life after debt. The first is the eternal life of capital. Derivative of this Christian genealogy, Capital is the Spirit and the Spirit is eternal. Though Marx famously saw the commodity, fetishized, as the mystification of the material relations of production, in truth the foundational narrative of modern Capital is of the Spirit that lives through all the wear and tear of materiality, that adds value to mere labor, that imbues products with meaning, that sanctifies the profanities of money. Since Capital is Spirit (in the Hegelian sense), the moving force behind History, it is worth reclaiming from its demystification by Marx.

Today, in the age of finance capital, where value is found in the buying and selling of values based on futurity, speculation, and volatility, the Hegelian sense of Spirit may be helpful to recall. It is the key to the laws of inheritance, investment, appreciation, and speculation, none of which could function without a sense that Capital is the supreme form of the Eternal.

This sense of Capital is anchored in the key ideological axiom of finance capital, which is the doctrine of liquidity. This doctrine is based on the idea that some assets are more easily converted to cash than others, and are thus more liquid than others. All capital in the age of financialization strives for liquidity, and the foundational legitimation principle of the major ideologies of banking, trading, and securitization is that they are the instruments that enable liquidity. From this point of view, the key to contemporary capitalism, which is the system that enacts the bodily life of the Spirit of Capital, is liquidity, the ability to melt all solids into the liquid form of cash.

And this is where debt comes in. Debt is the name of the search for liquidity among ordinary people, in their roles as students, workers, insurance buyers, loan seekers, mortgage holders, medical service customers, and shoppers of every type. Without entering into debt, we cannot be any of these things today in the age of debt as the link between the money we have and the money we need or want. And debt depends on the eternal life of Capital and the endless promise that debt can be piled on debt and that the day of reckoning can be indefinitely postponed.

Debt is also rewritten in the major narratives of neoliberalism as a kind of sacrificial act, in which we pay interest to preserve the larger cosmos of buying and being. As with sacrifice, there is an exchange between the humble sacrificer and the all-powerful receiver of what Georges Bataille called "the accursed share": the waste and excess generated by any economy or society, that part destined either to be spent luxuriously and without gain (in the arts, in nonprocreative sexuality, in spectacles and sumptuous monuments) or in outrageous and catastrophic outpourings (war, sacrifice, and religion). Debt unites the excesses and waste of the 1 percent with the petty credit slavery of the 99 percent, wrapping them both in an ideology of eternal life, sacrifice, and redemption, all anchored in the Spirit of Capitalism.

This soteriology of Capital links the little debt to the larger liquid Spirit, the small debtor to the big trader through what I have elsewhere called "the promise machine" (Appadurai and Alexander), the idea that a seamless world of utility, pleasure, convenience, and happiness is almost in our hands, provided we make the next payment, the next sacrifice, the next upgrade, the next liquid offering to the restless Spirit of Capital. Thus do we tolerate our mortal burdens and hope to find redemption in the guarantee of Life Eternal After Debt.

ARJUN APPADURAI is the Goddard Professor of Media, Culture, and Communication at New York University. His books include *Banking on Words: The Failure of Language in the Age of Derivative Finance* (University of Chicago Press, 2015), *The Future as Cultural Fact: Essays on the Global Condition* (Verso, 2013), *Fear of Small Numbers: An Essay on the Geography of Anger* (Duke University Press, 2006), and, with Neta Alexander, *Failure* (Polity Press, 2019). He is the coeditor of the journal *Public Culture*.

Works Cited

Appadurai, Arjun, and Neta Alexander. *Failure*. Cambridge: Polity, 2020.

Bataille, Georges. *The Accursed Share: An Essay on General Economy*. Vol. 1. Trans. Robert Hurley. New York: Zone, 1988.

Marx, Karl. *Capital: A Critique of Political Economy*. Vol. 1. Trans. Ben Fowkes. London: Penguin, 1976.

Schumpeter, Joseph. *Capitalism, Socialism, and Democracy*. London: Taylor and Francis, 2003.

Weber, Max. *The Protestant Ethic and the Spirit of Capitalism*. Trans. Talcott Parsons. New York: Routledge, 1992.

The Debt Chronotope

*D*ebt is a conspicuous and well-established motive in Western literature: it features debts to Gods, debts to ancestors, debts to landlords, debts to usurers. . . . The prominence of debt in literature indeed testifies to its primordial role in the history of civilization, where owing others and servicing one's debts stand out as perennial predicaments. Debt, in other words, is an important motive in literature because debt is an important factor in our lives. And why would we have literature, after all, if it were not to give us images of our lives—the hopes and fears, the joys and quandaries—through which we can contemplate and reflect on the way we live? We have literature, as Kenneth Burke once put it, as "an equipment for living."

When literature takes up a motive, when it pieces together an image of something of import to the lives of its contemporaries—debt, for instance—it not only refers to this thing by designating it or naming it. Literature has, in Anna Kornbluh's apt wording, a "propensity to abstract social relations into their essential configurations" (16). The value of literature does not reside most notably in its capacity to itemize whatever concerns us in our lives, but in the capacity to construct forms through which we

Volume 31, Number 3   DOI 10.1215/10407391-8744469

© 2020 by Brown University and d i f f e r e n c e s : A Journal of Feminist Cultural Studies

can construe such concerns *differently*, learning something about them that we don't learn when we address them in the discourses of, say, science, journalism, or everyday conversation. Hence the question: when literature addresses debt, how does this imply not only the recognition that debt does in fact impact forcefully on our lives but also a modification of the forms through which literature portrays such lives? What happens to narrative form in an age when debt has become a still more palpable burden for individuals and societies and where securitization of debt has itself become a source of capital accumulation?

In this essay, I hypothesize that debt is not only a highly noticeable motive in contemporary literature but also that we see the emerging contours of a new *debt chronotope*, an organization of narrative time and space that contributes to the understanding of life under the aegis of generalized indebtedness and to portraying the world-transforming clout of a debt-driven financial capitalism. I will start out by briefly recapitulating the main contours of Mikhail Bakhtin's somewhat elusive notion of chronotope as a nontrivial idea of representation, that is, of how literature invents models of time-space that can serve to symbolize particular historical experiences of time and space (I). The following two sections discuss the historical time-space of financial capitalism, that is, how financialization and the debt economy it entails change the time-space we perceive in the world around us (II), and how the operational logic of contemporary finance also eventually changes the ways we conceive of time and space (III). The literary chronotope changes historically with the different societal roles and functions of debt; after having charted some traditional forms of the debt chronotope in nineteenth-century realist fiction (IV), I will conclude by discussing three contemporary novels and the chronotopic forms they feature (V and VI).

I

Parts of the huge fascination exerted by Bakhtin's notion of *chronotope* undoubtedly go back to its lack of determination. At the beginning of his 1939 essay, "Forms of Time and of the Chronotope in the Novel," Bakhtin himself wryly suggested considering his use of the concept "almost as a metaphor (almost, but not entirely)" (84). Lack of determination thus doesn't signify some flaw—that conciseness or precision is amiss—but rather that the concept, like so many of Bakhtin's concepts (think about dialogism, heteroglossia, speech genre, to name a few), designates an entire problem field, a new aspect under which to consider otherwise well described phenomena, which invites us to gauge these phenomena anew and promises the eventual advent of entire subsets of new concepts and determinations. The particular invitation and promise that has made the chronotope a cherished notion in contemporary literary studies is the way in which Bakhtin combines three questions that in different ways pertain to matters of time and space and puts them into stimulating conversation with each other.

      The first question is about the presence of "real historical time and space" in literature. The important word here, of course, is "real": like other thinkers of his generation, Bakhtin insists on the experiential particularity of time and space and the immanence of these particulars in larger patterns of culture that include inherited world images, common understandings, and social habits. Bakhtin here echoes Martin Heidegger's vehement rejection of scientific and "vulgar" notions of time and space, as well as Ernst Cassirer's idea of time and space as highly variable historical symbolic forms. "Real" time and space here come to designate the actually lived temporalities and spatial distributions in different historical situations, local and highly contingent experiences of succession and sequence, of propinquity and positionality, thus not simply time and space, but so many versions of conceived and perceived times and spaces.

      If the first question is about the chronotope as *representamen*, that is, the historical reality recorded in literature, the second question pertains to the *representans*, the way in which the rendition of historically contingent experiences is organized in literary texts: a *what* and a *how*. As for the "how," Bakhtin ventures into an almost unlimited field of inquiry, nothing less, namely, than the examination of how time and space are rendered in the literary medium of text. And again, he cautiously avoids the obvious and well-trodden roads, in this case the one going back to Lessing's *Laokoon*, according to which literature is considered to be the medium of temporal succession, pinned against painting as the medium for spatial distribution. Contrary to such a default identification of literature and narrative, Bakhtin emphasizes the necessary *reciprocity* between time and space in the literary chronotope. In order to represent the particular historical chronotope of lived time and space, literature must reconstruct its specific spatiotemporal signature, that is, the way in which temporal sequences are always processes in a spatial setting, and conversely, how spatial distribution itself results from a temporal genealogy: "In the literary artistic chronotope, spatial and temporal indicators are fused into one carefully thought-out, concrete whole. Time, as it were, thickens, takes on flesh, becomes artistically visible:

likewise, space becomes charged and responsive to the movements of time" (84). The power of literature, for Bakhtin, resides in its ability to reconstruct artistically the spatiotemporal signature of a historical life-form: how we dwell in space, how we address and understand time, in short, the world-making that emerges from a particular set of cultural practices.

Chronotope thus designates two different things. The "historical chronotope" is a cultural life-world, the way time and space are lived in a historical context. And the "artistic chronotope" is a representational form, an image able to grasp and illuminate the time-space of a historical life-form by way of a particular literary organization of temporal and spatial markers. Historical chronotopes are ubiquitous, because life itself is chronotopic: because human agency creates patterns of time and space. Artistic chronotopes, on the other hand, are essentially rare, they are literary inventions, creating images that can retain the particular qualities of evanescent historical moments. Therefore, and this is the third qualification Bakhtin offers to characterize the chronotope: artistic chronotopes are seminal to the constitution of literary *genres.* At the heart of any genre or generic form lies a technique for representing a human time-space. And there are many time-spaces but few artistic chronotopes. Hence, any attempt to represent a historical aspect of life will take an existing chronotope as its point of departure in order to then modify, adapt, and repurpose it to a new context: exactly the way genre functions.

II

I have dwelt in such detail on Bakhtin's obdurately original notion because the three constituent parts of the concept actually invite us to hypothesize the existence of a chronotope of debt. As for the first part, the "historical chronotope," we should probably start by taking notice of what David Graeber has convincingly demonstrated in his bestselling monograph on debt: that it has taken many different guises in its first five thousand years and that there is thus not *one* historical chronotope of debt. Rather, debt is eminently prone to generate chronotopic configurations because of its efficacy at creating distributions of time and space. It is chronotopogenic.

In their comments to Nietzsche's analysis of debt in *On the Genealogy of Morality*, Gilles Deleuze and Félix Guattari specifically notice this quality. In the chapter of *Anti-Oedipus* dedicated to territorial representation, they reconstruct Nietzsche's idea of debt as the elementary mechanism of subjectivation and highlight how it serves "to breed man, to mark him in his flesh, to render him capable of alliance, to form him within the debtor-creditor relation" (189). And this mark, they contend, the mark through which subjectivity comes into being in the first place, crucially situates this emerging subject in a temporal and spatial context. Time emerges as the dimension of enforced answerability where present and future versions of a subject will be identifiable as *the same* subject, thus creating a memory of owing and an acceptance of the eventual demand to repay. And space concomitantly emerges through the "territorial inscription" instigated by the debt relation, delimiting what is yours and what is mine, where you belong, where you are admitted, where you are not. In this anthropological tale, debt is a violently enforced social relation through which subjectivity is created by marking a body and situating this body in a constraining time-space matrix, which combines a temporal distribution of expectation and a spatial distribution of possession and dispossession.

If debt is chronotopogenic, then, it is because the primitive relation at its core, the relation between a creditor and a debtor, immediately unfurls a full spatiotemporal universe. But it does so in many different ways; the historical chronotope of debt comes in different guises precisely because of the historical differences in the ways in which debt is mediated, socially, politically, and technologically. In this section, I will look into the operational logic of debt in twenty-first-century financialized capitalism to gauge its contemporary chronotopic profile.

Financialization is itself all about debt; among the many definitions of financialization in circulation, the one provided by German sociologist Wolfgang Streeck undergirds this relation. Against the backdrop of steadily diminishing returns in the production sector since the end of *les Trente Glorieuses* in the 1970s, he states, "The power elites of global capitalism would seem to be resigning themselves to low or no growth on aggregate for the foreseeable future." But, as Streeck cautiously adds: "This does not preclude high profits in the financial sector, essentially from speculative trading with cheap money supplied by central banks" (57). So, to maintain something that looks like growth, continuous and steady return on the fortunes of "the power elites of global capitalism," what is thrown in is debt, which comes in the guise of "cheap money." Because to be able to issue cheap money, one needs, as always with money, something to back it: money is credit, and credit invariably comes with its double, with debt. Cheap money can be provided through the issuing of state bonds, but it can be provided also by securitization of all kinds of societal values, transforming them into credit-yielding assets. Once a given societal value, like an infrastructure, a home, an education, or good health, can be translated into an asset by means of financial instruments, the credit they represent can be traded, invested in, speculated on. Hence the monumental buildup of debt, sovereign debt, mortgage debt, education debt, and so on. When the financial sector can still offer investors the harvest of a profit in the present, it is in exchange for debt positions piled up in the future.

This surge of debt that has accompanied the financialization of contemporary economies thus, of course, goes back to the politics of fiscal deficit, but it also goes back to growing private indebtedness, with generous provision of credit to individuals and households that have had to compensate for declining real wages with rollover debts. The production of money in exchange for future debt is premised on one vital mechanism of financialization, namely, the practice of securitization. Debt needs a security, whether a pound of flesh or a synthetic "collateralized debt obligation." This is why the financial sector has been so highly innovative in finding ways to transform what was just human or societal values into assets that can back tradable securities. Things and situations that were earlier just things and situations now in still greater number double as assets. Dwelling, living, and learning can be securitized, as can exploitable nature, critical infrastructure, and social order. What happens, though, when "cheap money" is created in this way, is that these assets henceforth are answerable for the debt issued in their names. This is the first notable characteristic of the historical debt chronotope in the twenty-first century: there is still less of the space we live in (and less lived space of activity) that is not a security for a debt—a debt to be collected in the future. Financialization is a new wave of enclosure, in Saskia Sassen's words, an "enclosure by financial firms of a country's resources and citizens' taxes," premised on "a capability to securitize just about everything in an economy and, in doing so, subject economies and governments to its own criteria for measuring success" (15, 118).

In a financialized world, the ground under our feet and the space of our lives are, if not scorched land, then securitized land. This kind of enclosure is not only a spatial one, however, but has an obvious temporal counterpart as well: that looming future when the debt is due. The time of debt, say Deleuze and Guattari, is "a memory—a memory directed towards the future" (189; translation modified), a temporal axis, in other words, where what is behind you is projected ahead of you, where the horizon of expectations is overwritten by what is already within the perimeter of experience. This radical, and radically counterintuitive, configuration of time, a temporality without transcendence, mirrors both Nietzsche's and Deleuze and Guattari's point: that debt is an eminent instrument of power, a power not only to mold subjectivity in a particular way but also to perennially clamp it to this form, so that the future is no longer a dimension of aspiration, but one of mere repetition. It is a general feature of debt that it disciplines aspiration, but this feature is crucially amplified by contemporary financialization in two respects. The first is in a purely quantitative way, when the sheer mass of debt being built up becomes monumental to a degree where it literally comes to block the view of any possible alternative. For a long time, the combination of tax cuts and expansive monetary policy have strained national budgets and extended sovereign debt while declining real wages and unrelenting austerity politics have made different forms of household debt a still more widespread prerequisite for social reproduction. But all the same, we remain—individually and collectively—obedient to the idea that debt is absolutely nonnegotiable. Second, also due to the quantitative explosion of debt, we now come to consider debt, in a somewhat qualitative way, as something we don't even imagine ever overcoming. Today, when credit is provided, it is no longer really a part of the understanding between creditor and debtor that the debt should actually be repaid; what is important is that it is continuously *serviced*. The creditors don't want their money back: they want a credit they can leverage and monetize on the market for derivatives. And the debtors, on their side, are incentivized to roll over, refinance, engage still further into the future, until this future gradually comes to aberrate still more from what we imagine a future to be. Money, in its traditional understanding, is a repository for storing past labor, "frozen labor." Debt, on the other hand, represents frozen *future* labor—and the more debt there is, the more perennial the predicament of indebtedness becomes, the more the future itself becomes enclosed.

III

According to Fernand Braudel, the long history of capitalism passes through a series of regularly occurring relays where abating rates of profit make capital owners look for new businesses. On such occasions, areas of social life that had hitherto been without import for capitalist accumulation are included into its sphere and hence subjugated to its logic: "nonmarkets" are transformed into markets proper. The wave of financialization that has transformed the world economy and social life at large over the last decades can be seen, through a Braudelian lens, as such an expansion, a foray into new spatiotemporal areas of the world through the enclosure of

new spaces, newly securitized distributed assets, and the preemptive enclosure of henceforth spoken-for futures. The historical chronotope changes
under the sway of financialization, and the time and space we perceive are
subordinated to a set of new and different rationales. Moreover, when debt
is retooled for a financialized economy, it also makes us *conceive* of time and
space differently; we operate and navigate in novel ways in this chronotope.

A core feature of financialization is a new way of mediating debt.
In its primitive form, debt is a relation between creditor and debtor—you and
me, here and there—and therefore it produces, as Deleuze and Guattari put
it, a "territorial inscription." Financialization intensifies this inscription
by securitizing still more credit-yielding assets and thus anchoring debt
relations everywhere; but on the other hand, it also blurs the relation by
mediating it differently. Key here is the attempt to *diversify* debtor-creditor
relations with new financial instruments, according to the procedures of
what Ivan Ascher has aptly baptized the "portfolio society."

The best-known example of diversifying financial engineering is
probably the instruments that fueled the subprime crisis of 2007–8. Innovative financiers launched techniques to stack large numbers of "asset-backed
securities" in order to slice them up into "collateralized debt obligations"
and eventually to insure them through "credit default swaps." These instruments were not only excellent at dissimulating what were, in fact, unten-
able debt positions (for a while, at least, until the surging defaults made the
entire edifice come down), they also—and more generally—served to dissolve
the tangible relation between creditor and debtor *and* to reassemble it in
a huge and dense tangle of more or less opaque relations. Mediated in this
way, the debt relation is no longer a relation between here and there, but
rather—from the debtor's perspective—a relation between here and a translocal industry issuing claims on servicing debt, or—from the creditor's perspective—between a revolving portfolio and an algorithmically constructed
volatility index based on finely ground market data. The contemporary debt
chronotope teaches us to refrain from conceiving of space—that is, gauging
the relation between here and there—in terms of an immediately given territory with tangible gradients of propinquity and distance. Instead, we are
situated vis-à-vis a ubiquitously present infrastructural order that relates
everything to everything else and constantly readjusts these relations in
real-time response to market interventions everywhere on the globe.

The ramification of debt relations and the resulting web of universal relatedness is, of course, premised on the unhindered global circulation of capital and on the consolidation of an information infrastructure

of immediate response. But the main operator of this licentious putting everything up against everything else is the *derivative contract*. Prices of assets and securities fluctuate, and their future oscillations are contingent on future events that remain, of course, unpredictable. Price contracts—swaps, futures, and forwards—are age-old remedies to the risk associated with price volatility that determine the conditions of a future deal in advance to prevent surprises. By ratifying the terms of a future exchange, the derivative contract calibrates the future present with the present future and thus hedges against future contingency, or neutralizes a risk. If the farmer has sold his crop at a predetermined price, he doesn't have to fear the risk of falling prices if the harvest is good, but neither can he profit from rising prices if the harvest is meagre. Now, if these derivative contracts are considered no longer just as contracts between judicious partners but also as securities in their own right that can be bought and sold in the securities markets, they become a means to price risk itself, as one is now betting on other people's bets, as it were, betting on how much the farmer would have lost or gained if he hadn't made the contract, on the gap between the future of the present and the present of the future. The use of derivatives as securities was heavily regulated up until the late twentieth century, but regulations have gradually been lifted on steady advice from neoclassical economists according to whom the pricing of risk and the eagerness to monetize every price deviation would purportedly stabilize prices by collectively reckoning their deviations. It is, of course, difficult to assess whether the boom of derivative contracts over the last decades has in fact provided just pricing, but it has for sure sparked the number of securities in circulation and thus contributed to the extraction of money in the present to be accounted for in the future. And it has been a propaedeutic to conceiving differently of time itself.

Crucially, derivatives have the ability to continuously shift the temporality of a given asset. New derivatives can be issued, modifying the past references and conjectural futures used to reference the given asset, and thereby creating different temporalities around it. Like an advanced exercise in speculative plotting, an asset—even an asset that is itself but a contractual bid on the future price of yet another asset—can be differently contextualized in terms of capturing points, parameters, and presuppositions, refracting its reality in different perspectives and eventually adjudicating its fate, its prospects, and its potentials. Devising different plots involving an asset is a matter of situating it in time, and the resulting tale is one of time as modeled on the basis of expectations of yield and exposure to risk. Lisa Adkins calls this a speculative time of "nonchronological pasts, presents, and futures":

Speculative time is a time in which pasts, presents, and futures stand not in a predetermined or pre-set relation to each other but are in a continuous state of movement, transformation, and unfolding. It is this form of time that belongs to the time of securitized debt. Thus, in the time of securitized debt, futures may remediate not only the present but also the past; the present and its relation to the past and the future may be reset in one action (via, for example, index rolling); pasts and presents can be forwarded and futures and presents backwarded. (96–97)

What is most striking about this plastic and malleable time is its *heteronomy.* In most of what we do and what happens in our lives, time is an unconditional variable, presenting us with moments to be seized, instances to be reckoned with. Here, however, time—the organization and sequencing of "nonchronological pasts, presents, and futures"—remains subordinate to a speculative practice, the plotting of assets' future prices in view of the price of risk and the exposure to volatility.

The historical debt chronotope in the age of financialized capitalism features many other characteristics in addition to the ones discussed so far; the brief analysis above should, however, provide an idea of both the *perceived* qualities of space and time under the aegis of contemporary finance—the experience of enclosure and colonization of surrounding spaces and times to come—and the new modes of *conceiving* of space and time that come with it as well, where spatial reality appears as ubiquitous relationality and interactional intensity, and where the experience of time has recursivity, repetition, and polychronicity as its hallmarks.

IV

What would be a literary form—or *artistic* chronotope—that corresponds to this historical chronotope? John Grisham, best-selling author of legal thrillers, a genre he has contributed seminally to define, recently published a novel that departed slightly from his usual design, the fast-paced unravelling of a crime through a dramatic judicial process. This novel, *The Rooster Bar*, displaces the focus from lawyers to law students, and particularly to student *debt.* It describes a low-ranking, for-profit law school that charges sizeable tuition fees covered by state-subsidized student loans and standardly produces not particularly employable lawyers with hefty debts. The novel follows a group of students that eventually sees the hopelessness of their venture and drops out of school to embark instead on a scam where they pretend to be lawyers and charge fees from clients they round up around police detentions. The scam is—of course—not viable, and its disentanglement is hardly a plot; rather, it comes through as a slightly burlesque pastime, and the novel exploits the lack of the thriller's habitual forward thrust to delve into different colorful crevices of legal, political, and educational life in today's America. The seasoned plotter of legal thrillers thus, somewhat improbably, probes the delight of a plot whose plot has itself come undone, become lost in time and space: "It was their first visit to Africa and neither ventured a guess as to how long it would last. Their pasts were a mess. Their futures were uncertain. So, somewhere along the way they decided to live in the present with no regrets. Life could be worse. They could be studying for the bar exam" (Grisham 373). Grisham's debt novel gives us a first hint of what happens to literary form under the pressure of a historical chronotope of finance that promulgates increasingly indiscriminate spaces and dizzyingly nonchronological versions of time: the order of the plot disintegrates. It is difficult to devise an intransigent and powerfully unfolding plot once the differences between here and there and between now and then lose their absolute qualities, and with them the quest, the ambition, the crusade, in short, the willful attempt to "prove [one's] soul," as Robert Browning had it, quoted by Lukács as epigraph to his late essay on Dostoevsky.

      This new situation noticeably departs from earlier instantiations of the debt chronotope. In the nineteenth century novel, amortization of debt is arguably one of the most efficient devices for plot configuration. In Balzac's *Lost Illusions*, everything that happens in the shrewdly construed double plot of David Séchard and Lucien de Rubempré is controlled and coordinated by way of debt positions. When the two protagonists, the frugal engineer and the extravagant poet, launch into their respective careers, they both do so on credit. From the outset this is a solid plot, and the simple question is whether their great aspirations will come to fruition before the debts are due. When Lucien's credit eventually dries up under the weight of his costly Parisian habits, he not only issues still more promissory notes but also fraudulently makes debt in David's name, forcing the latter to give up his revolutionizing business of paper production and leave the exploitation to the creditors. This master plot in place, Balzac artfully adorns it with subplots that in different ways intervene in the mesh of contracts, notes, and bills, propelled by a host of marginal characters all pursuing their particular pecuniary, political, or sentimental interests. One enters into the plot by picking a position in the amortization scheme of outstanding debt.

The debt chronotope in the realist novel is a tight, agonistic bolt between credit and solvency, amortization and self-realization. This dramatic potential is exploited with utmost verve by Flaubert in the third part of *Madame Bovary*, where the treacherous trader of luxury goods (with the no less treacherous name Lheureux) at a fatal moment sells the promissory notes Emma has issued and she is whirled into the crescendo of a feverish and futile quest to finance these cascading obligations, terminating in her inglorious death. In these instances, and countless others like them in the archive of realist literature, the amortization of debt is an ideal driver of plot. The sense of an ending is where the debt is due—which, to a novelist, is a perfect schematization of time, providing a dramatic time of fatality. In the age of financialization, however, when the fatal logic of amortization gives way to a perennial servicing of rolled-over debt, the race toward the end ceases to be the primary narrative trope. Instead lurks a sense of time as both always already and forever, and space as an infinitely interwoven surface: a new chronotope, a spacetime of spectrality and reversibility. To chart some of the compositional forms that come to characterize the new literary chronotope of nonprogressive time and translocal territorial grounding, I will briefly comment on three novels that offer different ways of responding to the contemporary time-space of financialized capitalism.

V

In an important study, *Heads or Tails: The Poetics of Money*, originally published in German in 1996, Jochen Hörisch discusses the nature of money from a media-historical perspective. Money, he claims, is one of three seminal "onto-semiotic" instruments at work in Western culture, the two others being the eucharist and television. Onto-semiotics is the way in which we associate being with signs, or, put differently, how we confer meaning onto being by associating it with a dimension where this being actually makes sense. This is, to be sure, a very accommodating definition, according to which almost the entire range of human activities involve practices of "onto-semiotics." But if the eucharist, money, and electronic image processing are historically *dominant* media, as Hörisch has it, it is because they are media that provide beings of the world with the allegedly most important features of meaning: those of transcendence, value, and representational appearance, respectively. Onto-semiotic media are devices of world making that provide shared standards for how to understand common societal life and symbolic systems through which individual experiences become compatible and comparable.

Daniel Kehlmann's humorous credit-crunch novel from 2013, *F*, echoes this idea in an allegorical tale of three brothers, a priest, a hedge fund manager, and a painter, and the triple crises of faith, finance, and forgery they live through on a warm summer day in 2008. The older brother tends to his religious office and distractedly gives out absolution and forgiveness, all while longing to resume his favorite pastime: solving his Rubik's Cube (when not eating, sinfully). The fund manager aggressively deals, amassing huge credit positions and leveraging them even more vertiginously. And the painter is engaged in his own clever contrivance, forging paintings that can be ascribed to a dead master and working the art market as a gallerist to manipulate the pricing of these paintings as they are released to the market. The three brothers, in other words, struggle to uphold the onto-semiotic functions of their professions, functions that are obviously under serious strain and in the process of divulging themselves as mere fictions (another F-word resonating in the title of the novel). Against this backdrop, the main action of the novel is three parallel stories where these fragile meaning-making enterprises eventually come to collapse.

Interestingly, what ensues in Kehlmann's universe when the onto-semiotic scaffolding of purportedly meaningful social understanding falters, is nothing less than a breakdown of spatiotemporal coordinates. When the priest finds himself unable to honor the demands on him—when he is approached by a believer in actual need of forgiveness—he succumbs to a violent seizure of claustrophobia where space itself somehow deflates and becomes unbreathable, unliveable. The investor in want of liquidity is taken by psychotic lightness and also loses himself in time and space, finding himself eerily out of pace with the action he takes part in and out of place in the urban flow around him, like an actor slightly misplaced on his set. The painter, finally, is mugged—perhaps the mugger is even the one who has come to seek absolution with the priest brother, albeit in a strange temporal loop—and mysteriously disappears into nothingness, literally melting into the matter surrounding him. This is a tale, then, of what happens when powerful onto-semiotic conventions topple and come out as mere fictions that nobody really believes in anymore and a tale that explores what happens to the time and space of a world that loses grip of its symbolic forms. Kehlmann gauges, half serious, half playful, the advent of a time out of joint and a space of wormholes as the hallmarks of the new topology that crops up when habitual onto-semiotic operations are put under stress and ultimately falter, and thus suggests, with a slant of fantasy, the contours of an alternative aesthetic chronotope to match the novel time-space of financialization.

A less playful—or differently playful—variation on the demise of our inherited sense of time and space can be found in Michel Houellebecq's magisterially boring exercise in resignation, *Sérotonine* (2019). Whereas Kehlmann outlines a chronotope in which convoluted time and folded space come to replace traditional notions like progression and extension, Houellebecq seems intent on retaining a traditional narrative pace and thus a sense of linear time, all while almost diabolically extirpating the very sense of time that unrolls: that of aspiration and eventual change. To this effect, *Sérotonine* explores and provocatively skews a prominent motive of narrative, the link between remembrance and longing, between past and future. The strand of remembrance here mostly consists of kitschy recollections of joy (unsurprisingly represented by selflessly loving and sexually serviceable women) and, as always in Houellebecq, leaves the reader perplexed as to whether this is an excruciatingly sad portrayal of our times or, on the contrary, an exquisite portrayal of our sad times. The narrative exploit in *Sérotonine*, however, is to have a protagonist who relentlessly works toward *preventing* such past experiences to turn into new expectations, thus effectively dismantling the bridge that should lead the way from the past into the future. The bulk of the novel is an exercise in not-wanting, and it displays a truly admirable stamina in aimlessly touring and duly describing the (admittedly bland) everyday time-space of France today, including the interspersed scenes of diffuse collective anger that famously prefigured the movement of the *gilets jaunes*. And in the midst of this is a protagonist who masters the Houellebecqian art of emotional noninvolvement save for a detached accounting rationality with an occasional spark of something like anger, only held in check by general spite. Houellebecq's protagonist has all the words necessary to describe this world but no longer the emotion to magnetize the words, as Musil once put it (1076).

If Houellebecq is indeed an economist, as Bernard Maris suggests, it is by way of this meticulously elaborated exercise in contemplating an infinite present of nonpromissory immanence. The obliteration of a meaningful plot and the systematic extermination of anything that could make something plot-like conceivable are the two main components of the Houellebecqian debt chronotope, a chronotope that monumentalizes an immobilized landscape of negative eternity. It divulges an insight into the contemporary nexus of credit and debt, namely, that if credit is a vehicle for making potential future value accessible already in the present, then it also leaves us with a future debt to be repaid, a work to be supplied in return for a remuneration that has already been spent.

VI

These two configurations of time, the tendency toward non-chronicity in Kehlmann and the enduring stasis in Houellebecq, are both in play in Zia Haider Rahman's *In the Light of What We Know* (2014). At face value, what is at stake in this novel is very straightforward: an account of a life. But it develops into an account where individual particulars are washed out and the temporality of agency curves into a strangely immobile vortex of complex and reciprocal relations.

The novel's first-person narrator is a descendant of Pakistani tycoons and ministers and the son of an acknowledged physicist, raised in Princeton and Oxford, where he himself has graduated as a mathematician before becoming a first-generation derivatives engineer on Wall Street and the Square Mile. His narrative starts in the late summer of 2008 when he spends long days alone in his Kensington house, suspended from his job, waiting for enquiries pending on his derivatives business, and de facto left by his banker wife whose businesses seem to keep her sempiternally away from home. In the midst of this professional and existential vacuum, a friend from the past shows up at his door, Zafar, a fellow student from Oxford whom he hasn't seen for more than a decade. The novel is essentially about filling this temporal gap, reconstructing Zafar's life since they lost contact in the general turmoil of busy adult lives. Zafar's trajectory is somehow the exact opposite of that of the narrator. A son of poor Bangladeshi immigrants, he has grown up in a London suburb and was only propelled out of an otherwise prescribed social destiny due to his talent for mathematics. The two South Asian boys meet at Oxford and both move on to the booming industry of finance as well-trained *quants*, before Zafar launches on a second career in humanitarian law, circulating between Afghanistan, Bangladesh, Pakistan, New York, and London.

Zafar's story is one of race and class: about his struggle to adapt to Oxford, his relationship to a high-bred British woman, his coming to terms with his own history (probably an offspring of the military rape campaigns around the time of Bangladeshi independence). It is also a story of the vicissitudes of humanitarian work in South Asia with U.N. compounds, military and mercenaries, and much more. And then, of course, it is a story of the world of finance, the math of finance, and indeed the view of the world in the light of finance. Altogether, an interesting late-twentieth-century life is reconstructed by his friend on the basis of their conversations in the warm fall of 2008, helped by Zafar's diaries and the narrator's own recollections. But it is also a narrative whose chronotopic structure has been thoroughly financialized. The relations between events in space are mostly derivative—indirect and obeying different logics of interaction—and relations in time are concomitantly curved, recursive, and generally recalcitrant to the steady, successive pace of an unfolding story.

The narrative is set on excavating and presenting Zafar's story. But it does so in a thoroughly nonlinear manner. The novelistic discourse rarely follows a neat sequence of temporally and causally organized events; from one paragraph to the next, we might well be in another location, at another time, or seeing with someone else's eyes. And the link that takes us from one sentence to the next might be an association, a digression, a parallel thought, a whim, even a ruse—all reminiscent of Proust's renowned technique, according to which the event of telling will always outweigh the events told. Eventually, action and reflection, information and conjecture, here and there, now and then bleed out and blend into the texture of the novel. When the relations unpacked in the narrative come to encompass such daunting leaps in time and space, it stresses the heterochronicity and translocality of the events themselves. To tell an interesting late-twentieth-century life, it is necessary to mobilize a batch of new relations and relation types that can reach beyond those of spatiotemporal situations, a new chronotope, in other words, through which we become able to gauge relations in an extended time-space, where everything is related in one way or another, and where time remains relative to stakes that others have in it.

In such a narrative, it ultimately becomes difficult also to appraise the protagonist, the *origo* of the narrative. While reading, one keeps asking, who is the first-person singular speaking here? The narrator in the act of telling? The narrator in earlier situations? Zafar talking to the narrator? Zafar writing in his diaries? These different "I"s blend, as the selves of writing, reading, talking, remembering. Rahman's technique of blended voices is reminiscent of the works of W. G. Sebald and, before him, Peter Weiss, where not only the discursive event takes the upper hand on the narrated event but where the subjectivities emerging from the discourse outdo the original subjects of enunciation. This is what Fredric Jameson at one point called a "dialogic agon" (396), a textual surface that hosts discursive events rather than personalized utterances. Annie McClanahan has perspicaciously noticed that characterization in Gary Shteyngart's *Super Sad True Love Story* verges astonishingly on caricature and stereotype and that this narrative technique can be linked to the changes in credit scoring techniques in the late twentieth century. Here, the until-then-prevalent narrative assessment of individual loan takers is abandoned in favor of an algorithmic weighing of predefined data points, no longer profiling the individual lender but assessing the composition of dividual qualities that can be statistically modeled. I think a similar point can be made for Rahman's novel: he is about to develop a narrative form that attenuates the individual voice and gives over to the dividual impulses that come to the fore in the event of narrating.

In an aside during an otherwise recurring discussion about maps, Zafar says about the London Underground map: "It never tells you [. . .] where on earth any given station is. In one sense, it is no map at all but a diagram; it's not topographical but topological; and the question is always: What use is imagined for the map?" (Rahman 54). *In the Light of What We Know* sets out to appropriate some of the new topological patterns that have become increasingly predominant in a financialized world—our historical debt chronotope—and accommodates them to relate an array of present-day experiences in a war-torn, debt-ridden, unequal, and insecure world. Like Kehlmann and Houellebecq, only more dauntingly, Rahman invents new chronotopic techniques to match present-day topologies. He shifts the narrative focus from events that take place in discrete locations to events that activate infrastructural relays and passages on a global grid of relations. He disarticulates the monodirectional and fatal biographical time and transforms it into a nonchronological and spectral time that intriguingly manages to accommodate and juxtapose different possible temporal sequences. And he downplays the novelistic dogma of the distinct and "rounded" character in order to make room for dividual impulses and propensities and to examine how they blend and merge in situations of collective fabulation.

Debt—and more broadly, the logic of contemporary finance—stands out as a discernible motif in Rahman's novel. It is less conspicuous in Kehlman and Houellebecq, but even if it did not really take center stage as a motif, one could still demonstrate its presence precisely in the chronotopic dimension, a dimension in which the three novels display a generic family resemblance as debt or finance fictions. The time and space of the contemporary debt economy and the everyday topologies of life under financialized capitalism here seem to have sparked new literary forms where arcane infrastructures of derivative relationality and strange metrics of algorithmic dividualization afford new kinds of writing, a financialized prose of affect and connectedness, through which what we know does in fact stand out in a somewhat different light.

FREDERIK TYGSTRUP is a professor of comparative literature at the University of Copenhagen and principal investigator of the research project Finance Fiction: Financialization and Culture in the Early 21st Century, sponsored by the Independent Research Fund Denmark, 2019–21.

Works Cited

Adkins, Lisa. *The Time of Money*. Stanford: Stanford UP, 2018.

Ascher, Ivan. *Portfolio Society: On the Capitalist Mode of Prediction*. New York: Zone, 2016.

Bakhtin, Mikhail. *The Dialogic Imagination*. Trans. Cheryl Emerson and Michael Holquist. Austin: U of Texas P, 1981.

Braudel, Fernand. *Civilization and Capitalism, 15th–18th Century*. Trans. Sian Reynolds. Berkeley: U of California P, 1992.

Burke, Kenneth. "Literature as Equipment for Living." *The Philosophy of Literary Form: Studies in Symbolic Action*. Baton Rouge: Louisiana State UP, 1941. 293–304.

Deleuze, Gilles, and Félix Guattari. *Anti-Oedipus*. Trans. Robert Hurley, Mark Seem, and Helen R. Lane. Minneapolis: U of Minnesota P, 1983.

Grisham, John. *The Rooster Bar*. New York: Doubleday, 2017.

Hörisch, Jochen. *Heads or Tails: The Poetics of Money*. Trans. Amy H. Marshall. Detroit: Wayne State UP, 2000.

Houellebecq, Michel. *Sérotonine*. Paris: Flammarion, 2019.

Jameson, Fredric. *The Modernist Papers*. London: Verso, 2007.

Kehlmann, Daniel. *F*. Hamburg: Rohwolt, 2013.

Kornbluh, Anna. *The Order of Forms: Realism, Formalism, and Social Space*. Chicago: U of Chicago P, 2019.

Lukács, Georg. "Dostoevsky." *Dostoevsky: A Collection of Critical Essays*. Ed. René Wellek. Englewood Cliffs: Prentice Hall, 1962. 146–58.

Maris, Bernard. *Houellebecq économiste*. Paris: Flammarion, 2014.

McClanahan, Annie. *Dead Pledges: Debt, Crisis, and Twenty-First Century Culture*. Stanford: Stanford UP, 2017.

Musil, Robert. "Das Hilflose Europa oder Reise vom Hundertsten ins Tausendste." (1922). *Gesammelte Werke*. Vol. 8. Hamburg: Rowohlt, 1978. 1075–94.

Rahman, Zia Haider. *In the Light of What We Know*. New York: Farrar, Straus and Giroux, 2014.

Sassen, Saskia. *Expulsions: Brutality and Complexity in the Global Economy.* Cambridge, MA: Harvard UP, 2014.

Streeck, Wolfgang. "How Will Capitalism End?" *New Left Review* 87 (2014): 35–64.

VINCENT MESSAGE

Translated by Cole Swensen

And Suddenly I Owed Nothing / Je ne devais plus rien

And Suddenly I Owed Nothing

*I*t was the morning of the seventh, and there was still a lot of money in my account. That seemed strange. My mortgage is paid on the fifth. The salary deposited at the very end of the month goes out just as it came in, to pay off the mortgage. I went online to check my account, but the lines had disappeared, the credit lines and the credit history. And given that banks are never late about such things, and given that they don't make mistakes, at least not in our favor, and given that I'm not naïve, I realized that a Russian hacker or perhaps an Anonymous hacker had gotten into the bank's system and erased from the bank's memory all traces of the intimate, or at least privileged, relationship that I'd developed with that bank. I knew neither his name nor his face. And he'd probably not done it in the dark of night, masked or wearing a balaclava, but perhaps had done it this very morning, sitting in front of his screen at breakfast in his Russian slouchwear, dipping his toast in his coffee with the little anonymous eyes of those to whom the world belongs.

I should have been happy, I who suddenly owed nothing, but in fact, I was completely unnerved.

Volume 31, Number 3   DOI 10.1215/10407391-8744483

I went out into the city; I went out for a walk.

In town, I met the one who owes nobody anything. The one who owes nobody anything did not owe me an explanation. But he must have thought I looked like a nice guy, as he took me aside and explained. His mother had nursed him because, having wanted him, she certainly owed him that. His nanny had taken good care of him because his parents had paid her to do so. The State had made him go to school because the State needs competent executives and enlightened citizens. On the day of his twenty-fifth birthday, his parents had given the one who owes nobody anything a bill detailing all the food, clothing, schooling, and medical expenses that his upbringing had entailed. The son had made his way in the world, worked hard, and paid it all back. He no longer sees his parents, he has no children, and he owes nobody anything. He is his own master; he has his own business, which is going pretty well and could even be really flourishing if taxes weren't ripping him off, if the State didn't abscond with all that money, which he'd made by the sweat of his brow—and for the explicitly stated reason of giving it to those who don't have any sweat on their brows. He who owes nobody anything does realize that he owes *a lot* to the tax accountants that he pays to keep him out of the clutches of the tax collectors. No two ways about it, he finds the tax men extremely taxing. And he advises me to get good advice. Bad advice, he says, and you get ripped off for sure. Good advice, and life can be palm-treed, islanded, and water-skied, lightly salted and slightly sandy.

I rushed off to the newsstand.

I opened the newspaper, and the paper said that the State accounts were all empty; there was no more money. And when the news agent told me that he was closing his doors for good, that he had no more business, I saw what it meant for the French baby. The French debt is around two thousand billion euros. Each French baby at birth, simply by virtue of having been born, takes on his or her little part of the debt, which is thirty thousand euros. But each French baby also owns his or her little part of the public wealth, which is worth fifty thousand euros. The French baby's balance sheet is in the black. The French baby is not starting off the worst in this life. And yet, the French baby is not someone who owes nobody anything. The French baby owes a lot but doesn't know to whom she owes it. About 60 percent of her debt is in fact held by investors who don't live in France. The French baby knows neither their names nor their faces. She doesn't know how they smell. The French baby's stroller is held by, who knows? maybe an insurance company in Germany. Her bed and play mat, perhaps by a bank in Qatar. Exploring the question further, the French baby, always perspicacious, realizes that the question cannot be explored further, that the Treasury has no way of knowing exactly who holds the Treasury's bonds, and to such an extent that, on a world map, no one knows exactly where the Treasury is. We need to mount a search.

I went to the library.

In my life up to that point, I hadn't wanted to think too much about money; it hadn't seemed like a good thing to think about. I had wanted to be worth more than that, to have other values, but I told myself that, all the same, money was there all around us, and it seemed strange to not know where it came from. I asked the Internet, and the Internet told me. I learned that it was the banks' giving credit that created the money through book-entry transactions. And that these transactions had been transacting since the beginning, since Mesopotamia, where clay tablets had first been used to keep accounts. And that writing had been invented so that no one could forget who owed what to whom. I learned that in times of war, when in the army, when watching an army file by, when traveling far, or when dealing with people that you'll probably never see again, it's best to pay cash. On the other hand, in times of peace, or at least times of relative calm, and when dealing with people that you know aren't going to simply up and disappear, people you know how to find again, or people you're actually related to, money is, above all, debt. I had to accept the fact that more financial documents have circulated in the world than love letters.

In the library cafeteria, I met a student who didn't have enough money for coffee. He'd given up law school. He lived on junk food and didn't take care of himself. He never went to the dentist or the eye doctor because he knew he'd never get reimbursed, and even though he got a housing allowance from the government, he was up to his neck in debt to his landlady and tried to avoid her. He was a young Russian student who'd come on an exchange program, a scrawny guy from the banks of the Neva who, from his earliest childhood, had gotten used to walking on ice and chopping firewood. He was pale, really pale, because you get pale when there's nothing to eat. I inspired his confidence; he wanted to confide in someone. He told me that, to make a bit of cash, he'd taken to pawning all his belongings, one by one. The other day, he'd sold a silver watch with a steel chain, for which he'd wanted four rubles, but the old woman wouldn't give him more than a ruble and a half, holding back the interest in advance. He spoke slowly, heavily; he didn't know how to live with the anxiety that he had to live with, and he had nowhere to go. He told me that, the other day, he'd taken a silver cigarette case to the pawnbroker, telling himself that as far as tobacco went, it was time to quit. And as she was looking the object over, he'd almost effort- lessly, almost mechanically, buried a hatchet in her skull. And when the old woman's sister walked in and saw the hatchet, he'd picked it up again and, in order to avoid complications, had split her head open as well. He told me that he'd thought, as he was committing this double murder, that he should probably not be doing what he was, in fact, doing. He said, you see what it is to have nowhere to go. I inspired his confidence; he wanted to advise me. He said don't trust Russian loans and don't trust the Russian media. Stay away from Russian winters, Russian hackers, and Russian prostitutes. Watch out for Russian novelists. Rebellion leads them to labor camps, and labor camps lead them to novels. A weakness for gambling leads them to casinos, casinos lead to debt, and debt leads to novels. Studies lead to debt, and debt leads to hatchets. Watch out for Rodion Romanovitch, he advised me. Rodion Raskolnikov. But when I asked him to spell it, he took out his cigarette case, found it empty, and said he'd be back—he was just going to the bar around the corner—he'd be right back.

Out on the street, I met an idealistic woman looking for a taxi, her hair disheveled from the light rain coming in off the Atlantic. She had desires, this idealistic woman, ambitions; she didn't want just to survive; she wanted to live with a certain degree of intensity. She was looking for a taxi. She'd wanted to get married in a stunning wedding gown, with a multitiered wedding cake and an acutely cool DJ; she'd wanted a beautiful house with a beautiful garden a bit outside of town, and a small motor boat to try waterskiing on that river they call the Seine and make waves. She'd wanted to feel like the owner rather than like someone who had to pay rent to a landlady that she'd want to avoid later. She'd been seduced by the pros- pect of watching the slow reduction of the percentage of interest and capital remaining due, even though she was fully aware that it was being reduced at exactly the same rate as the time she had left to live. While in the house, in order to forget the rain (for it rains sometimes in Normandy), she'd needed a porcelain dinner service, thick, spongy carpeting, and upholstery and clothing of the richest materials. When she went into town, she'd needed a horse-drawn carriage racing along the paving stones, and then the young lover who was so good at emptying glasses of champagne and having wild sex at the Hôtel de Boulogne. The idealistic woman had a suboptimal life but forced herself to maintain it at a certain degree of intensity. She no longer had any desire for her suboptimal husband, who ran around the country- side treating suboptimal patients who never remembered to pay. She liked to read love letters, not financial documents. She signed promissory notes without looking at their due dates, never read anything in fine print, and knew that there was a grace period but never had the grace to use it. She had desires, ambitions; she wanted to live with a certain degree of intensity. When I ran into her, she'd already been selling hats for some time, haggling with a rapacity more in line with the peasantry than the bourgeoisie, more a shopkeeper, to be frank, than a water-skier. She took her silver-gilt tea-spoons to the pawnshop so that she could keep on making love in carriages and drinking champagne at the Hôtel de Boulogne. She made the rounds of her lovers, who wouldn't give her a cent because they'd already screwed her, and the rounds of possible creditors, who'd only give her money if she'd sleep with them. The situation was suboptimal, not at the level of her desires and not as vivid as her dreams, which is the way things were when I found her looking for a taxi, or perhaps a handsome cab, or a horse-drawn carriage, to take her to the pharmacy, head down, her hair in disarray from the light rain, with the brilliant notion that stuffing herself with poison, that eating arsenic by the handful, would somehow help.

       I went to the bank to try to understand what was going on, who had deleted my lines of credit. I wasn't sure that I should be doing what I was, in fact, doing, but I suddenly owed nothing, and that unnerved me completely. You're lucky that I could meet with you without an appointment, said my banker, reproachfully. You're not the only person with a degree in the humanities and very few prospects that I've got on my plate, said my banker, reassuringly. As for your credit . . . she smiled. And, I feared, evasively. The banker plunked a beaker of Russian vodka down in front of me strong enough to split your skull and thaw your Neva. They aren't hackers, she said. They aren't Russian prostitutes. She poured herself a glass and downed it straight. It's the billionaires. You don't know it, you young humanities graduates with very few prospects, but billionaires have always been built in two stages. At the beginning of their lives, she said, smiling, at the beginning of their lives, they exploit: their social capital, the sweat of their brow, their intuition and insight, numerous loopholes, their family connections, their persuasive flair, politicians' appetite for lucre, other people's need of money, other people's strength, other people's work potential, other people's intuition and insight, and other people's professional conscience. She poured herself a glass and downed it straight. Billionaires have desires, ambitions. They don't want just to survive; they want to live with a certain degree of intensity. But once they have money, all that changes. Not always, but often. Ambition leads them to billions, and billions lead them to philanthropy. They wipe out malaria and polio; denounce growing inequalities; encourage, if not doctors in remote rural areas, then at least young cabinetmakers and graceful cellists; they argue for tax reductions for productive investments and foster the projects of great foundations that perch on our cities' edges like huge glass birds. And sometimes they come to us, without an appointment, open up our books, down a shot of vodka straight, close their eyes, and point to the debts that they'd like us to erase. They do that; they like doing that. And you, you young humanities graduates with very few prospects, you thankless curs, you have no idea, really, you have no idea what you owe them.

■

Je ne devais plus rien

Ce matin on était le 7 et il y avait encore plein d'argent sur mon compte. J'ai trouvé cela étrange. Le 5 du mois l'argent du crédit part. Le salaire tombé à la toute fin du mois repart comme il est venu pour rembourser le crédit. J'ai consulté mon compte en ligne mais les lignes avaient disparu, les lignes du crédit, l'historique du crédit. Et comme sur ces opérations les banques n'ont pas de retard, comme elles ne font pas d'erreur, ou pas en notre faveur, et comme je ne suis pas naïf, j'ai compris qu'un hacker russe ou anonymus s'était introduit dans le système de la banque et avait effacé de la mémoire de la banque tous les souvenirs de la relation intime ou en tout cas privilégiée que j'entretenais avec cette banque. Je ne connaissais ni son nom, ni son visage. Il n'avait peut-être en fin de compte pas fait ça nuitamment, masqué ou cagoulé, mais tôt ce matin plutôt, assis devant son écran et son petit-déjeuner, dans sa tenue de lose russe, en plongeant sa tartine dans un mug de café avec les petits yeux anonymus de ceux à qui le monde appartient.

J'aurais dû être content, moi qui ne devais plus rien, mais j'étais trop déboussolé.

Je suis sorti dans la ville, je suis sorti marcher.

En ville j'ai rencontré celui qui ne doit rien à personne. Celui qui ne doit rien à personne ne me devait pas d'explications. J'ai dû lui paraître sympathique, néanmoins, vu qu'il m'a pris à part et qu'il m'a expliqué. Sa mère l'a allaité parce que l'ayant voulu elle lui devait bien ça. Sa nourrice s'est occupée de lui parce que ses parents la payaient. L'État l'a obligé à aller à l'école car l'État a besoin de cadres compétents et de citoyens éclairés. Le jour de ses vingt-cinq ans, celui qui ne doit rien à personne s'est vu remettre par ses parents la liste des frais alimentaires, des frais vestimentaires, des frais scolaires et des frais médicaux engagés jusqu'alors pour son éducation. Le fils a travaillé, il a fait son chemin et a tout remboursé. Il ne voit plus ses parents et il n'a pas d'enfants, il ne doit rien à personne. Il est fils de ses œuvres, il est son propre chef, il a sa propre affaire qui ne marche pas trop mal, qui pourrait même marcher vraiment si les impôts le matraquaient moins, si l'État ne faisait pas preuve d'autant de sensiblerie en confisquant ce fric qu'il a acquis à la force du poignet, dans le but de le refiler à ceux qui n'ont pas de force dans les poignets. Celui qui ne doit rien à personne reconnaît devoir beaucoup aux fiscalistes qu'il paye pour lui mettre à l'abri ce que le fisc veut confisquer. Il me dit qu'il faut bien reconnaître que le fisc est confiscatoire. Il me conseille aussi de me faire conseiller. Mal conseillé, dit-il, c'est le matraquage assuré. Bien conseillé, la vie peut-être cocotière, insulaire et ski-nautiquière, délicatement salée et légèrement sablée.

J'ai couru jusqu'au kiosque.

J'ai ouvert les journaux et les journaux disaient que les caisses de l'État sont vides, qu'il n'y a plus d'argent. Et tandis que le kiosquier me racontait qu'il mettait la clé sous la porte, qu'il n'avait plus de clients, j'ai appris pour le bébé français. La dette française est d'environ deux mille milliards d'euros. Chaque bébé français quand il naît détient, pour s'être donné cette simple peine de naître, sa petite part de dette, qui est de trente mille euros. Mais chaque bébé français possède aussi sa petite part du patrimoine public, soit cinquante mille euros. Le solde du bébé français est positif. Le bébé français n'est pas celui qui part le plus mal dans la vie. Le bébé français néanmoins n'est pas quelqu'un qui ne doit rien à personne. Le bébé français doit beaucoup, mais ne sait pas à qui il doit. Sa dette en effet est détenue à soixante pour cent environ par des investisseurs qui ne résident pas en France. Le bébé français ne connaît ni leur nom, ni leur visage. Il ne connaît pas leur odeur. La poussette du bébé français est si ça se trouve détenue par un fonds d'assurance allemand. Son lit et son tapis d'éveil, par un fonds souverain qatari. En se renseignant mieux, le bébé français, très éveillé, a découvert qu'on ne pouvait pas se renseigner mieux, que le Trésor n'a pas le droit d'identifier précisément les détenteurs de bons du Trésor, si bien que sur la carte du monde on ne sait pas où est le Trésor : il faut chercher.

Je suis entré dans la bibliothèque.

Dans ma vie jusqu'alors je n'avais pas voulu trop penser à l'argent, je ne trouvais pas bien d'y penser, je voulais valoir mieux que ça, avoir d'autres valeurs, mais je me disais tout de même que l'argent était là partout autour de nous et je trouvais bizarre de ne pas savoir d'où il venait. J'ai demandé à internet et internet m'a dit. J'ai compris que c'étaient les banques accordant des crédits qui créaient la monnaie par un jeu d'écriture. Que ce jeu se jouait depuis le début, depuis la Mésopotamie où les tablettes servaient d'abord à tenir le compte des dettes. Que l'écriture s'était inventée pour que personne ne puisse oublier qui devait quoi à qui. J'ai appris qu'en période de guerre, quand on voyageait loin, qu'on était dans l'armée ou qu'on voyait passer l'armée et qu'on traitait avec des gens qu'on ne recroiserait jamais, il valait mieux payer comptant, en pièces sonnantes et trébuchantes. Mais que lorsque c'était la paix, ou un peu plus calme en tout cas, lorsqu'on faisait affaire avec des gens qui ne disparaissaient pas comme ça, qu'on savait où trouver, auxquels on était liés, l'argent c'était surtout la dette. J'ai dû me faire à l'idée qu'il circulait dans le monde plus de documents financiers que de lettres d'amour.

À la cafétéria de la bibliothèque, j'ai rencontré un étudiant qui n'avait pas d'argent pour s'offrir un café. Il décrochait de ses cours de droit. Il mangeait de la *junk food* et il se soignait mal. Ses frais optiques, ses frais dentaires étaient mal remboursés. Même s'il touchait les APL, il était endetté jusqu'au cou auprès de sa logeuse et ne voulait plus la croiser. C'était un jeune étudiant russe venu par un programme d'échange, un jeune mec efflanqué des bords de la Neva, habitué depuis gamin à marcher sur la glace et à fendre des bûches. Il était pâle, tout pâle parce qu'on est pâle quand il n'y a rien à manger. Je lui inspirais confiance, il voulait se confier. Il m'a dit que pour se faire du cash, il se dépouillait peu à peu de ses biens matériels chez une prêteuse sur gages. Il lui a apporté l'autre jour une montre en argent dont la chaînette était d'acier, dont il voulait quatre roubles, mais dont la vieille ne lui a donné qu'un rouble cinquante, en retenant les intérêts d'avance. Il avait la langue lourde, ne savait plus cohabiter avec l'angoisse qui l'habitait et n'avait nulle part où aller. Il m'a dit que l'autre jour, il a apporté à la vieille un porte-cigarettes en argent, en se disant que côté tabac ce serait l'occasion d'arrêter. Et pendant qu'elle regardait le gage, quasiment sans effort, presque machinalement, il a laissé retomber une hache sur son crâne. Et quand la sœur de la vieille est arrivée et a regardé la hache, il a levé de nouveau la hache et pour ne pas se créer de complications, a fendu son crâne également. Il m'a avoué qu'en perpétrant ce double assassinat, il avait pensé qu'il ne fallait peut-être pas du tout faire ce qu'il était en train de faire. Il m'a dit, vous savez ce que c'est, quand on n'a nulle part où aller. Je lui inspirais confiance, il voulait me conseiller. Il m'a dit ne faites confiance ni aux emprunts russes ni aux médias russes. Gardez-vous de l'hiver russe, des hackers russes et des prostituées russes. Méfiez-vous des romanciers russes. La rébellion les mène au bagne et le bagne au roman. Le goût du jeu les mène au casino, le casino à la dette et la dette au roman. Les études les mènent à la dette et la dette les mène à la hache. Méfiez-vous de Rodion Romanovitch, m'a-t-il avoué. Rodion Raskolnikov. Mais quand je lui ai demandé d'épeler, il a sorti son porte-cigarettes, s'est rendu compte qu'il était vide et m'a dit qu'il revenait, qu'il allait juste au bar-tabac et qu'ensuite il revenait.

Sur le boulevard, les cheveux défaits par le crachin qui venait de l'Atlantique, j'ai rencontré la femme idéaliste qui cherchait un taxi. Elle avait des désirs, la femme idéaliste, des ambitions, elle ne voulait pas survivre seulement mais vivre à un certain degré d'intensité, elle cherchait un taxi. Elle avait voulu le mariage avec la robe qui impressionne, la pièce montée étouffe-chrétienne et le DJ qui va bien, la belle maison avec le beau jardin à l'écart de la ville, le petit bateau à moteur pour s'essayer au ski nautique sur ce fleuve qui s'appelle la Seine et pour y faire des vagues. Cela la rehaussait de se sentir propriétaire plutôt que de verser un loyer à une logeuse qu'ensuite on n'aime pas trop croiser. Cela la séduisait de voir diminuer lentement la part des intérêts et le capital restant dû, même si elle avait pleine conscience que diminuait en même temps son espérance de vie. Lorsqu'elle était à la maison, il lui fallait pour oublier la pluie (parfois il pleut en Normandie) le service en porcelaine, le moelleux des tapis, l'étoffe pour les fauteuils et l'étoffe pour les robes. Quand elle allait en ville, il lui fallait le fiacre roulant à toute berzingue sur les pavés, puis le jeune amant qui va bien pour vider des coupes de champagne et s'envoyer en l'air à l'hôtel de Boulogne. La femme idéaliste avait une vie sous-optimale, mais s'efforçait de la maintenir à un certain degré d'intensité. Elle n'avait plus de désir pour son mari sous-optimal, qui battait la campagne pour des patients crasseux qui oubliaient de payer. Elle aimait lire des lettres d'amour, pas des documents financiers, elle signait les billets sans s'enquérir des échéances, ne regardait pas les conditions écrites en trop petits caractères, savait qu'elle avait le droit à un délai de rétractation mais ne se rétractait jamais. Elle avait des désirs, des ambitions, elle voulait vivre à un certain degré d'intensité. Quand je l'ai rencontrée, cela faisait longtemps déjà qu'elle vendait ses chapeaux en marchandant avec une rapacité paysanne plutôt que bourgeoise, boutiquière à vrai dire plus que ski-nautiquière. Elle portait au mont-de-piété des cuillères en vermeil pour continuer de faire l'amour dans les fiacres et de boire le champagne à l'hôtel de Boulogne. Elle faisait le tour de ses amants qui ne lui donnaient pas d'argent parce qu'ils l'avaient déjà sautée, le tour des créanciers possibles qui ne voulaient lui donner de l'argent que si elle consentait à baiser. Comme la situation était sous-optimale, pas à la hauteur de ses désirs et pas aux couleurs de ses rêves, telle que je la voyais elle cherchait un taxi, ou bien une diligence, un fiacre, pour filer à la pharmacie, la tête baissée, les cheveux défaits par le crachin, dans l'idée ingénieuse de s'empiffrer de poison, de manger à pleines poignées l'arsenic qui va bien.

Je me suis rendu à la banque pour essayer de comprendre ce qui se passait, qui avait effacé les lignes de mon crédit. Je n'étais pas du tout sûr qu'il fallait faire ce que j'étais en train de faire, mais je ne devais plus rien et j'étais trop déboussolé. Vous avez de la chance que je reçoive sans rendez-vous, m'a admonesté la banquière. Vous n'êtes pas le seul jeune client littéraire à faible potentiel de développement que j'ai en portefeuille, m'a rasséréné la banquière. Quant à votre crédit . . . m'a-t-elle souri. J'ai craint à ce moment-là une réponse de Normande. La banquière a poussé devant moi un shot de vodka russe à vous fendre le crâne et à vous dégeler la Neva. Ce ne sont pas les hackers, elle a dit. Ce ne sont pas les prostituées russes. Elle s'est servie un verre et elle l'a gobé sec. Ce sont les milliardaires. Vous ne savez pas ça, vous les jeunes clients littéraires à faible potentiel, mais les milliardaires de tout temps se sont construits en deux temps. Au début de leur vie, a-t-elle souri, au début de leur vie ils exploitent: leur capital social, la force de leurs poignets, leurs intuitions et eurêka, les failles réglementaires, le carnet d'adresses de leurs parents, le goût du lucre des politiques, leurs talents de persuasion, la force de travail des autres, le besoin vital d'argent des autres, la force physique des autres, les intuitions et eurêka des autres, la grande conscience professionnelle des autres. Elle s'est servie un verre et elle l'a gobé sec. Les milliardaires ont des désirs, des ambitions. Ils ne veulent pas survivre seulement mais vivre à un certain degré d'intensité. Une fois qu'ils ont l'argent, ça change. Pas tout le temps mais parfois. L'ambition les mène aux milliards et les milliards à la philanthropie. Ils éradiquent la malaria et la poliomyélite, dénoncent l'augmentation des inégalités, encouragent, si ce n'est les médecins de campagne, du moins les jeunes ébénistes et les gracieuses violoncellistes, plaident pour la suppression de l'impôt sur l'investissement productif, jettent les plans de fondations qui se posent au bord de nos villes sans faire de vagues, comme de grands oiseaux de verre. Parfois ils viennent chez nous sans prendre rendez-vous, ouvrent les livres de compte, gobent une vodka cul sec, ferment les yeux et pointent du doigt des dettes qu'ils nous demandent d'annuler. Ils font cela, ils aiment faire cela. Vous les jeunes clients littéraires à faible potentiel, vous êtes de beaux ingrats. Vous ne savez pas, vraiment, vous ne savez pas ce que vous leur devez.

VINCENT MESSAGE is an associate professor of comparative literature and creative writing at the University of Paris 8 Saint-Denis. His book *Romanciers pluralistes* (Seuil, 2013) is devoted to twentieth-century novels that stage value conflicts and aims to provide a basis for the notion of pluralism in literary theory. He has published three novels: *Les Veilleurs* (Seuil, 2009) was a finalist for the Goncourt for a Debut Novel; *Défaite des maîtres et possesseurs* (Points, 2016) was awarded the Orange Literature Prize; *Cora dans la spirale* (Seuil, 2019) was short listed for the Renaudot and Médicis prizes. His research deals with the social and environmental effects of capitalism and with the ways in which ecology makes it possible to renew the critique of capitalism.

COLE SWENSEN is a poet, translator, editor, and critical writer. She has won the PEN USA Award in Literary Translation and a number of awards for her own poetry, including the Iowa Poetry Prize and the San Francisco State University Poetry Center Book Award.

The Debt Narrative and the Credit Crunch of Democracy

A Rosetta Stone

*T*here are many good stories of debt, including some very famous ones. Everybody knows the story of the man who's long been absent for obscure professional reasons, and who realizes when he's back home that so-called suitors have tried to seduce his wife, chase off his son, harass his dog, and, above all, lay waste to his wealth (they are his debtors in so many ways). He takes revenge by slaughtering them (that's something they used to do at that time), which gets him into debt with all the big *patres familias* of the city, so he has to leave again, with an oar on his back. It's Odysseus, of course: the first indebted man at the birth of Literature. There is also the story of that other man who, assured of his impunity, never stops taking out debts, playing language tricks, and contracting mock marriages, till he has to face the fact that he's in debt not only to women and the whole of mankind but also to a transcendent authority, an archaic *deus ex machina* Commander-Father that he refuses to believe in. This is Dom Juan: hero and victim of the abiding play about belief. But my favorite story is the one about the gifted guy who frees a community of its rat scourge with a simple pipe; then, as no one would pay him back, he takes his fee by leading all

Volume 31, Number 3   DOI 10.1215/10407391-8744497

the children (except one) to *the sweet hereafter* of the promised land where all debts are settled. The Pied Piper of Hamelin. Take pity on the lame one who could not "dance the whole of the way," says Robert Browning in his poem (182): stuck in the real world, he can't hope for a better future, as Russell Banks put it in "Feeding Moloch: The Sacrifice of Children at the Altar of Capitalism," a beautiful lecture I had the privilege of attending at the Harvard Divinity School in November 2014.

Literature is a huge collection of narratives about debts—as are mythology and philosophy. "To Be or Not to Be in Debt" is a choice these fields have addressed since antiquity, and we may remember that Rabelais did so in the *Tiers livre*, when Pantagruel asks Panurge: "When will you be out of debt?"—"God forbid that I should ever be out of debt!" answers Panurge (qtd. in Graeber 126). According to David Graeber, "Panurge [. . .] serves as a fitting prophet for the world that was just beginning to emerge" (126).

All of Shakespeare's plays (including the somber to-be-or-not-be story of insolvent blood debts on the fringe of Europe) and the whole *Comédie humaine* by Balzac (*Gobseck, César Birotteau, La maison Nucingen, Eugénie Grandet, Le faiseur*, to name a few) are rife with debt narratives, which may still be accurate today—as Thomas Piketty argues in *Capital in the Twenty-First Century*—or may not be, if we consider that "credit-crisis" fiction can't be as realistic as it used to be.

Why Is This Debt Narrative So Essential?

According to the French theory of "primordial debt" (Michel Aglietta, André Orléan, Bruno Théret): "It's not that we owe 'society.' [. . .] Society *is* our debts" (Graeber 136).[1] Debt narrative is one of the primordial modes of causal representation of society and of textual embodiment of morality: "Arguments about who really owes what to whom have played a central role in shaping our basic vocabulary of right and wrong" (8). Narratives of debt are the way society tells its tale.

That's why the debt narrative strictly articulates the power of authority, the empire of calculation, and the practice of violence—as in Livy (*History of Rome*, book 2, chapter 23), when the debt slave shows the injuries on his body in order for them to amount to a repayment: the body itself becomes a narrative of debt and a plea for its cancellation (289–95).

As such, the debt narrative is not a simple figure of speech, literature, or thought: it acts powerfully in the real world. What is the Golden Legend of the *Conquista*? It is the mythical flipside of another story: that of a genocidal adventure led by indebted soldiers to erase what they owe and to provide infinite wealth to even more heavily indebted European kingdoms. Many wars can be narrated as debt exports. Colonization can be viewed as systemic debt slavery. And revolutions always "took the form of pleas for debt cancellation," notes Graeber, "the freeing of those in bondage and, usually, a more just reallocation of the land" (87). Ever since Solon, the first step of democracy in Europe has always been debt cancellation. And eighteenth-century French and American revolutionaries thought that the debts of one generation should not have to be a burden for the next. But on the other hand, narratives of colonial debt and "ecological debt" also tell us of irreducible debts, debts without the possibility of negotiation or redemption, for future generations burdened by the past.

So, let's consider the debt narrative as a sort of Rosetta Stone, like the one that allowed Champollion to decipher hieroglyphics by comparing three different versions of a single text, the first one written in hieroglyphics ("the language of the gods"), the second one in demotic Egyptian ("the language of documents"), and the third one in Greek ("the language of communication"): three versions of a decree (a statutory order) that settled the credit and debt accounts of the Ptolemaic Priests in Memphis.

Quite like the Rosetta Stone, the debt narrative is a historical, symbolic, and aesthetic way for us to decipher the interfaces between the three languages of economy, politics, and ethics.

To Repay or Not to Repay (That Is the Question)

At the very core of this Rosetta narrative lies the principle of the acknowledgment of debts: the famous IOU ("I Owe You"). The debt narrative is an *IOU narrative*. That's why literature likes it so much: it may model the interaction between the author and the reader right through the diegetic credit-and-debt plot—or its failure.[2] The IOU is the active ingredient of the debt narrative in any good causal story.[3]

But does the IOU imply the need for repayment? Graeber mentions "one puzzling aspect of the equation" that led Henry II to invent "the first successful modern central bank," the Bank of England: "Henry's IOU can operate as money only as long as Henry never pays his debt" (49). Becoming a debt-money narrative, the IOU ceased to imply a full repayment.

The general axiology of this (non)necessity of repayment is a complicated issue that has been around ever since Socrates, who argued on this matter with Cephalus and Polemarchus in the *Republic* (book 1, 331c) and concluded that justice can't simply be repaying one's debts (Shell 21–22). Let's think about the odd "morality" of repayment that prevails in the Sicilian or Neapolitan *vendetta*, still current today, which is represented as the inheritance of ancient "blood money." To repay one's debts can't be a strict guarantee of justice and the necessary end of all debt narratives because these narratives depend not only on guilt, power, and authority but also on violence, sexuality, and domination.

So: instead of "to be or not to be in debt" (who is not, after all?), we should rather say: "to repay or not to repay one's debt," that is the question. This is obvious in philosophical debates, especially in the post-Nietzschean critique of "infinite debt," as in Deleuze and Guattari's *Anti-Oedipus* or in Derrida's *Given Time* (which challenges Marcel Mauss's essay, *The Gift*),[4] and more recently in Maurizio Lazzarato's *The Making of the Indebted Man*.[5] On the other side of Mauss-inspired anthropology, Philippe Rospabé, in *La Dette de vie: aux origines de la monnaie sauvage*, argues that "primitive money is not originally a way to pay debts of any sort. It's a way of recognizing the existence of debts that cannot possibly be paid," like the *bride-wealth* (qtd. in Graeber 131). These debates also exist on the margins of law. For example, according to the formal doctrine of "odious debt," as Odette Lienau puts it in *Rethinking Sovereign Debt*, "a fallen regime's debt need not be repaid if it was not authorized by and did not benefit the underlying population"; such was the case of the repudiation of the tsarist debt after 1917. "In other words," says Lienau, "debt should not be continuous in some cases" (9). In any case, it seems to me that we could consider two different debt-narrative possibilities, two different ways for cultural forms to connect consumer debt experiences to global economies and to articulate *oikonomia*, *polis*, and *ethos* (domestic, political, and moral economies).

On the one hand: *to repay debts is an obligation* (that is, a necessity). This is manifest in the teleological story of debt as *Schuld*, the soteriology of repayment as ethical reparation (see Nietzsche 39–40). The *telos* of responsibility has two versions: there is the spiritual or religious one, modeled on the story of the Last Judgment with its overwhelming narrative posterity, which extends through to recent apocalyptic sci-fi stories; the other is secular and *bourgeois*, a morality of double-entry bookkeeping (Kluge and Vogl 30) leading to a naturalist, or a behaviorist, model that could still be "too omniscient to fail," as Annie McClanahan brilliantly puts it (42). On the other hand: unpaid debts create an obligation in the etymological sense of a literal *bond*;[6] and this implies other ways of representing time and redistributing the future: either valuing and "securitizing" risks, scoring credits, trafficking in insurance (cat bonds and credit default swaps included), as in the big-short stories of finance heroism; or facing at best the spirit of uncertainty that Arjun Appadurai argues in favor of (522–24)—a spirit, an *ethos*, or an imaginary of uncertainty, which is, in my opinion, the very principle of any true literary engagement (Bouju).

This may be the way the debt narratives of our times embody the anthropology of the global condition. And in "credit-crisis fiction" (McClanahan 16–18), they may be inventing a poetics of insolvency, or maybe a poetics as insolvency, if we consider that no author ever gives back to the reader what was initially promised and that it is precisely the profit of narrative credit to be liquidated with floating interest that one would never be able to "probabilize."

A New Abduction of Europe?

What happens today to the debt narrative in this Europe of the hard Brexit? Could the debt narrative still be useful to Europe as a way to address its foundations and values, its active principles and purposes (if they exist)? For the "debt crisis" is not only an economic, political, and ethical crisis of value, equality, and confidence, as I have mentioned; it is also a symbolic and aesthetic crisis.

It may be recalled, on that note, that the *symbolon* was invented precisely "as a token of agreement" in debt matters. As Marc Shell put it in *The Economy of Literature*: "*Symbola* were pledges, pawns, or covenants from an earlier understanding to bring together a part of something that had been divided specifically for the purpose of later comparison" (33). Such a *symbolon* could be a ring coin (*sphragis*): one that can easily be broken in two. Or later, as in Henry's times, when it served "as token of debt owed to the government," it could be in the shape of a tally stick, with a stock and a stub (of course).

So what we are facing today in Europe may be the political and symbolic confrontation between two leading debt narratives: the story of necessary repayment and the story of an inevitable cancellation of debts (or at least interest on debts), with in both cases a risk of breaking apart. This is, for instance, Thomas Piketty's argument: since the European Union was built on the *fiducia* of a cancellation (or a *sine die* postponement) of the odious French and (especially) German debts after World War II,[7] we cannot consider debt (especially Greek debt) outside the context of this fiduciary story about origins; and thus, we all need to face the possibility, if not cancellation, of at least *debt pooling* on the largest possible scale. Piketty suggests signing a new treaty for the democratization of the Eurozone ("Manifesto"),[8] which would decide the rhythm of repayment and, moreover, allow for relying on a special European tax system for funding higher education, social solidarity, and ecological transformations.

As for me, I'm trying to understand what part literature plays in this debate. How does it fight against the sophistic trend of political discourse and the neoliberal increase in inequality? How can it save us from the magical thinking of the financial ethos and help us imagine what a deep democracy—"a democracy of suffering and confidence," as Appadurai puts it (304–5)—could be in Europe today?

It can be seen that, in European novels today, the pressure of (sovereign and individual) debts is quite systematically related to a lack of credibility of, and credit for, democracy and the future: a crisis of "defuturization," as Joseph Vogl put it in *The Specter of Capital* (125), emphasizing the way neocapitalism captured the very word *future*, turning it into a financial product; an agonistic conflict between violent probability patterns and the fragility of possible engagements, linked to the algorithmic articulation of time; and a credit crunch of democratic institutions and representations, which forbids the reunification of all social *symbola*. Among the many European novelistic examples of this relationship, I would highlight *Resistance Is Useless* (*Resistere non serve a niente*, 2012) by Walter Siti: an imaginary biographical portrait of a genius in international finance (Tommaso Aricò), who is secretly working for the Calabrian mafia (the *'ndrangheta*).

Credit Crunch

The phrase *credit crunch* is used to designate the "tightening" of credit, a sudden sharp reduction in the availability of money from banks and institutional lenders due to an "unreasonable" rise of credit costs and to a lack of liquidities. In contemporary Europe, a credit crunch, as a crisis of sovereign debts that followed the global crash of subprime loans and derivative products, is weighing on the future of democracies. Even though the European Central Bank is trying to maintain low-interest loans to help systemically important banks keep their credit policies alive, the credibility of our economic sovereignty and solidarity has been seriously damaged— especially since the Greek crisis.[9]

This situation sets in motion an ancient mechanism: the one that lures individuals, companies, or communities to noninstitutional lenders during credit and liquidity crises. The large-scale practice of usury (usury and violence for recovering debts) is one of the most traditional and efficient businesses of mob organizations. And literature and narrative forms in general (see season 3 of the series *Fargo*) have, since Shylock, always been attracted to usurers and to usury-related plots.

But nowadays, the links between highly technologized finance and mafia have become deeply enmeshed—and this is one of the themes at the very core of Siti's *Resistance Is Useless*:

> *The mutation seemed to be minimal, but it included a change of strategy: to deal less with businesses and stocks [. . .] and ride the second-degree finance wave [nuotare nella finanza di secondo grado], between the fluctuations of the eurodollar and the jumps and starts of interbank loans [le capriole dei prestiti interbancari]; and to go after masterless money [inseguire denaro senza padrone], pure nominal values without origins [pura nominalità senza origine], "migrating money" ["soldi migratori"], as Boris used to say. "The world is indebted to itself, and we're going to take our cut." (Resistere 178; my translation)*

At one point, there is a conversation between Walter (who is the fictional alter ego of the writer) and the theoretician of the "new mafia," Morgan Lucchese. They talk about the link between covert mafia power and legally acquired wealth, a link that Roberto Saviano had already described in *Gomorra*. This link promises to become endlessly stronger with the advances of accelerated calculation systems and dematerialized finance:

> *The wave of fear that descended upon the markets after 9/11 (the crisis of airline companies, the suspended consumption) was decisive for the organization of the Web. And what is the Internet if not a web? That is the answer for the new century: no more battleships or blockades, but agile structures, knots linked together by spider webs. The remedies for the crisis are sivs, structured investment vehicles, and dark pools, platforms where money can pass through without leaving any trace. Whose money is it? Impossible to know in this misty bunch of acronyms [lì la titolarità dei Fondi sfuma in un polverio di sigle], of nested companies [società inscatolate], of risks to be eliminated and self-generating money through leverage operations [di azzardi da far sparire e di denaro che si autogenera mediante successive operazioni in leva]. (Resistere 256)*

It's not only a matter of marginal exploitation of the loopholes of neocapitalism by a few covert organizations: it's also a question of the very form that constitutes the contemporary economy, where the erasing (or the unreadability) of the traces of any transaction, and the noninstitutional financing of liquidities, allow for the "natural" insertion of mafias into the political texture of our societies and for the perversion of the democratic contract. As Lucchese says: "We have to become a background noise, not a metastasis but the normal tissue of the economy [*dobbiamo diventare un rumore di fondo, non una metastasi ma il tessuto normale dell'economia*] [. . .]. The future belongs to enlightened oligarchies that pass over the frontiers and the laws of any single State [*il futuro appartiene alle oligarchie illuminate che scavalcano i confini e le leggi dei singoli Stati*]" (*Resistere* 240–42).

One of Siti's goals is thus to cast light on this threat hanging over our democracies by writing the fictional biography of a gifted trader, Tommaso Aricò, who has been involved in the mafia since his childhood: his father had to repay his debt to the *famiglia* by killing a traitor (the scene occurs in the prologue, titled "Before and After, Forever" ["Prima e dopo, per sempre"]). Tommaso, who thinks he therefore has "a debt to collect" (*un credito da riscuotere*), seeks protection from the 'ndrangheta that finances his advanced studies in mathematics. Eventually, he secretly works for the organization under the cover of a job at a hedge fund called Persona: his mask has become his true face.

Siti chooses to tell us about the contemporary truth of our masked reality through the character of Tommaso: it's a matter of putting a face on the mask, as Leonardo Sciascia would say. (*Il volto sulla maschera* [English translation: *The Face on the Mask*] is the title of a book published by Sciascia in 1980.) Siti's novel is a bildungsroman of the secretly *mafioso* constitution of late-capitalist economics.

In order to reach this goal, Siti has to find the right balance between theory and story. As in Saviano's *Gomorra*, but with very different stylistic and narrative solutions, he seeks an embodiment of the neocapitalist covert economy: he needs a body to incarnate the abstract technology of money circulation in the era of transnational Internet spaces. So, unlike Saviano, Siti chooses the protective screen of a fictional character but without sacrificing the polemical power of the essayistic form, which in this novel culminates in a *theorem* of neofascism:

> *Morgan knows, he's at the core of the theorem [*nel cuore del teorema*]: he hopes (like many others, more or less powerful than*

he is, more or less aware, all around the world) for a mixed, transnational regime, in which pop stars, drug lords, food cartels feel as though they were part of the same category of winners, the ones who knew how to make a profit from obligatory pleasure. An emerging desire layered on top of the fossilized desire of the old properties. No traceability whatsoever of personal wealth: dirty or clean, financiers will be the new prophets [direttori di coscienza]. *(Resistere 281)*

In this *teorema* of our times, Siti inherits Pasolini's fight against "the disappearance of the fireflies." It's not just a matter of fighting against the abstract and disembodied global power of high finance; it's a matter of fighting against the way this power weighs on the common body of democratic subjects:

Their superiority over a sublimated and self-referring finance consisted and consists in not losing contact with the material economy [non perdere il contatto con l'economia concreta]: *ruined factories, unemployment, blood and land, the hopes and wastes of global desire* [le speranze e i rifiuti del desiderio globale]. *"We are the fulfilled formal model of finance* [Siamo il modello formale compiuto della finanza]. *Or its perfect complement: derivatives are phantom money* [i derivati sono soldi fantasma], *funeral shrouds looking for bodies* [lenzuoli che necessitano di un corpo]; *we are the bodies looking for a shroud."* (Resistere 260)

At stake here is the neofascist turn of formal democracies, accelerated by the secret art of speculation, whose phantom incarnation is Tommaso. Tommaso was born and raised under the empire of calculation: his father's debt has been converted, thanks to his superior gifts in mathematics, into an "infinite credit" under the auspices of the mafia. He seems to be the only one capable of understanding the enigmatic logics of derivative titles and CDSS (Credit Default Swaps) in the wake of the 2007 crisis; but he is also a libidinal monster whose devouring desires reflect the dynamics of finance. According to him: "risk-management models [. . .] are the very same mathematical models that demonstrate how atoms of calcium penetrate into the bones [*il penetrare degli atomi di calcio nelle ossa*]. Just like large-scale financial cycles obey the Fibonacci spiral ('we're at the core of nature'). Finance is mathematical like music: it's the music of desire when desire becomes concrete [*è la musica del desiderio quando il desiderio diventa concreto*]"

(*Resistere* 35). Tommaso is the golden ratio of underground finance; he's the exact flip side of McClanahan's "Living Indebted." His infinite credit balances the infinite debt of the democratic subject. He's the living incarnation of the ideology of antidemocratic indebtedness Graeber addressed when he wrote: "What is a debt, anyway? A debt is just the perversion of a promise. It is a promise corrupted by both math and violence" (391).

Tommaso is also a literary construction: inventing a "true" character, a multidimensional and ambiguous illegal creditor, is not only an achievement of the *'ndrangheta*; it is also a novelistic achievement that manages to make visible the "grey zone" and make audible the "background noise" (*rumore di fondo*) of the underground economy. But if, on the one hand, the presupposition that this is fiction allows us to think that this emblematic character is a literary object, constructed and fleshed out purely in writing, then on the other hand, the whole narrative is inserted into a kind of autobiographical story that incriminates the author and makes him dependent on his own creation.

The "invention" of Tommaso is a lesson in the anatomy of political economy and also a literary anatomy lesson. Siti draws on Sciascia (*L'Affaire Moro*), whose denunciation of the links between mafia power and the political culture of secrecy and corruption was based on his theory of "black on black" writing: "writing in black on the black page of reality [*nera scrittura sulla nera pagina della realtà*]," as he used to say, in order to allow us to see the nearly invisible patterns of fake democracy (Sciascia, *Nero su nero*). Sciascia thought that only the rational irony of literature could fight against the blinding power of the perversion of democracy.

This is exactly what Siti does right from the start, since his title (*Resistance Is Useless*, or "futile") can be read both literally and as an antiphrasis: the novel tells of the fight, word for word and body for body, of its writer against disqualification from democracy at the hands of neofascists:

> *The individual is no longer the "qualified subject" of English empiricism; the informational delusion (which nobody is brave enough to evade) makes any private individual's conscious decision about the common good completely illusory [*rende chimerica per i privati qualunque decisione consapevole sul bene comune*]. If the modern individual vanishes, his corollary, democracy, doesn't make sense anymore either—although we continue wearily to partake in it during obligatory celebrations around the fetish that is the ballot box [*intorno al feticcio dell'urna elettorale*].*

> *Democracy is the fallen god of modernity who survives as an idol made of papier mâché [la democrazia è il dio morto della modernità che sopravvive come idolo di cartapesta]. The babbling of political analysts is an indication of their embarrassment regarding a funeral rite that cannot be celebrated [l'imbarazzo per un rito funebre che non si può celebrare]: that's why they cling to the last vestiges of insurrectional democracy, in underdeveloped regions or in the heart of cities. But democracy can't be (or can no longer be) mass poetry [la democrazia non può essere (non più) un poema di massa]. (Resistere 280)*

Resistance Is Useless is not mass poetry, or a thesis novel: it's the story of an ironic combat in favor of an alleged eidolon of papier mâché.

This is clear from the beginning of the novel, with its three prologues. "Before and After, Forever [*Prima e dopo, per sempre*]" is a frightening vendetta and execution story as well as the scene of the origin of Tommaso's bond to the 'ndrangheta, since the killer is his father, who is being forced to show his obedience to the organization. The second prologue, "The Perception of Prostitution [*La prostituzione percepita*]," is a fictional article by a professor from Yale about an ethological experiment involving a sort of prostitution practice among capuchin monkeys: it helps the narrator of the novel (who admits to being the author of this false article) introduce a motif that will become central to the novel—that of the relationship between voluntary servitude and a "universal mediator" (*mediatore universale*) such as money or sex. This double prologue, both narrative and theoretical, leads to a third one, which takes the form of a first-person repentance on the part of the author and also serves to establish the novel's authorial contract: the author is meant to be one of the personae, one of the masks in the whole story: he is the exact counterbalance, the antagonist of the creditor, of the antidemocratic subject whose hedge fund is called, fittingly, Persona.

The aging, desiring author, Walter, is advised by his editor to quit "writing books for sissies [*per froci*]" and wants to earn enough money to renovate his crumbling house, so he agrees to write a potentially profitable nonfiction novel, a biography of Tommaso, who commissioned it himself. "Who am I to you [*che cosa sono io per te*]?" says Tommaso to Walter (*Resistere* 49).

What does this imply? Is it a kind of Faustian pact? Can he write on credit for the prince of calculation—in exchange for an advance that makes him the capuchin monkey of the genius mobster-financier?

One of the virtues of Walter Siti's novel is to keep in plain sight the ambiguity, the perversion even, of the writing process: the "portraitist," the contemporary equivalent of the court painter, is contracted, and the diversion that fiction creates seems to serve as a transparent "protection," or a necessary hypocrisy (*persona*):

> —*Aren't you afraid of appearing as my accomplice [*risultare il mio complice*]? Do you need more money?*
> —*Money? I had some, I spent it the wrong way, and if I had more I would spend it even worse.*
> —*Listen, Walter, can I ask you a stupid question?*
> —*Stupidity is my favorite game.*
> —*Who am I to you? I mean, what do I represent, why did you commit . . . ?*
> —*I asked myself the same question [. . .] maybe you are my stunt double, the one who does the dangerous scenes for me [. . .] a prototype of mutation [. . .] or maybe, on a deeper level, you're my avenger [. . .].*
> —*Everybody will say you've sold yourself to organized crime; you should keep away from a guy like me.*
> —*I'll pretend you're a figment of my imagination [. . .] that's the advantage of novels [*questo è il vantaggio dei romanzi*] [. . .]. I delegated you to live themes that are mine [*ti ho delegato a vivere temi che sono i miei*] [. . .] in short, I'm going to write a novel by proxy [*un romanzo per procura*]. (*Resistere 313–14*)*

We shouldn't read this literally, though: Siti knows that fiction is not a real protection by proxy, neither for the mafia nor the publisher. It is, rather, the necessary detour that allows one to focus on reality and tie together its loose ends, no matter the risk:

> —*The question is: how much can I say about all this? Too many dark shades eventually risk ruining the portrait [*il ritratto*].*
> —*Why should I care? I'm going to hell no matter what. The important thing is that the big picture is clear [*che risulti chiaro il quadro d'insieme*]. (*Resistere 290*)*

The novel is the compromise of a writer in the service of a deeper reality—his aging and his disqualification from democracy—represented metaphorically by his dilapidated house (which was bought on credit):

*Here I am, with this "omniscient narrator" project that I've always been ashamed of [*questo progetto di "narrator onnisciente" che m'ha sempre fatto arrossire*]; the only "omniscient" being would be God, if he existed. In order to pose as an omniscient narrator, one must either be highly presumptuous or expect splendor from your epoch [*richiedere splendore alla tua epoca*]. But I have to act in order to save my poor apartment, whose plaster bubbles pulsate as though they were veins—or scars: my house is more alive than I am. I'll be the rhetorical tool by which facts are purified and take on meaning while also becoming distorted: a fool in the service of things [*un pagliaccio al servizio delle cose*]. (*Resistere 50–51*)

And so, as the fool concludes, the epilogue, the "afterword" of the novel, replies to the prologue: "Forced to choose between justice and truth, I chose truth (even if truth took on unpalatable, sectarian, and intransmissible forms) [*dovendo scegliere tra giustizia e verità, ho preferito la seconda (pur presentandosi la verità in forme indigeste, settarie e non transmissibili)*]" (*Resistere* 319). This is one of the most interesting difficulties of Siti's writing: the way the unbearable financier Tommaso (or any other character belonging to a corrupted reality) embodies the truth as an alter ego of the writer:

We were chatting about everything, his work and mine:

*—Kafka said it and he was right: literature is wage-labor in the service of the Devil [*la letteratura è il salario per il servizio del diavolo*].*
*—You don't necessarily have to possess goods to sell them [. . .] you can sell money that doesn't exist, that for the moment is just a hole [*che per ora è solo un buco*] [. . .].*
*—You also prefer the possible to the real [. . .]. You're breathing life into the infinite [*date fiato all'infinito*], you're not just the Geiger counter of the will-to-power. (*Resistere 46*)*

Tommaso, Prince of Possibilities, is the accursed share of Walter, whose "fascination with evil is obscure even to himself [*la mia fascinazione per il male è oscura anche a me stesso*]," according to the afterword. The fact that the novel is "written on credit" creates a "debt to the truth [*un debito da pagare alla verità*]" that the author wishes to repay (*Resistere* 316), and he does so by waging a war of detail and precision against the mob democracy—black on black, fiction against Fiction.

Resistance Is Useless is a political fiction in the sense Emily Apter and I have suggested, that is, a narrative form of political theory or political relation (Apter and Bouju). This novel by Siti (along with others, like the great *Contagio*) is structured as a debt economy (secrecy/truth), and the very possibility of telling the true story of underground, undercover finance relies on an intimate battle between the old "qualified subject" of democracy and the new Prince of Calculation, a battle in which high-wire finance is planning the credit crunch of democracy itself, as if it were making an idol of papier mâché. But also: a battle in which denunciation—the writer's reporting on this crisis—turns the paper eidolon that is the novel into one of the last vestiges of democracy.

Epilogue

"Europe expiring *in media insanitate*!"
"*Fiducia* devouring her children"
(Justice, Truth, etc.).
—Valéry

What has the narrative of Europe turned into in our times of debt: A tale of the Minotaur at the center of a labyrinth of nations? The story of *Fiducia* devouring her children (like the Commander did with Dom Juan)? An "article 50" Pied Piper leading us to the delusion of a sweet hereafter?[10] What has become of the ring-of-stars symbol more than sixty years after the Treaty of Rome?

In Robert Menasse's latest novel, *The Capital*, there is a story that takes place in a tattoo parlor (called "Mystical Bodies") in Brussels. The old progressive ("heterodox," as we say in France) German economist, Professor Erhart, wants to get a twelve-star circle tattoo around a bruise in the shape of Europe. "No. I'm not going to do it," says the tattoo artist; "in a few weeks' time it'll have vanished anyway" (234). "So no stars for a vanishing Europe?" the professor asks, in this tragicomedy of the EU, which tells of the structural impossibility of any (economic, political, or moral) debt pooling in Europe.

When literature focuses on the dissent of any democratic subject, it addresses the contemporary crisis of political, economic, moral, or aesthetic credibility and helps the reader become aware of the major, essential conflict between truth and secrecy, power and justice, calculation and unconditionality. Let us hope—at a time when great demagogues are in charge almost everywhere—that new narratives of debts will manage to make the symbol of Europe a real ring of solidarity, and not a bunch of euro-stubs without stocks, or a broken Pied Piper IOU pipe.

EMMANUEL BOUJU is a professor of comparative literature at the Université de la Sorbonne Nouvelle and a senior member of the Institut Universitaire de France. He has been a visiting professor at Indiana University Bloomington and at Harvard University. Professor Bouju's publications include *Épimodernes. Nouvelles "leçons américaines" sur l'actualité du roman* (Codicille, 2020), *Fragments d'un discours théorique* (Éditions Nouvelles Cécile Defaut, 2016), and *La transcription de l'histoire. Essai sur le roman européen de la fin du vingtième siècle* (Presses universitaires de Rennes, 2006).

Notes

1   See also Graeber 56: "Governments use taxes to create money, and they are able to do so because they have become the guardians of the debt that all citizens have to one another. This debt is the essence of society itself. It exists long before money and markets, and money and markets themselves are simply ways of chopping pieces of it up."

2   On the causal model and its possible post-"crash" topicality, see Kluge and Vogl.

3   See John Lanchester's nonfiction account of the crisis (*IOU*) and Annie McClanahan's comment and critique (40).

4   See the critique of Derrida's argument at the very beginning of Arjun Appadurai's "The Ghost in the Financial Machine" in *The Future as Cultural Fact* 233.

5   Lazzarato's theory powerfully echoes in the "coda" of McClanahan's *Dead Pledges*, dedicated to "The Living Indebted," after she criticizes it in chapter 2 because "it misses much of what is specifically new in contemporary credit relations"—namely, their normalization for economic survival and the "new forms of impersonal structural violence that operate on the debtor's body" (79–80).

6   Recall that in Rome, at a time when debt slavery no longer existed, insolvent debtors were attached, bonded (*nexi*).

7   The London Conference in 1953 decided that the repayment of the German debt would be postponed to a hypothetical reunification of Germany, but it was eventually cancelled in 1991, officially because there wasn't any calculation mechanism for inflation and GDP proportionality.

8   See "Manifesto." See also Bouju et al.

9   The Greek crisis forms the backdrop of Rhea Galanaki's *Utmost Humiliation* and Christos Chrissopoulos's *The Parthenon Bomber*.

10 Article 50 of the Treaty on European Union, enacted by the Treaty of Lisbon on December 1, 2009, introduced a procedure for a member-state to withdraw from the European Union.

Works Cited

Appadurai, Arjun. *The Future as Cultural Fact: Essays on the Global Condition.* London: Verso, 2013.

Apter, Emily, and Emmanuel Bouju, eds. *La fiction politique (XIX–XXI siècles)*. *Raison-Publique.fr* 4 May 2014. https://www.raison-publique.fr/article706.html.

Banks, Russell. "Feeding Moloch: The Sacrifice of Children on the Altar of Capitalism." Lecture. 5 Nov. 2014. Harvard Divinity School. Cambridge, MA.

Bouju, Emmanuel, ed. *L'engagement littéraire*. Rennes: Presses Universitaires de Rennes, 2005.

Bouju, Manon, et al. *Changer l'Europe, c'est possible!* Paris: Seuil, 2019.

Browning, Robert. *Selected Poems*. New York: Routledge, 2013.

Chrissopoulos, Christos. *The Parthenon Bomber*. Trans. John Cullen. New York: Other Press, 2017.

Deleuze, Gilles, and Félix Guattari. *Anti-Oedipus: Capitalism and Schizophrenia*. Trans. Robert Hurley, Mark Seem, and Helen R. Lane. Minneapolis: U of Minnesota P, 1983.

Derrida, Jacques. *Given Time: 1. Counterfeit Money*. Trans. Peggy Kamuf. Chicago: U of Chicago P, 1992.

Galanaki, Rhea. *L'ultime humiliation*. Trans. Loïc Marcou. Paris: Galaade, 2016.

Graeber, David. *Debt: The First 5,000 Years*. London: Melville, 2011.

Kluge, Alexander, and Joseph Vogl. *Crédit et debit*. Trans. Magali Jourdan and Mathilde Sobottke. Paris: Diaphanes, 2013.

Lanchester, John. *IOU: Or Why Everyone Owes Everyone and No One Can Pay*. New York: Simon and Schuster, 2010.

Lazzarato, Maurizio. *The Making of the Indebted Man: An Essay on the Neoliberal Condition*. Trans. Joshua David Jordan. Los Angeles: Semiotext(e), 2012.

Lienau, Odette. *Rethinking Sovereign Debt: Politics, Reputation, and Legitimacy in Modern Finance*. Cambridge, MA: Harvard UP, 2014.

Livy. *History of Rome*. Vol. 1. Trans. B. O. Foster. Cambridge, MA: Harvard UP, 1919.

"Manifesto for the Democratization of Europe." http://tdem.eu/en/manifesto/ (accessed 10 July 2020).

McClanahan, Annie. *Dead Pledges: Debt, Crisis, and Twenty-First Century's Culture*. Stanford: Stanford UP, 2017.

Menasse, Robert. *The Capital*. Trans. Jamie Bulloch. New York: Norton, 2019.

Nietzsche, Friedrich. *On the Genealogy of Morality*. Trans. Carol Diethe. Cambridge: Cambridge UP, 2008.

Pasolini, Pier Paolo. "Disappearance of the Fireflies." Trans. Christopher Mott. *Diagonal Thoughts* 23 June 2014. http://www.diagonalthoughts.com/?p=2107.

Piketty, Thomas. *Capital in the Twenty-First Century*. Trans. Arthur Goldhammer. Cambridge, MA: Harvard UP, 2014.

Rospabé, Philippe. *La dette de vie: Aux origines de la monnaie sauvage*. Paris: La Découverte/Mauss, 1995.

Saviano, Roberto. *Gomorrah: A Personal Journey into the Violent International Empire of Naples' Organized Crime System*. Trans. Virginia Jewiss. London: Picador, 2008.

Sciascia, Leonardo. *L'affaire Moro*. Milan: Adelphi, 1994.

——————. *Nero su nero*. Milan: Adelphi, 1991.

——————. *Noir sur noir*. Trans. Nino Frank and Corinne Lucas. Paris: Maurice Nadeau/ Papyrus, 1981.

Shell, Marc. *The Economy of Literature*. Baltimore: Johns Hopkins UP, 1978.

Siti, Walter. *Resistere non serve a niente*. Milan: Rizzoli, 2012.

Valéry, Paul. "The Island of Xiphos." *Poems in the Rough*. Trans. Hilary Corke. *Collected Works of Paul Valéry*. Vol. 2. Princeton: Princeton UP, 1969. 118–34.

Vogl, Joseph. *The Specter of Capital*. Trans. Joachim Redner and Robert Savage. Stanford: Stanford UP, 2015.

The Utopia of Bankruptcy

Don't be afraid, there's nothing left to
lose.
—Catastrophe

*A*t the end of his bestselling essay *Debt: The First 5000 Years*,
David Graeber unsurprisingly pleads for the advent of a world free of debt:
"Nothing would be more important than to wipe the slate clean for everyone, mark a break with our accustomed morality, and start again" (391).[1] In
Graeber's radical perspective, to "start again" doesn't amount to resetting
the meter, but means that we should free ourselves for good from the very
assumption that debts have to be repaid. In order to shake off the burden of
debt, one need not simply redirect the sense of debt or erase odious debts but
"challenge the principle of debt itself" (390–91), which is more moral than
economical. Like many other critics of capitalism, Graeber invites us to
imagine a new world of "genuinely free men and women" who may be able
to "make real promises to one another" (391). What would this new world
look like? What would these "real promises" be? Graeber honestly admits
that "at this point we can't even say. It's more a question of how we can get
to a place that will allow us to find out."

Why is it so difficult for anyone to answer Graeber's questions?
Why does such a powerful account of the destructive powers of public

Volume 31, Number 3   DOI 10.1215/10407391-8744511

and private debt stop at the threshold of utopia? Of course, it takes a lot of imagination to picture a debt-free world in a time when debt weighs so heavily on our lives, our conception of time, and our discussions about politics and morality. But even in times when debt was not as crucial for economic governance, Graeber argues that its necessity was never seriously questioned. Because debt is not just a variable component of economic systems; it is one of those background beliefs so deeply enshrined in our notion of any kind of economy that it seems impossible to find a way out. So even if Graeber tries to emancipate his reader from the moral premise that makes the burden of debt possible, his book's title suggests it might be another few thousand years before we find a way of making the radical move it calls for.

The Bankrupt Phoenix

In this article, I would like to offer a literary answer to Graeber's questions by digging into a recent novel by Benjamin Markovits, *You Don't Have to Live Like This*. Markovits's narrative is rooted not in the mythical realm of a post-debt-jubilee world, but in the historical reality of a bankrupt city, namely Detroit. Detroit's fate has been an object of international fascination for the past decade. It has epitomized the failure of the American dream and the eternal renaissance of the American phoenix, the end of capitalism and its ability to profit from crisis. It has inspired countless documentaries, novels, movies, memoirs, essays, and articles about the lost ideal of Fordism and the utopian promise of urban farms.[2] Bankruptcy was a metaphor for its economic meltdown before it became a grim legal reality for a municipality too indebted to pay its bills.

The city of Detroit filed for Chapter 9 federal bankruptcy protection on July 18, 2013. It was declared bankrupt five months later with liabilities estimated at 18.5 billion dollars. While it was one among many cities going bankrupt in the years following the financial collapse of 2008, it was by far the largest city and the most spectacular case in American history. And with Detroit being commonly represented as a symbol of a bygone prosperity, this massive failure was also immediately depicted as a national symbol, echoing the tremendous number of personal bankruptcies and house evictions everywhere in the country.

The news of Detroit's bankruptcy, however shocking, wasn't surprising for people familiar with images of blight that had already been widely circulating at that point: Detroit had been the poster child for urban decline long before the financial crisis hit. Municipal bankruptcy therefore only seemed to give the final blow to a city plagued by a long series of crises triggered by debt, whether private, corporate, or public. In the shrinking city, foreclosures, mortgage delinquencies, and short sales had been all too frequent long before the housing market bubble collapsed nationwide in 2008. In 2009, the debt of multinational corporations became equally evident when the "Big 3" (Chrysler, Ford, and GM) asked Congress for a 50 billion dollar bailout. This seemingly general insolvency caused multiple tragedies: family homes lost to anonymous LLCs, water and electricity shutoffs, cuts in jobs, wages, and pensions. As the French writer Tanguy Viel ironically stated in a novel published a few months before municipal bankruptcy, Detroit looked "like a sort of modern Pompei, whose lava wouldn't come from burning rock, but rather from credits and debts" (14).[3]

Unlike Pompei, though, Detroit had an emergency manager, Kevyn Orr. For twenty-one months, this bankruptcy lawyer supervised elected officials and was allowed to sell city properties, cut services, and redefine the contracts and pensions of the city's employees. This dramatic suspension of democracy was advertised as a chance to transition from debt to credit, from past liabilities to future investments, from agony to rebirth. Though it came at a high cost, the Lazarean narrative of bankruptcy was all the more powerful since it blended with the comforting myth of Detroit as a phoenix rising from the ashes after every disaster, whether natural or financial.[4] Comparing the Great Fire of 1805 and the Great Crisis of 2008, the accounting firm Ernst and Young, which participated in the drawing up of Detroit's restructuring plan, summed up the optimistic moral of the capitalist fairytale: "Detroit rose from the ashes once more, emerging from bankruptcy in December 2014. Its liabilities have been restructured and the city is now on course for a second revival" (Malhotra 12).

It would be easy to ironize on the cheap mythology of corporate storytelling and its underlying ideology of creative destruction. But interestingly enough, Ernst and Young's accounting has the unintended virtue of laying bare the ambiguity of the promise of bankruptcy laws. While *revival* may seem to announce a clean slate, the phoenix myth reminds us of the cyclical nature of debt crises: Detroit has emerged from the ashes only to be able to get new loans, some of them used to reimburse its past creditors during emergency management. Thus bankruptcy does not emancipate from the obligation to pay one's debts; it enforces it. It does not end a decades-long crisis; it makes the cycle of debt and credit endless. One could argue that the resurrected phoenix looks very much like the agonizing debtor.

In this context, to present Detroit's all too real bankruptcy as a utopia may seem not only morally dubious but simply wrong. Far from contradicting Graeber's law of debt's inescapability, the story of Detroit's municipal bankruptcy is a cautionary tale of the impossibility of getting clear of debts. Or, to put it in Walter Benjamin's terms, it exemplifies the ability of capitalism to render debt infinite.[5] In what sense, then, can a situation of generalized insolvency be said to pave the way for the utopia of a debt-free world? Avoiding the easy symbolism that so often transforms Detroit and its inhabitants into an exciting thought experiment (see Leary), Markovits's novel offers a nuanced answer to this question, calling for a closer examination of the potentials of life in a ruined city.

"Starting-from-Scratch-in-America": The Promised Land of Bankruptcy

Greg Marnier, known as Marny, is the main character as well as the narrator of *You Don't Have to Live Like This*. He's an adjunct professor of American colonial history in his early thirties who, after years of academic precarity and no possibility of tenure, returns to live with his parents in Baton Rouge. Like most of his college friends from Yale and Oxford, he has been through the cycle of expectations and disillusions awaiting talented graduates after they enter the job market, "[w]orking harder than they wanted to, making less money, living somewhere they didn't want to live" (5). In a reunion of ex-Yalies, he meets one of his former friends, Robert James, who has made a fortune in the digital economy and is about to start a new project called "Starting-from-Scratch-in-America." Marny doesn't really know what to do with his life and is looking for "a better test of who (he is) than middle-class American life" (4). He accepts the invitation to move to Detroit, a place depicted by Robert James as "a war zone" where "[p]eople are burning down houses," but also as a land of opportunities: "[T]here are still some beautiful big houses standing empty. You could do whatever you want with them, set up any kind of society" (17).

Markovits finely exposes the mix of idealism and cynicism that defines the program: a "small experiment in regeneration" (56) as much as a "kind of Groupon model for gentrification" (17) meant to get national media attention while Detroit, with the Big 3 bailout, is "all over the news" (17). In practice, people from various backgrounds, most of them white, many of them having gone through personal bankruptcy, carrying student debt, or otherwise struggling with money issues, organize via Facebook to submit offers to take over a neighborhood. Robert James sees them as heirs to the "early settlers" of America who "people forget [. . .] were shipped over by private companies; it was a business venture" (53). He claims his economic model must be profitable so that it can be reproduced beyond Detroit, "in Cleveland, Buffalo, Erie, Milwaukie, east Baltimore, etc." (57). As a typical businessman, he thinks solutions to social problems are as scalable as resources: "[I]f you can fix it here, you can fix it anywhere" (56). But above all, he is trying to do "something high-profile" (17) that will be noticed by the new Obama administration.

Barack Obama himself, or at least his fictional double, appears in the novel. He comes to Detroit for a Democratic Party fundraiser organized by Robert James. The title of the novel, *You Don't Have to Live Like This*, in an excerpt from the president's fictional speech:

> *"Now I know there are folks here today who don't agree with everything I do, and I don't expect you to. But there are things we can agree on. That the American Experiment ain't over yet. And that's not because we're sitting around on our butts, waiting for the results to come in. The people rebuilding Detroit, and some of you are in this room right now, are still tinkering with it, still adapting it, still moving forward. You have come here from Albuquerque and Chicago, from Queens and from Cleveland and from San Diego. You have come from Mexico and Poland and Sudan and from right here in Detroit. You have come because you lost your job or you couldn't get a job or you had to work three jobs just to put food on the table. Because your health insurance ran out or your mortgage was worth more than your home. Because the school you sent your kids to couldn't afford to buy books or because the part-time job you got in college turned out to be the best thing you could find after earning your degree. You have come because there was a voice in your head saying,* You don't have to live like this. There's a better way to live. *This voice has called people to America for over four hundred years. It calls to us now . . ." and so on. (179)*

Detroit figures here as the modern equivalent of the promised land that immigrants longed for when they came to the United States.[6] But while the speech explicitly echoes the American dream of a better life ("the American Experiment"), it is also, obviously, a degraded version of it. While one hundred years ago, people from all over the world came to Detroit because

Henry Ford offered wages twice as high as the average national salary, they are now attracted by a metropolis so ruined one can hope to survive on cheap rent and a DIY economy. Moreover, what these newcomers are trying to get away from isn't the Old World or the Third World; it's the broken promises of the American dream itself: the broken promise of student credit that leaves thousands of young people with a part-time job that won't cover their loan, the broken promise of a mortgage that ends up worth more than the house it was meant to buy, the broken promise of health insurance, with its infinite list of preconditions that excludes so many sick people from being covered. They won't find these promises fulfilled in Detroit, but they might find a place broke enough to survive without them.

Nothing to Lose: The Utopia of the Dispossessed

The sentence "You don't have to live like this," then, takes another meaning, criticizing the American Experiment less because it failed than because it promoted a purely economic conception of life. *You don't have to live in debt*, always in fear of going bankrupt, turns into *You don't have to live on credit*, constantly working to accumulate commodities you don't need. In the novel, a precarious and forcefully frugal Marny confronts his brother Brad, a hard-working lawyer with an affluent lifestyle, claiming, "Not everybody wants to live the way you live" (267). When Brad asks him "what the people want," he goes on to explain: "What people want is basically pretty simple [. . .]. Shelter, food and community. None of these has to cost much. You read *Walden* in college, you know what I'm talking about" (268).[7] Paradoxically, in a city so indebted that it has lost all hope of reimbursing its creditors, everyone can try to escape the "quiet desperation" of the indebted man described by Thoreau in a famous paragraph:

> *Some of you, we all know, are poor, find it hard to live, are some-times, as it were, gasping for breath. I have no doubt that some of you who read this book are unable to pay for all the dinners which you have actually eaten, or for the coats and shoes which are fast wearing or are already worn out, and have come to this page to spend borrowed or stolen time, robbing your creditors of an hour. It is very evident what mean and sneaking lives many of you live, for my sight has been whetted by experience; always on the limits, trying to get into business and trying to get out of debt, a very ancient slough, called by the Latins* aes alienum, *another's*

brass, for some of their coins were made of brass; still living, and
dying, and buried by this other's brass; always promising to pay,
promising to pay, tomorrow, and dying today, insolvent; seeking
to curry favor, to get custom, by how many modes, only not state-
prison offenses; lying, flattering, voting, contracting yourselves
into a nutshell of civility, or dilating into an atmosphere of thin
and vaporous generosity, that you may persuade your neighbor
to let you make his shoes, or his hat, or his coat, or his carriage,
or import his groceries for him; making yourselves sick, that you
may lay up something against a sick day, something to be tucked
away in an old chest, or in a stocking behind the plastering, or,
more safely, in the brick bank; no matter where, no matter how
much or how little. (5–6)

The indebted man depicted by Thoreau borrows less money than he borrows time: he comes and goes between future and past, savings and liabilities, "trying to get into business and trying to get out of debt." He depends on others to find a job or to believe in his promises that he'll be able to pay tomorrow. He doesn't have room for today, except when he dies, inevitably insolvent. Frugality, conversely, allows him not only to be independent but to be present. Being free from debt means one can make promises but *they don't need to be believed.* The frenetic pleasure of capitalist accumulation is replaced by the luxury of mastering time, the responsibilities toward parents and children by the far less demanding bonds of friendship, the abstraction of credit by the material anchor of an autonomous life lived day to day.

We may be more sympathetic to this frugal version of the American dream, but Markovits is smart enough to cast a shadow on this counterutopia. While Thoreau explained how he came to the woods to live "Spartan-like" in order to "elevate (his) life by a conscious endeavor" (88), most of the people coming to Detroit are eager to find a place where they may "sit on their tushes" (Markovits 126) and "live on the cheap" (101). They do not welcome every morning as "a cheerful invitation to make [their] life of equal simplicity, and I may say innocence, with Nature herself" (Thoreau 86), but spend their days on trivial modern occupations like watching TV, looking after kids, or patrolling the streets for the local Neighborhood Watch (Markovits 126–29). To be fair, even if they wanted to be, like Thoreau, "worshipper(s) of Aurora" (86), Detroit's urban prairies are not as pristine as Walden Pond. As it turns out, nature in Detroit is contaminated, DIY is just another name for dire precarity, and the revitalization of local communities is made possible by evicting former residents. Once more, the repetition exposes the flaws of the original ideal. As Brad pointedly asserts, Thoreau "didn't give a damn about community" and he "didn't have any kids" (Markovits 268). Thoreau's ideal of a debt-free life may not be the best way to understand what is at stake in a ruined metropolis.

"Unreal Estate": The Precarious Utopia of the Commons

The sentence "There's a better way to live" points to the messianic ideal of a free market of unlimited commodities or to the regressive ideal of a premarket economy, where humans could be independent and connected to nature. Bankruptcy allows for these dreams to be revived even though it eventually destroys them: Detroit is not a blank slate where one could write the story of life after debt or before credit. One of the main lessons of Markovits's amoral novel might, then, confirm Graeber's conclusion that a world without debt can be dreamed of but certainly not achieved. This is, after all, the common critique of utopia: that it has to remain unreal or must end in disaster.

But such a conclusion would be far too simplistic. Detroit is not, and will never be, the promised land where one could start the colonial epics of the New World conquest over or go back to the Thoreauesque freedom of a frugal life without bonds or debts. Still, as Andrew Herscher, an urbanist at the University of Michigan, points out in his *Unreal Estate Guide to Detroit*, it is the very devaluation of the city and its inhabitants that places Detroit "in a time of conjoined precarity and possibility."[8] The breakdown of the city has allowed for large parts of the urban territory to fall out of the market economy. As they cannot be sold or rented, devalued houses cease to exist in the eyes of market agents except as obstacles to the valuation of other assets. Herscher proposes to requalify these "dead zones for both free market capitalism and formal politics" (12) as "unreal estate":

> The values of unreal estate are unreal from the perspective of the market economy—they are liabilities, or unvalues that hinder property's circulation through that market. But it is precisely as property is rendered valueless according to the dominant regime of value that it becomes available for other forms of thought, activity and occupation—in short, for other value systems.
>
> Unreal estate emerges when the exchange value of property falls to a point when that property can assume use values

unrecognized by the market economy. The extraction of capital from Detroit, then, has not only yielded the massive devaluation of real estate that has been amply documented but also, and concurrently, an explosive production of unreal estate, of value-less, abandoned or vacant urban property serving as site of and instrument for the imagination and practice of an informal and sometimes alternative urbanism.

Unreal estate is less a negation of real estate than a supplement of it, located both inside and outside of real estate's political economy. [. . .] Unreal estate may thus be understood as a term that fits within what J. K. Gibson-Graham calls "a land-scape of economic difference, populated by various capitalist and non-capitalist institutions and practices," the latter not simply absences of the former but singularities with their own particular forms and possibilities. (9)

The extraction of capital has created the unintended possibility for "new sorts of commons" whose very existence challenges the constant move forward of debt and credit: their value is not "based on *investments* that pay off in a better-world-to-come, whether within or beyond the market economy," but rather, "on expenditures in the present moment, critically refusing to mortgage that moment for another, different future" (14). Herscher gives many examples of these commons in his guide: a shared garden in a vacant lot providing fresh products to the residents of a block, a "Mower Gang" dedicated to the upkeep of public parks, or a nonprofit organization disassembling buildings into reusable parts, such as doors, windows and fixtures. Unlike activists who occupy places to prevent privatization and development, these groups invent public uses of formerly developed spaces now abandoned by capital. But like activists, they tend to demonstrate not only that other ways of living are possible but that they are already real.

"Unreal estate," therefore, is not unreal in the same way as utopia is unreal.[9] It is not a promised land to be longed for or a thought experiment to be used as a critical tool to escape and oppose our TINA reality.[10] Instead, unreal estate points to the fact that in a globalized world that doesn't allow us to think of otherworldly territory, there are actually many alternatives existing within capitalist economies. While utopia has been written and theorized as a fictional territory that doesn't share any common background with the political space it opposes, the commons arising in bankruptcy are grounded in an existing place and are constantly affected by it. Of course, this is also what makes them so vulnerable: "commons-in-the-making," Herscher warns, exist only in a spatial and temporal interval, "constantly susceptible not only to further deterioration, but also to further 'betterment' as defined by a value regime that equates improvement with profitability" (10).

It is no surprise then that, like more conventional urban guides, this one should be updated to reflect the changing patches of unreal and real estate in Detroit over the recent years. Many of the initiatives listed in Herscher's book have disappeared, either replaced by others or reclaimed by public and private operators. In that sense, the commons' present vulnerability is opposed to the messianic time of utopia: they arise in conditions of poverty no one should romanticize, they remain experimental in their making, and they can always be appropriated or destroyed by capital. In Detroit, the urban farms movement has been internationally praised as a practical solution providing fresh food and independence to low-income residents as well as a small-scale alternative to extractivism and an easy-credit economy.[11] But revolutionary as it may be, the promise of bankruptcy presents itself as a very unsettling version of the kingdom, one in which, to quote Rebecca Solnit, mostly black people "are being forced to undertake an experiment in utopian post-urbanism that appears to be uncomfortably similar to the sharecropping past their parents and grandparents sought to escape" (73).

Still, when Graeber wonders "how we can get to a place that will allow us to find out" what life without debt would be like, he may overlook some already existing spaces where alternative economies and values arise outside the dominant circuits of debt and credit. Almost insignificant from the perspective of market actors, these local experiments have gained visibility in the social sciences as ways of "envisioning real utopias" in the interstices of market economies (Wright), describing "emerging temporalities" that escape presentism (Baschet), and thinking about "collaborative survival" and "latent commons" in the ruins of capitalism (Tsing 4; 255). The alternative to a casino economy no longer lies in a bright future that the present society should try to get closer to; it lies in the here and now, "in the spaces and cracks" of capitalist economies (Wright 322). Breaking down the downward spiral of debt as much as the crazy growth of an economy based on credit derivation, insolvency paves the way for worlds of precarious possibilities where mutual aid and autonomy go hand in hand with greater vulnerability.

If we confront Graeber's question—"What sorts of promises might genuinely free men and women make to one another?" (391)—with the precarious reality of these alternatives, we may find it difficult to answer. The urban farmers of Detroit, the mushroom pickers of Oregon,[12] the nomad workers walking away from their mortgage to live in a van (see Bruder): they are free from past debts and skeptical of credit, but they continue to depend, at least occasionally, on capitalist circuits that take advantage of their precarity. By hoping for a "clean slate" and "genuine" freedom, Graeber may replicate the common mistake of narrations of bankruptcy, carrying the idea of a radical break from the past when the reality of life without debt is heterogeneous, impure, and swiftly changing.

It may be easier to imagine resurrection, fresh starts, and jubilees to come than to document the complexity of what is already happening in the ruins produced by debt and credit governance. In his final remarks to the adjustment plan allowing the city to exit emergency management, Judge Steven W. Rhodes, from the United States Bankruptcy Court, compared the Detroit bankruptcy case to "the other 30,609 bankruptcy cases that were filed in our court in 2013. In every case, we have a debtor who needs help, who made mistakes, who took unwarranted risks, who accepted bad advice, who exercised bad judgment, who was too long in denial, or who had just plain bad luck. But no matter, our society holds dear the value of a fresh start and of second chances" (qtd. in *Daily Detroit*). The dominant narrative of bankruptcy is not only simplistic; it is as scalable as capitalism itself. Its moral premises apply in a standardized fashion to impoverished cities as to individual debtors. The precarious utopias of bankruptcy, on the other hand, are grounded in particular contexts and cannot be easily reproduced. Their vulnerability and diversity pose a serious challenge not only to the very logics of capitalist tales of debt but to social sciences' narratives of alternatives to debt: Detroit is neither an American phoenix whose renaissance demonstrates the ability of capitalism to triumph from crises nor a laboratory of the possible futures of a postindustrial world. It is a site of precarious experiments that any scalable narrative, aimed at producing systematic or duplicable knowledge, might betray.

Insolvent Narrations

After the riots that put an end to the "Starting-from-Scratch-in-America" project, Marny chooses to stay in Detroit, where he survives by "going through some of the burned-out houses and looking for things other people overlook" (388). He hasn't got a job, but he does "some day labor, fruit picking, furniture removal, leafleting, yard work" (389), and occasionally he sneaks into a farm to glean "things to eat" (388). In other words, he is a modern-day *chiffonnier*. The neighborhood looks more or less the way it did before it was taken over: most of the "settlers" have gone, and Marny, once again, contemplates whether it might be possible to "start over" (391) in New York. His life has lost its direction, like his narrative, which keeps enumerating his shifting thoughts and actions. The novel itself seems to have achieved a full circle back to the initial situation when Marny was an academic drifter hoping for a better life and a self-proclaimed incompetent storyteller:

> *When I was younger I was never much good at telling stories. If I scored a goal at Pee Wee soccer, which didn't happen often, I used to try and describe it for my brother over lunch, over the hot dogs and potato chips. Then he kicked it there and I ran here and he passed it to me there. My brother called these my "this and then this and then this" stories. I don't know that I've gotten any better at it. (1)*

Before reading *You Don't Have to Live Like This*, I may have been skeptical of the possibility of telling a story as complex, long, and politically loaded as this one in the manner of a soccer game told by a preschooler. But when it comes to questioning the dominant forms of life and the craft of storytelling that supports them, I certainly underestimated the politics of enumeration. While Thoreau would start his plea for frugality with a long chapter on the economics of life in the woods, Marny's narration, conversely, mirrors his childlike insolvency, recounting tragic and mundane facts in the same fashion, willfully reluctant to engage in any kind of accountability. As carefree and mostly idle as the child he used to be, he does not need to connect past and future, money owed and money gained, causes and consequences. He survives on small gains and petty thefts, unable to save but with no need to spend: he lives, to reverse Thoreau's quote, "inevitably insolvent." It might be a wise life emancipated from the excessive work and worries of the indebted man or a wasted life resulting from the inability to grow up and take responsibilities. "Maybe my brother is right," Marny concludes. "Worrying about money is what you pay for. It stops you from worrying about everything else" (391).

    The undecidability of Markovits's narrative is by no means a consequence of the childlike incompetence of his narrator. Or better: this childlike incompetence is precisely what allows us to capture the complex reality of lives relieved from the burden of debt but exposed to discomfort, uncertainty, shifting bonds and feelings, and even, in Marny's case, moral guilt when he faces the deadly consequences of the colonial endeavor he has been a part of. Enumeration, in Markovits's novel, accounts for an ethics of presence that has less to do with the bliss of the Thoreauesque awakening to the "essential facts of life" (Thoreau 88) than with the uncomfortable understanding of the impossibility of reducing any life to essential facts. In that sense, Marny's static trajectory is either a farewell to the utopia of bankruptcy, with its "clean slate" and its too simple freedom to start over, or a call to redefine utopias as all but perfect alternatives. Indeed, if there is such a thing as the utopia of bankruptcy, it is necessarily an impure one, a utopia in which it is difficult to determine whether one is happy or depressed, free or indolent, child or adult, dependent on the market or free from its chains. Such a utopia has the ability to question not only the quiet despair of the indebted man—that of the poor perpetually in debt as well as that of the rich perpetually in search of credit—but also the classical alternatives to the assumed sadness of these lives: the capitalist narrative of a new beginning after bankruptcy, the frontier narrative of a new world free from the old world's debts, and finally, the moralizing narrative of self-sufficiency. All these classical alternatives are attractive because they seem to promise the security of a life forever free from the anxiety of financial collapse. Precarious utopias, conversely, don't promise any world to come; their precarity may even make promises impossible to keep. But as Jacques Mesrine, a famous French bandit, once said, "[T]here is no other world. There's just another way to live."[13]

RAPHAËLLE GUIDÉE is an associate professor of comparative literature at the University of Poitiers (France) and a junior member of the Institut Universitaire de France (IUF). Her research interests include the writing of utopia, representations of disasters, and political imagination in literature, arts, and social sciences. Her book *Mémoires de l'oubli* (Classiques Garnier, 2017) focuses on narratives of mourning and debt toward those whose memory has been lost or erased. She has also coedited several interdisciplinary collections of articles about contemporary literature, including *L'Apocalypse, une imagination politique* (Presses universitaires de Rennes, 2018), *Dire les inégalités* (Presses universitaires de Rennes, 2016), and *Utopie et catastrophe* (Presses universitaires de Rennes, 2015).

Notes

1   Catastrophe, quoted in the epigraph to this article, is a French collective of young writers and musicians. This is the last sentence of their manifesto, "Puisque tout est fini, alors tout est permis," published in the daily newspaper *Libération* on September 22, 2016. The epigraph in the original French reads "N'ayez pas peur, il n'y a plus rien à perdre." The English translation is mine.

2   See Dora Apel's excellent *Beautiful Terrible Ruins: Detroit and the Anxiety of Decline* for a full list and a thorough analysis of anglophone texts, movies, and art exhibitions up to 2015.

3   "En fait, Detroit ressemble à une sorte de Pompéi moderne, dont la lave ne proviendrait pas d'une roche incandescente, plutôt des crédits et des dettes" (my translation).

4   See the city's motto, *Speramus meliora, Resurget cineribus* ("We hope for better things, It shall rise from the ashes"), a leitmotif in narratives about Detroit.

5   See Benjamin's "Capitalism as Religion." For a luminous explanation of this rather obscure fragment, see Löwy.

6   See Safransky for a convincing critique of the "frontier narrative" in Detroit.

7   Marny alludes to a famous quote from *Walden*, even though, significantly, Thoreau never mentions community as one of the necessities of life: "None of the brute creation requires more than Food and Shelter. The necessaries of life for man in this climate may, accurately enough, be distributed under the several heads of Food, Shelter, Clothing, and Fuel; for not till we have secured these are we prepared to entertain the true problems of life with freedom and a prospect of success" (Thoreau 12).

8   Herscher, back cover. The "unreal estate agency" was initially a collective project of urban studies academics at the University of Michigan. I am very grateful to Peter J. Hammer, director of Detroit Equity Action Laboratory (Wayne State University), for introducing the project to me and to Mireille Roddier, who was a cofounder of the Unreal Estate Agency, for taking the time to explain at length the collective inquiry behind the book.

9   Even though most of the examples sampled in the guide are authentic, Herscher explains that his book "encompasses invention of many sorts" and hopes to provoke questions "about what the parameters of the 'real' are or could be" (16).

10   TINA is an acronym for "There Is No Alternative." It refers to a slogan often used by Prime Minister Margaret Thatcher in the eighties and has become a rather commonly used expression in anticapitalist circles.

11   Grace Lee Boggs, Detroit's most famous activist, has described the urban agriculture movement and its resonance in *The Next American Revolution: Sustainable Activism for the Twenty-First Century*.

12   See Tsing, esp. chapters 4 and 5.

13   This quotation is the epigraph of *To Our Friends*, an anarchist reading of recent crises by The Invisible Committee.

Works Cited

Apel, Dora. *Beautiful Terrible Ruins: Detroit and the Anxiety of Decline.* New Brunswick: Rutgers UP, 2015.

Baschet, Jérôme. *Défaire la tyrannie du présent. Temporalités émergentes et futurs inédits.* Paris: La Découverte, 2019.

Benjamin, Walter. "Capitalism as Religion." Trans. Rodney Livingstone. *Selected Writings, 1913–1926.* Vol. 1. Ed. Marcus Bullock and Michael W. Jennings. Cambridge, MA: Harvard UP, 2004. 288–91.

Boggs, Grace Lee, with Scott Kurashige. *The Next American Revolution: Sustainable Activism for the Twenty-First Century.* Berkeley: U of California P, 2012.

Bruder, Jessica. *Nomadland: Surviving America in the Twenty-First Century*. New York: Norton, 2017.

Catastrophe. "Puisque tout est fini, alors tout est permis." *Libération* 22 Sept. 2016. https://www.liberation.fr/debats/2016/09/22/puisque-tout-est-fini-alors-tout-est-permis_1506625.

Daily Detroit. "'It's Your City'—Bankruptcy Judge Steven Rhodes' Conclusion Is a Letter to Detroiters." *Daily Detroit* 9 Nov. 2014. http://www.dailydetroit.com/2014/11/09/it-is-your-city-bankruptcy-judge-steven-rhodes-conclusion-is-a-letter-to-detroiters/.

Graeber, David. *Debt: The First 5000 Years*. New York: Melville, 2011.

Herscher, Andrew. *Unreal Estate Guide to Detroit*. Ann Arbor: U of Michigan P, 2012.

The Invisible Committee. *To Our Friends*. Trans. Robert Hurley. South Pasadena: Semiotext(e), 2015.

Leary, Patrick D. "Detroitism: What Does 'Ruin Porn' Tell Us about the Motor City?" *Guernica* 15 Jan. 2011. https://www.guernicamag.com/leary_1_15_11/.

Löwy, Michaël. "Le capitalisme comme religion: Walter Benjamin et Max Weber." *Raisons politiques* 23 (August 2006): 203–19.

Malhotra, Gaurav. "Rising from the Ashes Once More." *Citizen Today* 20 (August 2015): 12–15.

Markovits, Benjamin. *You Don't Have to Live Like This*. New York: HarperCollins, 2015.

Safransky, Sarah. "Greening the Urban Frontier: Race, Property, and Resettlement in Detroit." *Geoforum* 56 (2014): 237–48.

Solnit, Rebecca. "Detroit Arcadia: Exploring the Post-American Landscape." *Harper's* (July 2007): 65–73.

Thoreau, Henry D. *Walden*. Ed. Jeffrey S. Cramer. New Haven: Yale UP, 2004.

Tsing, Anna Lowenhaupt. *The Mushroom at the End of the World: On the Possibility of Life in Capitalist Ruins*. Princeton: Princeton UP, 2015.

Viel, Tanguy. *La disparition de Jim Sullivan*. Paris: Minuit, 2013.

Wright, Erik Olin. *Envisioning Real Utopias*. London: Verso, 2010.

William Gaddis's *J R* and the Many Faces of Junk Bonds

*A*yad Akhtar's play *Junk*, which premiered in August 2016, is about a specific kind of financial product: junk bonds, or high-yield bonds, and the mania of hostile takeovers that this product made possible in, primarily but not only, the 1980s. Based on actual characters (the protagonist Robert Merkin is modeled on junk-bond king Michael Milken) as well as on actual events (the Revlon and RJR Nabisco deals of that particular decade), "[T]he world evoked in the events depicted—the origins of debt financing—are not just a matter of the past," as Akhtar himself points out in a note to the 2017 book publication of the play, "but represent an ethos and an ontology very much central to what we call the world today" (9). In an interview, included in the published book as a sort of postscript, Akhtar elaborates that even though the play is called *Junk*, "[I]t's not just about junk bonds. The play is about the moment in American history when our relationship to debt changed" (154). One might add: one of many moments. And when Akhtar, in the same interview, says that he has tried to expose what he calls "corporate fiscal dictatorship" but that he hesitates to use the word *dictatorship* because he is afraid that it will make him sound "like a commie"—and he is not, he

Volume 31, Number 3   DOI 10.1215/10407391-8744525
© 2020 by Brown University and d i f f e r e n c e s : **A Journal of Feminist Cultural Studies**

hastens to clarify, "a communist" (156)—I for one have no such fears. More importantly, though, this fear of communism, which is not exactly a new phenomenon, has, as we will come to see in due time, profound implications for the critique of capitalism and the phenomenon of junk bonds.

Nevertheless, Akhtar's play and (some of) his comments remain a useful, contemporary point of departure for this article, which will travel back to the 1970s, not the 1980s. There is little disagreement among scholars that the contemporary era of financialization (what I mean by this phrase should be clear from what follows), not to mention the crisis that we still find ourselves in, can be traced back to the beginning of the 1970s. The year 1973, in particular, stands out as an exceptional year when it comes to financial history. This "annus horribilis" (Clover 11), which marked the end of the three golden decades of seemingly endless growth and the beginning of stagflation, was the year when the gold standard was finally abandoned and the Bretton Woods system thus effectively abolished;[1] when a severe oil crisis hit the world; when Robert Merton published "Theory of Rational Option Pricing," and Black and Scholes wrote their "The Pricing of Options and Corporate Liabilities," which introduced the formula for pricing options, a formula that now only goes by the name the Black-Scholes formula;[2] when the Chicago Board Options Exchange opened (at long last!) on April 16, after immense lobbying from the Chicago School economists led by Milton Friedman; and when American investment bank Drexel merged with Burnham and Company to form Drexel Burnham in 1973, which is where Michael Milken worked and wreaked havoc.

Paraphrasing Fredric Jameson on Peter Weiss, there is no exaggeration in claiming that 1973 constitutes a monument of radical, financial instants ("Foreword").[3] Naturally, countless other events are worth mentioning, regardless of their having taken place in 1973 or not, but I'll restrict myself to three, since they all have a bearing on issues that I will touch on below: the Employee Retirement Income Security Act of 1974 (ERISA),[4] the fiscal crisis in New York City and its near bankruptcy in 1975, and the deregulation of brokerage commissions in 1975. In terms of broader economic history, the beginning of the 1970s was also the beginning of what Robert Brenner has called the long downturn, a crisis in profitability and a transition from a Fordist and industrial to a so-called post-Fordist, deindustrialized, globalized, and financialized economy. It was, in so many words, the beginning of what Jameson would famously call late capitalism (with its cultural other, postmodernism [*Postmodernism*]), or what David Harvey refers to as neoliberalism (*Brief*).[5]

As for this current, autumnal phase or cycle of financial expansion, from the 1970s onward,[6] we find countless literary works that deal with the historical transformation of the economy and the new world of finance. The birth of the financial thriller with the publication of Paul Erdman's *The Billion Dollar Sure Thing* in 1973 is but one example (which I have dealt with elsewhere: see Frantzen, Tygstrup, and Andreasen). The postcrisis novel is another. In what follows, however, I will focus on William Gaddis's 1975 novel *J R* as a way of probing the relation between finance and fiction—between economy and literature—in the 1970s. While the 1970s have received ample attention with regard to economic and financial history, the same is not true with regard to the literary history (of finance fictions) of the decade.[7] Yet Gaddis is an exception. The scholarship on *J R* alone could fill libraries,[8] and while I am indebted to numerous studies within this body of work, I also draw the analysis in another direction: I will show that Gaddis's satirical novel is related to the revolution of the junk bond market in the 1970s and 1980s, as personified by the junk bond king, Michael Milken, and also to the ideological fictions that inhere in this historical transformation (the fictions of corporate democracy, people's capitalism, and the so-called socialization of finance). As such, junk bonds—which came into being in the 1970s, had their heyday in the 1980s and still, despite various scandals, indictments, and crashes, permeate the financial world today—become a reference point for assessing more general issues, most notably what Akhtar termed "the origins of debt financing," above. The question of junk bonds may appear to have little purchase on the question of debt, and on the much bigger story of the changes in and of the financialized economy since the 1970s, yet I will argue that it is not an epiphenomenon, nor of little significance; in fact, I will suggest that junk bonds are integral to the transformation of the finance economy in the direction of an entirely debt-driven one.[9] By the same token, my argument rests on the premise that a literary work such as Gaddis's novel may indeed offer an insight, however complex and convoluted, into this particular past, which is also to say, into our present. Like Akhtar, Gaddis provides "an origin myth for the economy that we've inherited" (Akhtar 153), only *before* the fact (in 1975) rather than *after* (in 2016). And like Akhtar, Gaddis also feared sounding like a commie.

Holy Shit! An Introduction to William Gaddis and J R

J R was published in 1975 and won the National Book Award in 1976. Despite its complexity and length, it was thus a success in a way that his previous book, the debut *The Recognitions*, was not. In the two decades that passed between his first and second book, Gaddis worked for the government and big business: he made contract films for the United States Army until the scandal of Vietnam made him move to Eastman Kodak, IBM, Ford Foundation, the pharmaceutical company Pfizer, and so on, where he worked as a freelancer doing public relations work and writing speeches for executives (Walker). He used these experiences to write *J R*, but the idea for this particular novel was there from very early on. Almost twenty years prior to its publication, Gaddis presented his idea for a novel to be named either *Sensation* or *jr* in a letter to himself:

> *In very brief it is this: a young boy, ten or eleven or so years of age, "goes into business" and makes a business fortune, by developing and following through the basically very simple procedures needed to assemble extensive financial interests, to build a "big business" in a system of comparative free enterprise employing the numerous (again basically simple) encouragements (as tax benefits &c) which are so prominent in the business world of America today. (qtd. in Swenson 93)*

At one point, he considered a subtitle that stated that it was a "novel about futures," but ultimately he rejected this idea, opting for just *J R* instead (Moore 89). It is perhaps a bit surprising that *J R* was showered in praise, as it is a demanding read. Its 726 pages are written almost entirely in dialogue, with no indication of who is speaking and no chapter breaks either. The fact that the narrator is only very sporadically present means that there are only around fifty pages of description (see Black 171).[10] As one reviewer put it in November 1975: "The rest is talk: conversation, monologue, harangue; voices on telephones, intercoms, radios, TV; sound tracks; the slang of schoolchildren and hipsters; the doublequackduckspeak of commissars, of law, science, business, PR, and education; the broken poetry of drunkenness and nervous breakdown—all interrupting each other" (Stade).[11] The rest is indeed talk, broken conversations on the telephone, noise, and basically, to quote Don DeLillo's finance novel *Cosmopolis* from 2003, just money "talking to itself" (77).

    The story takes place in the last half of 1972 in Massapequa, Long Island, and in New York (Moore 81). Like Melville's *Bartleby*, *J R* is a story of Wall Street, but unlike Bartleby, who would prefer not to, its main character JR, an eleven-year-old boy, is a very illustrious character, full of vigor and resourcefulness. With a soiled handkerchief over the receiver in the school phone booth (to hide his true age), JR starts speculating, calling in orders, doing trades. Before long—and with the additional help of one Edward Bast, a struggling artist and musician who teaches at the school JR goes to—the titular protagonist has built up a huge economic conglomerate: The J R Family of Companies. At its zenith, this family includes a brewery, a publishing house, a shipping line, a nursing home, a funeral parlor, and so on.[12] The web of this empire ropes in every character in the novel; like Borges's famous map, it eventually covers the whole world. In the last part of the novel, the paper empire crumbles, or rather crashes like the proverbial house of cards, yet JR is, at the very end, totally prepared to begin another adventure and start a new empire.

This is the story, in so many words. It is, in short, a story about *money*. (It is also, it should be noted parenthetically, a book about divorces, car accidents, suicide, mental breakdown, and so on. Even an article less myopic than this one couldn't do justice to all the entanglements of the plot and the innumerable subplots.) As Stephen Moore writes: "Asked by an interviewer in 1968 what his work in progress was about, Gaddis answered, 'Well . . . ah, just tell them it's about money'" (81–82). Or as Peter Dempsey argues: "Gaddis's novels are basically satires. At root, they are about money. Money as a medium of exchange grew up with capitalism, and Gaddis's novels are relentless in their criticism of the way contemporary capitalism corrupts and distorts human creativity and personal relationships."

Indeed, Gaddis's novels are all about money, how money talks, corrupts, spreads like a virus, destroys all values (I will take issue with and problematize parts of this in the latter section of this article). So is the spoof, "Trickle-Up Economics: JR Goes to Washington," published on October 25, 1987 in the *New York Times*. Here, an older JR appears on a Congressional hearing about the Federal budget:

> So that's where you need these cheap inflation dollars so everybody can pay everybody back, right? See we had this neat idea of this here trickle down theory only it didn't work out so good, I mean it all like got stuck at the top where 15 years ago this richest 1 percent of the nation held 27 percent of the wealth now they've got almost 36 percent, I mean it mostly like trickled up. And see where the Administration's goal was to end inflation it worked so good that this sudden massive collapse of it brought these terrific budget deficits so like now we're this world's biggest debtor nation where if these here Japanese weren't like buying $60 billion in Treasury bonds a year we couldn't hardly pay the gas bill, right?

But none of the novels engages with the question of money more deeply than *J R*, the first word of which is, simply, *money.*

> *—Money . . . ? in a voice that rustled.*
> *—Paper, yes.*
> *—And we'd never seen it. Paper money.*
> *—We never saw paper money till we came east.*
> *—It looked so strange the first time we saw it. Lifeless.*
> *—You couldn't believe it was worth a thing.*
> *—Not after Father jingling his change.*
> *—Those were silver dollars.*
> *—And silver halves, yes and quarters Julia. The ones from his pupils. I can hear him now . . . (3)*

The passage is a dialogue—between Edward Bast's two aunts, Anne and Julia Bast—about money. However, the novel is not so much about paper money or silver coins as it is about stocks and bonds, penny stocks and junk bonds, that kind of "money," that kind of "fictitious capital" (Marx 525). Money as debt, money as junk (bonds). Or to quote JR and his favorite expletive: money as "holy shit."[13]

JR's first real speculation scheme involves buying nine thousand wooden forks from the Army and reselling them to the Navy. Then, he buys a lot of bonds in a textile mill called Eagle Mills, located in the town of Union Falls. In general, it is a very complicated financial plot, as evidenced by the following dialogue between JR and his unwilling accomplice and co-conspirator, Bast (with JR being the first speaker, Bast the second):

> *—Look I'm trying to put all your crap over here and you keep getting it mixed up with mine again that eagle thing, right under there with the eagle on give it here . . .*
> *—What this? What's . . .*
> *—Give it here.*
> *—What is it some more debenture crap? What's this here thousand in the corner shares?*
> *—Dollars boy that's how much you know, it's this here bond.*
> *—What you paid a thousand dollars for a bond? I bet boy . . .*
> *—That's the whole thing you get them real cheap because they owe all this here interest.*
> *—Who does, they owe who.*
> *—Me, this here Eagle Mills they owe me.*

—A thousand dollars?
—Plus all this here interest. (170)

This is one of JR's main strategies in building up his "paper empire," as it is called in the novel (651): he buys these "real cheap" bonds in a company—in this case Eagle Mills—which is also to say, he buys its debt, and Eagle Mills thus not only has to pay him back but to pay him back with interest. Eventually this operation allows him to realize a hostile takeover of the company, raiding it before dismantling it bit by bit. In this specific way, JR as a person and *J R* as a novel "anticipated the *junk-bond* market of the 1980s" (Coe). We might even say the same thing about JR that people used to say about Michael Milken who made a killing in the 1980s: JR *is* the market (Bruck 95). If we are to understand the novel in general and these financial intricacies in particular, it is necessary to leave Gaddis's dialogues behind for a moment to understand what junk bonds are.

Junk Bonds, Hostile Takeovers, Michael Milken's Trading Bonanza

The information provided here will probably strike the uninitiated reader as tedious and laborious while the professional trader will find them hurried and superficial. Junk bonds are bonds that are below investment grade (below BBB—triple A is the highest). They are low-grade, high-yielding bonds, much cheaper that investment-grade bonds, and much riskier, which also means that the potential profit, the yield, is higher than it would otherwise be. A regular bond is a loan that the bondholder makes to the bond issuer, and the main thing to understand about the difference between stocks and (corporate) bonds is that when you buy stocks in a company, you *buy* a piece of the company; when you buy bonds in a company (or from the state, in the form of government bonds, also called Treasuries), you *lend* it money: what you own in this case is the company's debt, and for this you get an annual yield. From the company's perspective, to sell bonds is to borrow money from the market. It is thus a way for a company to raise capital. There are, generally speaking, three ways of raising money: borrow from a bank; sell shares; or sell bonds (Lanchester 58 and 73). The appeal of junk bonds is that if you are a newly established company or a company in crisis, then you probably can't borrow money from the bank and people might not want to buy your stocks because you're unable to get an investment grade, since such a rating (courtesy of infamous institutions like Standard and Poor's and Moody's) presupposes that your company has a relatively low risk of default. Which you do not. Which does not mean that you cannot raise capital or sell your bonds. You can. It just means that you have to go on the junk bond market.

Because of banking deregulations, in particular the deregulation of brokerage commissions in 1975, and a new monetary policy, in particular the so-called Volcker shock in 1979, the bond market had become unusually volatile by the 1980s. Before that, the bond market was considered a market "for women," as a character actually says in *J R* (67), or a "boring" market, as Adam Smith (a more obvious pseudonym is hard to find) wrote in the bestselling book *The Money Game* (1968): "Active investors do not pursue bonds [. . .]. It isn't that one can't make money with these instruments, it's that they lack romance enough to be part of the game; they are boring. It is very hard to get excited over a bond basis book, where your index finger traces along a column until it gets to the proper degree of safety and yield" (20). But this was no longer the opinion in the 1980s. As Paul Erdman states in his *Money Guide* from 1984: "These days bonds are no more 'forever' than diamonds" (150).[14] Junk bonds in particular were a smash hit in the 1980s, with the American bond market shooting through the roof, in the words of Michael Lewis (*Liar's* 191), and they naturally played a role in the stock crash of 1987. They were also popular as a way of financing hostile takeovers and leveraged buyouts (LBOs), meaning, to buy companies more or less against their will. This is of course the controversial part of the securitization process of junk bonds and junk bond financing, but as Roger Miller, codirector of mergers and acquisitions at Salomon, told the *New York Times* in 1985: "Junk bonds are the Holy Grail for hostile takeovers, at least for now" (qtd. in Bleakley). This was reflected not only in mainstream media but also in popular culture, in Hollywood films. Think, for instance, of Michael Douglas as Gordon Gekko in *Wall Street* (1987), think of the airline company that he raids by using so-called greenmailing tactics (like JR, he is very interested in its pension fund). Or think of Richard Gere as the ruthless but charming corporate raider Edward Lewis in *Pretty Woman* (the first line in this 1990 movie is: "It's all about money"), and think of Mr. Morse's ship manufacturing company, which Lewis is about to raid but then, because of Vivian (the prostitute played, as most people remember, by Julia Roberts), he thinks better of it and decides instead, as a final moral gesture, to go into business with the old man, who strides out of the meeting announcing proudly: "Mr. Lewis and I are going to build ships together, great big ships." But think mainly of Michael Milken.

The story of Michael Milken (b. 1946) is the story of a man who revolutionized Wall Street and the world of finance in the 1970s and 1980s. He worked at the Drexel Burnham company in New York in the beginning of the 1970s, gradually getting into, or inventing, really, the market of junk bonds until he moved his high-yield operations to Los Angeles in 1978. He had made his first junk bond financing in April 1977 (a $30 million bond for Texas International, a small oil exploration company). Prior to this date, the market had mainly consisted of so-called fallen angels, bonds whose rating was lowered at some point but not below BBB to begin with. But Milken saw a golden opportunity in high-yield bonds, and using portfolio theories of diversification, it really did not matter if some companies (whose debt you had bought) defaulted on the bonds, that is, if some of the junk bonds, as the jargon goes, blew up in your face. And so, in 1977, his trading bonanza was already taking off. Despite the soaring interest rates after 1979, Milken was killing the market (he was the market). Why? Because he was very creative with the financial products and instruments he offered for sale—so creative, in fact, that the Securities and Exchange Commission (SEC) charged Milken and Drexel Burnham Lambert with insider trading and securities fraud in the late 1980s. In 1990, after several years of investigation and prosecution, Milken agreed to plead guilty to six charges.[15]

A Democratization of Capital and Credit?

As Connie Bruck writes in her book *The Predator's Ball*, at the end of the 1980s, with the stock market crash in 1987 and the lawsuits against Boesky and Milken, "obituaries for junk began to appear in the press. But they were wrong" (345). Drexel Burnham tried as hard as it could to turn the sentiment of Congress and of the public around. It launched its own massive PR campaign in 1987, making music videos and selling T-shirts with slogans such as: "Junk Bonds Keep America Fit."

The message from Drexel was that not only do junk bonds keep America fit, they also bring about a total and unheard-of democratization of credit and financial speculation. Drexel claimed in the same 1987 ad campaign that it had, indeed, "furthered the '*democratization of capital*'" (qtd. in Bruck 350; my emphasis). It had given mainstream America access to the public and corporate debt market, prompting or pushing the belief that anybody can make it, here and now, on the junk bond market. Small fish can eat the big fish, or: "Small corporations can go big-game hunting," as the already mentioned article in the *New York Times* had it in 1985 (Bleakley).

This fiction, or fantasy, was prevalent at the time and inherent to the trading of junk bonds. As Glenn Yago writes in *Junk Bonds: How High Yield Securities Restructured Corporate America* (a book in which he offers his warmest thanks to Milken, acknowledging that the book "owes an enormous intellectual debt" to him): "With the growth in the *availability* of capital, junk bonds have created *access* to capital for small and medium-sized companies that had been economically disenfranchised from participating in the capital markets" (9). Quoting one of Milken's business partners, Nelson Peltz ("The thing about capital is, if you don't inherit it, you have to borrow it"), Yago goes on to argue that "junk bonds applied the same logic that gave millions of Americans homes, automobiles, and higher education to provide loans for business ownership and development" (9). For all the flaws in his analysis and his extremely biased view of junk bonds, Yago does draw a correct parallel to the housing market, where Lewis Ranieri at Salomon Brothers developed the mortgage-backed securities intended to realize the "democratic" idea that everybody should have the right to own a house.[16]

This is the American dream 2.0. And it is more than a purely individualistic dream: it is a collective, democratic dream. Or, to refer to Peter Drucker's book, with its telling if somewhat derogatory title, *The Unseen Revolution: How Pension Fund Socialism Came to America*, it is a *socialist* dream. In the book, Drucker is preoccupied with the revolution in pension funds, which goes back to when General Motors established a pension fund for its workers in 1950. This "revolution" deserves a few words in passing, since it is emblematic of what Christian Marazzi has called the socialization of finance. It is socialism, Drucker claims, because workers come to own the means of production, or part of the company, through the pension funds: "In terms of Socialist theory, the employees are the only true 'owners' of the means of production. Through their pension funds they are the only true 'capitalists' around, owning, controlling, and directing the country's 'capital fund.' The 'means of production,' that is, the American economy—again with agriculture the only important exception—is being run for the benefit of the country's employees" (5).[17] However outrageous this analysis might sound,[18] similar ideas were introduced in Denmark, albeit as a positive project. In 1973, the social democratic government and prime minister Anker Jørgensen proposed a model called ØD, "Økonomisk demokrati" (literally meaning "economic democracy"), based on a report from the Danish Confederation of Trade Unions. As far as pension funds in the u.s. are concerned, it was, in the words of the anonymous *Kirkus* review of Drucker's book, "nothing short of a unique and salutary American brand of socialism—the ultimate ownership of the nation's business by the nation's workers, as beneficiaries of pension trusts [. . .]. The Dickensian clerk, the assembly-line worker, you, I, and the rest of the proletariat have become men and women, not of property, but of expectations" ("Unseen").

Back to J R: Realism and Critique in Gaddis's Novel

To return to *J R*, we are now in a position to appreciate what is at stake in the novel. When Marazzi, in *Capital and Language*, defines the process of financialization that took off in the early 1970s as "the diversion of savings from household economies to stocks and securities" (21), isn't this precisely what *J R* is about? When he writes about a "paradoxical anthropological metamorphosis of the postmodern citizen" (22), can we find a more apt characterization of the novel's child protagonist, JR? Marazzi continues: "With their savings invested in securities, workers are no longer separate from capital, as they are, by virtue of its legal definition, in the salary relationship. As shareholders they are tied to the ups and downs of the markets and so they are *co-interested* in the 'good operation' of capital *in general*" (37). Doesn't JR take this co-interest in the good operation of capital to the extreme and absurd?

The answer to these rhetorical questions is, as is hopefully clear by now, yes. And it is on the basis of this affirmation that the *realism* of *J R* as a novel can also be understood, the ways in which the novel indexes a new financial reality and ideology. Obviously, this is made clear not only at the level of content but at the level of form as well. If JR as a character, "a natural spokesperson for capital," in the words of Ralph Clare, is "not so much speaking for capital as capital is speaking through him" (120), the novel as a whole, or the voice of the novel, so to speak, is also to be regarded, or heard, as the very voice of capital, the noise of incessant speculation, money talking to itself. By the same token, the novel's formal complexity, its strange temporalities and almost excessive levels of abstraction, should also be viewed less as postmodern playfulness and more as a kind of literary realism, a mimetic device meant to capture and reflect, for instance, the hall of mirrors of the junk bond market, its dense, jungle-like web of information and interaction (or, if these traits are traits of postmodernism, if *J R* is indeed a postmodern novel, then it is postmodern to the extent that capital has itself become postmodern).[19]

Speaking of finance and fiction within an overall framework of realism, it is in any case clear that there can be no clear-cut representation of finance for the simple reason that finance as such entails and embodies *a crisis of representation*. In the 1970s this crisis of representation was also, I would contend, a crisis of genre. According to Mary Poovey, while economic and literary writing share "an engagement with the problematic of representation" (5), a system of representation is experienced as problematic only when it no longer works, which was clearly the case in the 1970s. One new system of representation, or one new genre, was the financial thriller, mentioned above. It should come as no surprise that the logics and effects of financial capitalism circulate and structure aesthetic genres: they have done so throughout history and will continue do so, as cultural systems of representation struggle to grasp the economic reality of their times (see Adkins 175).[20]

If the majority of financial thrillers in the 1970s were about oil, gold, and currency speculation as related to the abolition of the Bretton Woods system in 1971–73 (Erdman again comes to mind), Gaddis's novel is prompted by a concern with junk bonds, hostile takeovers, and leveraged buyouts. In terms of genre, it is perhaps most accurate to say that *J R* provides a *satire* of the embryonic junk bond market and its concomitant fantasies: the fantasy of the democratization of finance; the fantasy that workers can become or have already become shareholders, that discount brokers can become big swinging dicks, and pawns can become kings or queens; the fantasy that the proletariat has already been transformed into men and women of expectations, citizens into speculators, and ordinary people into owners of real estate and, indeed, owners of the nation's businesses as beneficiaries of pension trusts. This is, to Gaddis, a matter of satire, a matter of both realism and critique.

At the outset of the novel, JR and his class are going on a field trip with their teacher, Mrs. Joubert. As she tells her pupils: "We're taking a field trip in to the Stock Exchange to buy a share of stock," to "buy a share in America" (18). In New York, the class ends up buying shares in a company called Diamond Cable. Buying a share helps America, they are told, "turn the promise of tomorrow into the reality of today": "that's what people's capitalism is, isn't it everybody," Mister Davidoff, a corporate public relations executive, asks them (92). Even if the deregulation of brokerage commissions (the so-called mayday of 1975) made it possible for smaller players to compete on the market,[21] even if the introduction of junk bonds provided easier access to credit, Gaddis clearly wants to answer (and have his readers join him in answering): No. This is not what people's capitalism is about. This is not a democracy. Or, as Gaddis puts it himself, more elaborately and eloquently, in an interview from 1987: "I'd always been intrigued by the charade of the so-called free market, so-called free enterprise system, the stock market conceived of as what was called a 'people's capitalism' where you 'owned a part of the company' and so forth. All of which is true; you own shares in a company, so you literally do own part of the assets. But if you own a hundred shares out of six or sixty or six hundred million, you're not going to influence things very much" (Interview 277).

From JR to Michael Milken to Jonathan Lebed

In the same interview, Gaddis goes on to say that in hindsight the novel seems to have been rather prophetic. The point here is not to claim that *J R* is an act of prophecy or to hail Gaddis, uncritically, as a seer,[22] although it must be admitted that Gaddis had an acute understanding of the ongoing changes in and of capitalism and that he even included references to Milken in the novel (in the guise of a character named Senator Miliken). It must also be admitted, more curiously, that some twenty years after the publication of the novel, in the late nineties, Jonathan Lebed (b. 1984) actually emerged as a real-life JR, carrying out financial transactions from his bedroom in his parents' house in New Jersey. Using penny stocks, not junk bonds, as his main weapon, Lebed was the first minor ever to be prosecuted by the SEC (the Securities and Exchange Commission), in 2000. According to Lewis, who writes about the case in *Next: The Future Just Happened*, Lebed "used the Internet to promote stocks from his bedroom in Cedar Grove, New Jersey. Armed only with accounts at AOL and E-Trade, the kid had bought stock, then using 'Multiple fictitious names,' posted hundreds of messages on Yahoo Finance message boards recommending that stock to others" (27–28).[23] Jonathan made $800,000 trading online during a six-month period, and was precisely eleven years old when he got his first AOL account and started trading (Lewis, *Next* 195)! Of course, the media couldn't help describing him as a "stock whiz kid" (*Bloomberg*), but when asked in the SEC investigation, "Where did you learn your technique for day trading?" Jonathan simply answered, "Just on TV, Internet." And when the obvious follow-up question came, "What TV shows?," Jonathan's answer couldn't have been more laconic: "CNBC mostly—basically CNBC is what I watch all the time" (Lewis, *Next* 46–47; Taylor 197).

This is Gaddis's satire and critique, whether prophetic or not: by letting an eleven-year-old kill the junk bond market, he satirizes the

idea that anybody can now play the game, while also taking the idea seriously in the sense that, well, maybe anybody can do it. In his portrait of
JR, Gaddis avoids the kind of mythologization that befell Milken who, in
his heyday, received the praise of being "a one-man revolution" (*Forbes*)
and "a world-class financial wizard" (*California Business Magazine*; qtd.
in Bruck 270). JR is no such thing. He is perfectly average and ordinary.
He is the kid next door, and not, as Gaddis himself stresses, "one of these
computer-wizard brilliant kids" (Interview 287). He is not a genius; he is
you and me. In this reading, you do not have to be the Mozart of the money
markets to make a killing. You can be an eleven-year-old kid (reality eventually confirmed this).

  Economists, traders, and politicians usually tell a different story
than this one. They tell us, the public, that the financial world and its intri-
cate instruments, like junk bonds, are so incredibly complex that no one
outside this selfsame world will be able to understand it, let alone criticize
it, and that we should therefore leave the "players" alone and let them do
their thing (and occasionally bail them out). But maybe, Gaddis seems to
say to his readers, it is not that complicated after all. Maybe we could all
understand the system if we really wanted to. And Gaddis wants us to. In *J R*,
in the course of a dialogue between the stockbroker Crawley and newcomer
Bast, the former teaches the latter about the idioms and colloquialisms of
Wall Street: "[W]hen we say at the market we mean at the market price."
Crawley then asks Bast, in relation to Eagle Mills: "Wallpaper Mister Bast,
wallpaper. Know what wallpaper is?" "Well I thought I . . ." (197). But no, Bast
doesn't know. Crawley doesn't provide an answer to his own question, but
Investopedia does: "*Wallpaper* is the name given to stocks, bonds, and other
securities that have become worthless" (Kenton). With regard to the novel,
the pedagogical point seems to be that readers have to achieve a certain
degree of financial literacy. What *J R* wants, then, is for the reader to learn
the language of finance capital (not just the jargon and the colloquialisms).
This is a matter of education (a key term and topic in Gaddis's oeuvre), and
it seems to be a precondition for engaging critically with finance, whether
in a novel or in the real world. Like JR, we have to become acquainted with
the words and worlds of finance, but unlike JR, the goal is not to make a
profit but to offer resistance to the capitalist system that we have come to
learn but not love.

Critical Remarks on Gaddis's Critique of Capitalism

The scene with Bast and Crawley ends on a deeply satirical note, with Crawley wanting to commission the economically destitute Bast to write some "zebra music" for a film he has produced (202). The whole discussion around wallpaper is also a bit of a joke, which is only emphasized when the character named Duncan appears in the book, since Duncan actually has a wallpaper firm that sells wallpaper in the everyday sense of the word. This is perhaps the problem with the novel and with satire in general: that it relies on an atmosphere of helplessness, that it remains a discourse and a form that arises out of an impotent, if not cynical, position. We can certainly make fun of Milken, JR, and the junk bond raiders, laugh at their T-shirts and their megalomania. But can we do more than that? Can Gaddis? It is not a rhetorical question; it is indeed uncertain.

What is certain is that Gaddis, in his pedagogical project, clearly strives to expose and ridicule the by now familiar fiction of a people's democracy that was integral to the junk bond market from its embryonic stage, saying, as in the interview, that "if you own a hundred shares out of six or sixty or six hundred million, you're not going to influence things very much." Of course, it isn't a real democracy; capitalism is not democratic. There's no such thing as a free enterprise system—which is why, in the novel, this phrase is always cut short: "the whole God damned free enter . . ." (406), "a real lesson in what the free ent . . ." (461). It is total fantasy, an ideological fiction. But even if it is a fiction, it surely has material consequences for real people, as Bast tries to tell JR in a later dialogue about Eagle Mills.

It is an absolutely crucial scene, yet the tone between Bast and JR is less friendly than in the scene analyzed above. They are at the Met in New York, discussing Eagle Mills. Having succeeded in his takeover of the company, JR now wants to sell everything off, even though Bast has just travelled to Eagle Mills and told the people there, the workers, that they don't have to worry. "[Y]ou can't," Bast quite reasonably protests, "you can't just dismantle the company." "How come?" JR asks. "Because," Bast says, "these are real people up there that's how come! A lot of them who owned the stock still can't believe it's not worth anything and even the ones who owned bonds, a lot of them are old and when they first bought the bonds it was almost like they were lending money to, to someone in the family. And the ones who work there, even if you could sell their ballfield and put their offices in the mills how long do you think they'd . . ." (296). But JR is unaffected and unmoved: "[T]his isn't a popularity contest" (296). Then he begins to talk about "depreciated acceleration," which is another joke, since the proper financial term is accelerated depreciation. JR emphasizes that Eagle Mills has a really nice pension fund, with a lot of equity, and thus leverage! Again, Bast objects: "[D]id it ever occur to you that a lot of them might be getting real old along with everything else?" (298). The workers at Eagle Mills, Bast continues, are "almost ready to retire and draw their pensions, what do you think a pension fund is for" (298). It is for something else, JR declares, it is for profit, "tax credits" (298), and "capital gains" (299). "Stop it," Bast insists, "these people [have] worked all their lives for miserable wages so they can finally retire on a miserable pension" (298). But JR is adamant:

> —No but holy, I mean listen I'm the one that has to figure things up and like make these here decisions with these risks [. . .]. But what am I suppose to do! his foot came to the floor and he got the other one free of the radiator,—I mean who asked them for their lousy mills? All I did was buy these bonds for this here investment and mind my own business and then they turn around and dump all these wrecked up buildings and people and stuff on me and what do they expect me to do, build them a park? I mean holy shit [. . .] he ripped a paper towel down and worked it at his nose,—I have this here investment which I have to protect it don't I? [. . .] You can't just play to play because the rules are only for if you're playing to win which that's the only rules there are. (300–301)

Here, one could go on at length about the novel's formal qualities, JR's colloquialisms, his repeated use of phrases such as "no but," and his favorite expletive, "holy shit!" (as Freud emphasized, money and shit go hand in hand). One could also elaborate on the conflict that emerges in this dialogue (a conflict also staged in a number of films mentioned above) as a conflict between production and speculation, between building in order to create things and building in order to create nothing at all. As Chairman of U.S. Steel James Roderick broadcasted already in 1979: "The duty of management is to make money, not steel" (qtd in Harvey, *Conditions* 158). Or as Matthew McConaughey's character Mark Hanna says to Jordan Belfort (Leonardo DiCaprio) in *The Wolf of Wall Street* (2013): "We don't create shit; we don't build anything." (It could, of course, be argued that what these people create is nothing but shit.)

Akhtar's *Junk* displays another version of the same conflict, where the hostile takeover bid, financed by junk bonds, concerns a steel company, Everson Steel and United, with its chief executive Thomas Everson, Jr. hammering the message home: "That's what this company is about. Making steel" (24). The decline brought about and accelerated by the raiders and their weapons of mass destruction, junk bonds, is merely a sign of a more general decline in American industry, at least according to the old(er) generation, here personified by Leo Tresler, a private equity magnate who refuses to deal in junk: "*What's he* [the corporate villain Merkin] *doing.* What *is* he doing? We used to be a country that paid our bills. Made things. This guy comes along and says he's *manufacturing debt*" (26)—whereas he, Tresler, is "a real man with real money. No crummy notes, no crazy paper" (82).

Of course, both Tresler and Merkin are wrong, caught as they are in this somewhat false ideological conflict between the realer than real economy and the unreal, speculative, and financial economy.[24] The pivotal point is that the conflict is based on a question of reality (what kind of capital is "real" and what kind "fictitious") and also a question of morality (which version of capitalism is better and to be preferred, morally speaking). This is exactly where we find reason to expose Gaddis's critique of financial capitalism to critique. While it is unsurprising that a lot of Hollywood films—as well as almost all the financial thrillers of the 1970s—reduce or move politics to ethics, it is perhaps somewhat unexpected that Gaddis, in *J R*, falls into the same trap. Like Leo Tresler, he seems to nourish a certain nostalgia for the good old less speculative days of capitalism.

Despite his critical concern with accelerating financialization—the financialization of everything, as Harvey puts it (*Brief* 33)—and the privatization of public infrastructure, education, healthcare, and so on, Gaddis's critique of the capitalist society remains a moral, even conservative one.[25] He is first and foremost preoccupied with and lamenting the moral decline, as it is phrased repeatedly in the novel, from status to contract.[25] And we, as readers, are meant to perceive JR the protagonist as a symptom, or the infantile embodiment, of capital as such, but only to the extent that he embodies the "simple cheerful greed" inherent, according to Gaddis, to the system (Interview 287).[26] Gaddis is adamant that greed is the cause of the crisis of capitalism: the immoral and scrupulous actions of individuals, the abuses of the system—not the system itself. As Gaddis says:

> *I'm frequently seen in the conservative press as being out there on the barricades shouting: Down with capitalism! I do see it in the end as really the most workable system we've produced. So what we're talking about is not the system itself, but its abuses.*

> *I don't mean criminal but the abundant abuses just* within *the*
> *letter of the law. The essential question is whether it can survive*
> *these abuses given free rein and whether these abuses are inher-*
> *ent in the system itself. I should think it is perfectly clear in my*
> *work—calling attention, satirizing these abuses—that our best*
> *hope lies in bringing things under better and more equitable*
> *control, cutting back the temptations to unmitigated greed and*
> *bemused dishonesty [. . .] in other words that these abuses the*
> *system has fostered are not essential, but running out of moral or*
> *ethical control can certainly threaten its survival. (286)*

If this is our best hope, then we have to agree with Kafka, modifying his
famous saying ever so slightly: there is hope, only not for us who live in the
capitalist system of debt and financial speculation.[28]

Concluding Remarks on Gaddis's Story of a "Nickel and Dime Takeover of a Broken Down Mill"

I have focused on William Gaddis's *J R* as a story anatomizing
and anticipating the junk bond market that reached its zenith in the 1980s,
especially when these junkiest of bonds became the predominant way of
financing leveraged buyouts and hostile takeovers. With the benefit of hindsight, Christopher Walker, a reviewer for *The Observer*, was able twenty
years later to elaborate that *J R* is "a brilliant, anarchic comedy about the
infantile nature of American business" and that "Gaddis was ahead of his
time. His 11-year-old speculator was a short-pants version of the infamous
1980s junk-bond dealer, Michael Milken." Alluding to Jonathan Lebed rather
than Milken, Mark C. Taylor writes that "it took almost two decades for
the world William Gaddis imagined in *J R* to become a 'reality'" (191). As a
novel about junk bonds and an eleven-year-old kid killing the market, *J R*
is indeed some fiction: a fiction made real.

Naturally, other topics and themes in *J R* could have been chosen
as worthy of consideration: inheritance as depicted in the parts about the
Bast family; education in relation to the school where a lot of the action takes
place; art and writing as represented not only by Edward Bast but also by
the character named Thomas Eigen, who wrote an important novel once
but now works as a speech writer (a life trajectory not unlike Gaddis's own);
New York in the 1970s, the fiscal crisis in "Fear City," and the apartment
in which the aforementioned Eigen and his friend Jack Gibbs spend quite

some time;[29] or the issue of comedy, of entropy, of information and technology. I might have connected Gaddis's satirical novel to the emergence of the financial thriller in the 1970s, a genre that, in contrast to the fate of *J R*, dominated the bestseller lists of the decade (in particular, Paul Erdman's *The Billion Dollar Sure Thing* and Arthur Hailey's *The Moneychangers*). So many *other* stories, but the story of junk bonds is the one that I, for better or worse, have chosen to (let Gaddis) tell.

As Susan Strange notes in *Mad Money*, however, "[T]he junk bond story has been told many times as a highly coloured tale of the players who came from nowhere, dazzled the financial scene—and then came to grief." But, she adds, "from a systemic angle, it can also be seen as part of a broader political economy story in which the inflation of the 1970s, fueled by the Vietnam War and the oil price rise, and the cumulative revolution in banking both played a part" (33). In this sense, then, the story about a "nickel and dime takeover of a broken down mill" (*J R* 431)—a story that may appear small and insignificant even if highly intriguing—is part of a bigger story about the revolution not only of Wall Street but of financial capitalism as such. The story about junk bonds that Gaddis tells in his 1975 novel is a story about debt and credit, about how everyone suddenly had access to credit and how debt was transformed into an asset. In Akhtar's *Junk*, the character based on Michael Milken, Robert Merkin, states that "debt signifies new beginnings" (66). Paraphrasing the (in)famous speech made not by Milken but by Michael Douglas playing Gordon Gekko in *Wall Street*, we could say that in this brave new world, debt is good.

And in this world, it is difficult to distinguish fact from fiction, the "real" economy from the "fictitious" and speculative one, and real-life actors from movie stars playing roles. In these muddy waters, Gaddis sails with JR as his wild and inexperienced captain. Gaddis's interest in the novel is not only in the junk bonds but also in the fiction that inheres in them. This fiction or fantasy has been called the democratization of capital and credit, and it is a persistent fiction. When William D. Cohan, institutional investor, told Milken's life story for *Business Insider* in 2017, he wrote that the "greatest innovation in the recent history of finance" is "the junk bond" and that this innovation or invention "has done nothing less than bring about the democratization of finance."

For all the novel's merits—in terms of realistically and critically registering new levels of financialization, its ideological fictions and real, material effects—*J R* has, as I have shown, at least one serious shortcoming. At the end of the day, Gaddis's critique of capitalism remains a moral and ethical one, bemoaning the greed of JR (greed is not good) and the decline from status to contract that runs in tandem with the changes in and of the economy. Like Akhtar, Gaddis was too afraid of being labeled a communist to really face the system in its totality, and he was thus also incapable of imagining and depicting any way of resisting it *at that level.* Instead of talking about the system, he talks about the abuses of the system. Instead of talking about, or at least hinting at the possibility of, abolishing debt, Gaddis calls for more "moral and ethical control," that is, for "bringing things under better and more equitable control, cutting back the temptations to unmitigated greed and bemused dishonesty" (*Interview* 286). This is a fiction—perhaps more essential to capitalism than any other—that Gaddis does not see for what it is: that things would be better, or more acceptable, if only we had more control, if only bankers behaved a bit more responsibly and people in general did not succumb to the temptation of greed.

MIKKEL KRAUSE FRANTZEN is a postdoctoral fellow in the Department of Arts and Cultural Studies at the University of Copenhagen. He is affiliated with the collective research project Finance Fiction—Financialization and Culture in the Early 21st Century. The author of *Going Nowhere, Slow—The Aesthetics and Politics of Depression* (Zer0, 2019), his work has appeared in *Critique: Studies in Contemporary Fiction,* the *Journal of Austrian Studies, Studies in American Fiction, boundary 2,* the *Los Angeles Review of Books,* and *Theory, Culture, and Society.*

Notes

1 After Nixon made his announcement, Leo Melamed, new chairman of the International Monetary Market in Chicago, quickly called Milton Friedman (who already in 1953 wrote the essay "The Case for Flexible Exchange Rates") and got him to write a paper, "The Need for Futures Markets in Currencies," which would serve, as Perry Mehrling puts it in *Fischer Black and the Revolutionary Idea of Finance,* "as the intellectual backing for the new markets he [Melamed] would propose" (169).

2 In 1997 Merton and Scholes (Black was no longer alive at this point) received the Nobel Prize for their pioneering formula and for facilitating "new types of financial instruments" and "more efficient risk management in society" (Mehrling 3). It ought to be mentioned here that the title for this article is borrowed from the title of an article Fischer Black wrote in 1995 called "The Many Faces of Derivatives."

3 As Max Haiven writes, "[T]here is a substantial hazard in electing to frame financialization as a periodizing concept and additionally to trying to peg it to a specific year" (88), yet he, like so many others, chooses 1973 as a "particularly telling moment" in history, when a lot of seismic changes occurred. See also Clover 11; and Finch 731.

4 See Mehrling 222: "Pension money was big money, and getting bigger every day as a result of ERISA."

5 Obviously, there are differences and disagreements among these histories and periodizations, but what they do not disagree on is the significance of the year 1973.

6   Here, I am implicitly referring to yet another one of the influential thinkers of the history of capitalism, Giovanni Arrighi, who is famous for describing capitalism's systemic cycles of accumulation, cycles that not only alternate between material and financial expansion but also between geographical epicenters. It is the phase of financial expansion, when profits tend to come from speculation and fictitious capital (according to Marx's formula M–M'), that Arrighi calls an autumnal phase.

7   Of course there are (a few) exceptions, like Finch or Marsh.

8   From seminal works such as the anthology *In Recognition of William Gaddis* (Kuehl and Moore) and Steven Moore's *William Gaddis: Expanded Edition* to articles from the last couple of years, for example, Allan; and Kessous.

9   While I am writing this, the coronavirus pandemic has hit the world, and as a result the economy is suffering in ways that eclipse the financial crisis of 2007–8. One key area presently is corporate debt and junk bonds. On April 9, 2020, the *Financial Times* reported that the Federal Reserve has deemed it necessary to enter "new territory with support for risky debt," that is to say, to support junk bonds by buying debt from risky companies (Rennison et al.). Why? Because the corporate bond market is a bubble that could burst any day now. Or as Jonathan Tepper wrote a couple of weeks earlier, on March 20, 2020:

    Corporate debt has doubled in the decade since the financial crisis, non-financial companies now owe a record $9.6 trillion in the United States. Globally, companies have issued $13 trillion in bonds. Much of the debt is Chinese, and their companies will struggle to repay any of it given the lockdown and the breakdown in supply chains. We have not even begun to see the full extent of the corporate bond market meltdown. One little discussed problem is that a large proportion of the debt is "junk," i.e., lowly rated. An astonishing $3.6 trillion in bonds are rated "BBB," which is only one rating above junk. These borderline bonds account for 54% of investment-grade corporate bonds, up from 30% in 2008. When recessions happen, these will be downgraded and fall into junk category. Many funds that cannot own junk bonds will become forced sellers. We will see an absolute carnage of forced selling when the downgrades happen. Again, the illusion of safety and liquidity will be exposed by the coronavirus.

10 John Johnston writes: "[N]o dialogue is possible simply because this is not a human being talking, but money itself; and it is not the language of money but the speech of money, the flux of capital as it enters into and becomes part of verbal communications" (169).

11 For more on the acoustics, or aural aspects, of the novel, see Kessous.

12 Eagle Mills, Alberta and Western Power Company, Ace Development Company, Nobili Pharmaceuticals, Frigicom, J R Shipping Corporation, the magazine *She*, and so on.

13 The many views on the intimate relation between money and shit, between the sacred and the scatological have been well rehearsed, so I won't do so again here. For readings of *J R* that venture in this direction, see Moore on the excremental and religious origin of money (81) and the intertextual reference to Wagner's *Ring des Nibelungen* ("Rhine [. . .] GOLD" [*J R* 32]); and Taylor on how money is, at the same time, worthless (like shit) and priceless (like gold) (57).

14 But Erdman still doesn't give much for bonds, junk or otherwise. Speaking of bonds and gilts (government bonds), he writes: "[Y]ou will never make a killing," but "you will not lose your shirt either" (*Paul* 157).

15 It was, in fact, Milken's longtime business partner Ivan Boesky who, as part of a plea in his own case, implicated Milken, who, by the way, was recently pardoned by Donald Trump. Before that, however, Milken held annual conventions at the Beverly Hilton Hotel in Los Angeles, known as the Predator's Ball, featuring, as Will Kenton writes, "some of the nation's most prominent corporate raiders and financiers who were also Drexel clients. After the first convention in 1979, these conventions became increasingly focused on setting up leveraged buyouts and hostile takeovers using junk bonds." In recent years, the Milken Institute, a think tank founded by Michael Milken in 1991, has continued the tradition, although, for obvious reasons, under another name. In 2019, Ivanka Trump was in the audience for a conference that revealed "anxiety over 'class war' and 'revolution'" (Edgecliffe-Johnson et al.). Milken is still very much in vogue and is as rich as ever, it would seem. His trademark operations—the junk bonds that were used for hostile takeovers— "have become a mainstream financing tool for almost any healthy company of any size, and a standard portfolio asset even for retail investors," as Charles Morris puts it in *The Two Trillion Dollar Meltdown* (123), an updated version of *The Trillion-Dollar Meltdown*. For more on the present state of junk bonds, see note 10.

16 In "William Gaddis's Aesthetic Economy," Angela S. Allan is also preoccupied with the democratic fantasies of Milton Friedman and his fantasy of democratizing the economic as such *via* the free market (229).

17 For a good article on Gaddis that uses Marazzi and also quotes this specific passage by Drucker, see Kessous.

18 In *Pension Fund Capitalism*, Gordon L. Clark notes "the astonishing growth of Anglo-American pension fund assets over the past thirty years" (1) and states that "the idea of 'pension fund socialism' is an exercise in political rhetoric rather than reality" (43). Similarly, Michael Hudson has written about how the revolution in pension funds is far from a socialist and/or democratic project but is, on the contrary, just another capitalist and/or financial way of exploiting labor (439).

19 This understanding of realism, as intimately connected to a novel's formal and fictional qualities, relies heavily on Anna Kornbluh's *Realizing Capital*.

20 I am indebted to my colleague Torsten Andreasen for this point.

21 Connie Bruck talks about "a band of mainly small-time entrepreneurs, raiders, green mailers, the have-nots of the corporate world" (20).

22 Moore writes that "[i]n interviews in later years, Gaddis half-seriously boasted of warning an unheeding society of the junk-bond eighties and the crash of 1987" (123). In *The Paris Review Interviews*, Gaddis thus proclaims: "Looking around us now with a two-trillion-dollar federal deficit and billions of private debt and the banks, the farms, basic industry all in serious trouble, it seems to have been rather prophetic" (Interview 277).

23 Mark Taylor also brings in Lebed (and Lewis) in his reading of *J R*: "Two decades after the publication of Gaddis's novel, Jonathan Lebed became a real-life JR; he created a virtual empire by trading stocks and publicizing his picks on his Web site, Stock-Dogs.com" (9).

24 As Finch writes: "The fictionality of finance is, of course, a fiction itself" (731).

25 This is hardly news to readers of Gaddis, so I am not making an original point here. Lee Konstantinou, who also lends an attentive ear to the dialogues between JR and Bast, writes:

What is evil about private equity and finance capital is structural, not personal [. . .]. Though Gaddis has said that what he was writing against was a corrupted version of capitalism—not capitalism per se—his rendition of J R might give us reason to wonder. Does capitalism with a human face humanize capitalism or simply conceal the indifferent, playfully destructive, inhuman heart of the system? Is Gaddis obligated to give a positive account of what a decent system might look like, or is critique enough?

See also Kessous 14.

26 A lot could be said about the novel's thematization of this transition, or decline, from status to contract. As the character named Gibbs asks another character called Beamish: "[T]he whole God damned problem's the decline from status to contract right Beamish? Whole God damned

problem right?" (393, as well as 396, 509, 595, and 698). See also Konstatinou; and Moore 83–84).

27 Some readings of *J R* follow Gaddis in his own reading of JR as motivated by simple greed. See, for instance, Allan 227.

28 See Kafka's reply to Max Brod: "plenty of hope, an infinite amount of hope—but not for us" (qtd. in Benjamin 798).

29 The story about New York in the 1970s was and is also a story about bonds and pension funds and the relation between the public and the private. Harvey writes that the New York City fiscal crisis is an "iconic case" of the broader crisis of capital accumulation: "Capitalist restructuring and deindustrialization had for several years been eroding the economic base of the city, and rapid suburbanization had left much of the central city impoverished" (45). This is precisely what Garth Risk Hallberg's 2015 novel *City on Fire* is about; it tells the story in the form of fiction. While Kim Phillips-Fein's *Fear City* is not fiction but a historical, documentary work, it too describes how the city of New York "turned to debt" at this particular moment in history and how "[i]n retrospect, the expansion of New York City debt seems of a piece with the broader economic patterns of the late 1960s and early 1970s: a turn to finance and speculation during the 'go-go-years' at the end of the long postwar boom, followed by a contraction when this bubble popped" (6, 76).

Works Cited

Adkins, Lisa. *The Time of Money*. Stanford: Stanford UP, 2018.

Akhtar, Ayad. *Junk*. New York: Back Bay, 2017.

Allan, Angela S. "William Gaddis's Aesthetic Economy." *Studies in American Fiction* 42.2 (2015): 219–41.

Arrighi, Giovanni. *The Long Twentieth Century: Money, Power, and the Origins of Our Times.* London: Verso, 2010.

Benjamin, Walter. "Franz Kafka: On the Tenth Anniversary of His Death." 1934. *Selected Writings.* Vol. 2. Trans. Harry Zohn. Cambridge, MA: Harvard UP, 2005. 794–818.

Black, Joel Dana. "The Paper Empires and Empirical Fictions of William Gaddis." Kuehl and Moore 162–73.

Bleakley, Fred R. "The Power and the Perils of Junk Bonds." *New York Times* 14 Apr. 1985. https://www.nytimes.com/1985/04/14/business/the-power-and-the-perils-of-junk-bonds.html.

Brenner, Robert. *The Economics of Global Turbulence: The Advanced Capitalist Economies from Long Boom to Long Downturn, 1945–2005.* London: Verso, 2006.

Bruck, Connie. *Predator's Ball: The Inside Story of Drexel Burnham and the Rise of the Junk Bond Raiders.* London: Penguin, 1988.

Clare, Ralph. "Family Incorporated: William Gaddis's *J R* and the Embodiment of Capitalism." *Studies in the Novel* 45.1 (2013): 102–22.

Clark, Gordon L. *Pension Fund Capitalism.* Oxford: Oxford UP, 2000.

Clover, Joshua. "*Retcon*: Value and Temporality in Poetics." *Representations* 126 (2014): 9–30.

Coe, Jonathan. *Marginal Notes, Doubtful Statements: Non-fiction, 1990–2013.* Kindle ed. London: Penguin, 2013.

Cohan, William D. "Michael Milken Invented the Modern Junk Bond, Went to Prison, and Then Became One of the Most Respected People on Wall Street." *Business Insider* 2 May 2017. https://www.businessinsider.com/michael-milken-life-story-2017-5?r=US&IR=T.

DeLillo, Don. *Cosmopolis: A Novel.* New York: Scribner, 2003.

Dempsey, Peter. "William Gaddis. Life and Work." 17 Dec. 1998. https://www.williamgaddis.org/life&work.shtml.

Drucker, Peter F. *The Unseen Revolution: How Pension Fund Socialism Came to America.* London: Heinemann, 1976.

Edgecliffe-Johnson, Andrew, Lindsay Fortado, and James Fontanella-Khan. "Elite Gathering Reveals Anxiety over 'Class War' and 'Revolution.'" *Financial Times* 2 May 2019. https://www.ft.com/content/0f9cf638-6c28-11e9-80c7-60ee53e6681d.

Erdman, Paul. *The Billion Dollar Sure Thing.* New York: Charles Scribner, 1973.

——————. *Paul Erdman's Money Guide.* London: Sphere, 1985.

Finch, Laura. "The Un-real Deal: Financial Fiction, Fictional Finance, and the Financial Crisis." *Journal of American Studies* 49 (2015): 731–53.

Frantzen, Mikkel, Frederik Tygstrup, and Torsten Andreasen. "Finance Fiction." *The Routledge Handbook to Critical Finance Studies.* Ed. Christian Borch and Robert Wosnitzer. London: Routledge, 2020.

Gaddis, William. Interview. *The Paris Review Interviews 2: Wisdom from the World's Literary Masters.* London: Picador, 2007. 272–305.

——————. *J R*. New York: Knopf, 1975.

——————. "Trickle-Up Economics: JR Goes to Washington." *New York Times* 25 Oct. 1987. https://www.nytimes.com/1987/10/25/books/books-and-business-trickle-up-economics-j-r -goes-to-washington.html.

Hailey, Arthur. *The Moneychangers*. New York: Doubleday, 1975.

Haiven, Max. *Art after Money, Money after Art: Creative Strategies against Financialization*. London: Pluto, 2018.

Hallberg, Garth Risk. *City on Fire*. New York: Knopf, 2015.

Harvey, David. *A Brief History of Neoliberalism*. Oxford: Oxford UP, 2005.

——————. *The Conditions of Postmodernity: An Enquiry into the Origins of Cultural Change*. Oxford: Blackwell, 1990.

Hudson, Michael. "From Marx to Goldman Sachs: The Fictions of Fictitious Capital, and the Financialization of Industry." *Critique* 38.3 (2010): 419–44.

Jameson, Fredric. "Foreword: A Monument to Radical Instants." *The Aesthetics of Resistance*. Vol. 1. By Peter Weiss. Trans. Joachim Neugroschel. Durham: Duke UP, 2005. vii–xlix.

——————. *Postmodernism; or, The Cultural Logic of Late Capitalism*. Durham: Duke UP, 1991.

Johnston, John. "'JR' and the Flux of Capital." *Revue française d'études américaines* 45 (1990): 161–71.

Kenton, Will. "Predator's Ball." *Investopedia* 26 Jun. 2018. https://www.investopedia.com /terms/p/predators-ball.asp.

Kessous, Sadek. "The Sound of Finance: Noise, Music, and Pension Fund Capitalism in William Gaddis's JR." *Textual Practice* 18 Feb. 2019. https://doi.org/10.1080/0950236X.2019.1580214.

Konstantinou, Lee. "The Playful Destruction of J R." *Los Angeles Review of Books* 17 Jul. 2012. http://tumblr.lareviewofbooks.org/post/27412313005/the-playful-destruction-of-j-r.

Kornbluh, Anna. *Realizing Capital: Financial and Psychic Economies in Victorian Form*. New York: Fordham UP, 2014.

Kuehl, John Richard, and Steven Moore. *In Recognition of William Gaddis*. Syracuse: Syracuse UP, 1984.

Lanchester, John. *I.O.U.: Why Everyone Owes Everyone and No One Can Pay*. New York: Simon and Schuster, 2010.

Lewis, Michael. *Liar's Poker*. New York: Norton, 1989.

——————. *Next: The Future Just Happened*. New York: Norton, 2001.

Marazzi, Christian. *Capital and Language: From the New Economy to the War Economy*. Los Angeles: Semiotext(e), 2008.

Marsh, Nicky. *Money, Speculation, and Finance in Contemporary British Fiction*. London: Bloomsbury, 2007.

Marx, Karl. *Capital.* Vol. 3. Trans. David Fernbach. London: Penguin, 1991.

Mehrling, Perry. *Fisher Black and the Revolutionary Idea of Finance.* Hoboken: Wiley, 2011.

Moore, Steven. *William Gaddis: Expanded Edition.* New York: Bloomsbury Academic, 2015.

Morris, Charles. *The Two Trillion Dollar Meltdown.* New York: PublicAffairs, 2008.

Phillips-Fein, Kim. *Fear City: New York's Fiscal Crisis and the Rise of Austerity Politics.* New York: Metropolitan, 2017.

Poovey, Mary. *Genres of the Credit Economy: Mediating Value in Eighteenth- and Nineteenth-Century Britain.* Chicago: Chicago UP, 2008.

Pretty Woman. Dir. Garry Marshall. Touchstone Pictures, 1990.

Rennison, Joe, Robin Wigglesworth, and Colby Smith. "Federal Reserve Enters New Territory with Support for Risky Debt." *Financial Times* 9 Apr. 2020. https://www.ft.com/content/c0b78bc9-0ea8-461c-a5a2-89067ca94ea4.

Smith, Adam (George Goodman). *The Money Game.* London: Pan, 1970.

Stade, George. "William Gaddis's Frigicom." *New York Times Book Review* 9 Nov. 1975. https://www.nytimes.com/1975/11/09/archives/jr-jr-jr.html.

Strange, Susan. *Mad Money: When Markets Outgrow Governments.* Ann Arbor: U of Michigan P, 1998.

Swenson, Brynnar. "Immanent Realism: Time and Corporate Form in William Gaddis's *J R*" *Literature and the Encounter with Immanence.* Ed. Brynnar Swenson. Leiden: Brill/Rodopi, 2017. 92–105.

Taylor, Mark C. *Confidence Games: Money and Markets in a World without Redemption.* Chicago: Chicago UP, 2004.

Tepper, Jonathan. "Covid-19 Has Exposed Our Financial Fragility." *UnHerd* 20 Mar. 2020. https://unherd.com/2020/03/covid-19-has-exposed-our-financial-fragility/.

"The Unseen Revolution. How Pension Fund Socialism Came to America." *Kirkus Review* 1 Jun. 1976 (posted online 16 May 2012). https://www.kirkusreviews.com/book-reviews/peter-f-drucker/unseen-revolution/.

Walker, Christopher. "All in Order, Thanks." *Observer* 27 Feb. 1994. http://www.williamgaddis.org/frolic/frolicrevcwalker.shtml.

The Wolf of Wall Street. Dir. Martin Scorsese. Red Granite Pictures, 2013.

Yago, Glenn. *Junk Bonds: How High Yield Securities Restructured Corporate America.* Oxford: Oxford UP, 1990.

SILVIA FEDERICI

Edited and introduced by Arlen Austin

Nigerian Writings (Fragments)

Journals of Originary Accumulation:
Introduction to Silvia Federici's Nigerian Writings

*A*sked to account for the political and economic situation she encountered upon arrival to teach philosophy at the University of Port Harcourt in 1984, Silvia Federici invoked an inaugural moment in 1979, a great creation *ex nihilo* of a "third world debt crisis" when, with the stroke of a pen, Paul Volcker, chairman of the Federal Reserve, raised interest rates to astonishing highs of nearly 20 percent. Her analysis was accompanied by certain sound effects:

> [T]he Nigerian civilian government had not managed to discon-
> nect from the European and American economic systems—the bulk
> of their loans were contracted at variable interest rates in U.S.
> dollars. So, when the Feds raised interest rates, the debts exploded
> and their currency crashed. It was pure recolonization, a manu-
> factured debt crisis. Then came the IMF, the cavalry, clip-clop,
> clip-clop, clip-clop, bom-baaa! and they said, "no problem, here

Volume 31, Number 3   DOI 10.1215/10407391-8744553

© 2020 by Brown University and d i f f e r e n c e s : A Journal of Feminist Cultural Studies

are some new loans; you just have to submit to recolonization, total control." (Federici and Caffentzis, interview)

The short-lived civilian government of Nigeria's Second Republic, under president Shehu Shagari (1979–83), saw the ballooning of publicly held foreign debt, driven by the "Volcker shock" and compounded by the oil glut and price collapse of the early 1980s (Falola and Ihonvbere). The principal of the nation's debt nearly tripled in these four short years, reaching over 18.5 billion USD by 1983 while annual interest payments rose from $440 million in 1980 to over $1250 million by the time the nominal democracy fell to the military coup of Muhammadu Buhari on New Year's Eve of 1983. By the end of the decade following significant "structural adjustment," foreign debt would constitute an insurmountable 115 percent of Nigeria's GDP.[1]

It may come as a surprise, then, that Nigeria was considered "under-borrowed" in the mystical parlance of the World Bank and International Monetary Fund (IMF) throughout the 1970s. As Federici remarks in one of the texts reproduced below, "[C]apital has not forgotten the lessons of the Catholic Church, which has always spoken Latin when explaining to the masses the principles of the faith" (124). The prodigious oil wealth of the Niger Delta had been largely siphoned off by U.S. and European corporations before nationalization, and subsequently, following the formation of the Federal Ministry of Petroleum Resources in 1971, the nation's coffers were significantly pillaged by the fraud and embezzlement of a series of military leaders and bureaucrats. Still, enormous wealth was produced, buoyed by the oil crises of 1973 and 1979. The modicum of surplus retained left Nigeria less in need of the loans desperately required for postindependence infrastructure projects than most countries on the continent. However impressively maleficent, the corruption of local strongmen would pale in scale relative to the expropriation of resources through the debt mechanisms implemented by the IMF and World Bank in the 1980s and 1990s.

The first major loan foisted on Nigeria was part of the great alchemy by which the IMF and World Bank transmogrified surpluses into debts throughout the continent by recycling the petrodollars of OPEC nations as variable interest loans. In 1977, 1 billion USD was given to the military regime of Olusegun Obasanjo "without conditionalities" (Fajana 17)—the euphemism for foisting unregulated loans on countries to foster economic dependency. To be sure, these absent "conditionalities" would soon return as "structural adjustments," including the defunding of higher education, required in managing and refinancing the debt. Thus Nigeria was set on the path of austerity, repression, and immiseration through the very "liquidity" of its own natural resources.

Silvia Federici and her partner George Caffentzis describe their move to Nigeria as impelled by the experience of austerity and unemployment in New York and the political retrenchment and stagnation of the early Reagan years. The movements in which they had played such pivotal roles had fragmented; both the Zerowork collective of which Caffentzis had been a founding member and the Wages for Housework movement for which Federici's work was so crucial had largely dissolved as international endeavors by the late 1970s (Cleaver; Toupin 126–28). The crushing austerity imposed after the city's near bankruptcy in 1975 represented a profound curtailment of gains won by social movements of the 1960s.[2] As Federici would later write, the same year that the New York Wages For Housework Committee had established its community presence with a storefront space, "a reign of terror fell on the city with the arrival of a troika sent from Albany to replace the mayor and the local government. Contracts were reopened, wages frozen, spies were stationed in telephone booths to check whether public employees actually punched in and out at 9 and 5, commandos followed the garbage collectors at night to see if they actually cleaned the streets or slept in their trucks" (Introduction 23). The forms of manipulation through debt dependency, already put into play in Latin America, Asia, and Africa, had come in force to the metropolis. By the fall of 1983, Caffentzis had managed to secure a position teaching at the University of Calabar, from which he advocated for Federici's hiring. Federici remained in Brooklyn, the lone tenant in her building following the death of her landlady and the eviction of her neighbors. After the new landlord disconnected her heat, she recalls sleeping in her winter coat, the door unlocked and propped open with a cinder block to allow ease of escape should the landlord forgo the process of legal eviction and start a fire.

When hired to teach philosophy at the University of Port Harcourt in 1984, Federici arrived on a campus brought to a standstill by anti-austerity protests. On New Year's Eve of the previous year, the military coup of Buhari had ended the civilian government of the Second Republic. The IMF and World Bank were urging debt refinancing on the country, entailing massive cutbacks in social services and a whole neocolonial administrative regime. One of Federici's first memories on arriving at the University of Port Harcourt was an encounter with striking students holding placards reading "IMF DEATH PILL" and the local press amplifying the deadly nature of the austerity that the nation was being forced to swallow. In response, the Buhari regime would come to implement its notorious "war against indiscipline," accusing the preceding civilian government of egregious corruption, which (although often descriptively accurate) deferred blame from the international capitalist investment that had precipitated and structured the crisis. Possessed of a hubris rivaling that of Trump, Buhari's own hypocrisy was proportional to the grandiosity of his moralizing claims. As minister of oil under Obasanjo when the first loans from the IMF and World Bank were arranged, Buhari's "disciplined" eye had overseen the disappearance of approximately 2.8 billion dollars from the national coffers.[3] Buhari's regime developed a perverse reworking of neonationalist anticolonialism; he would refuse the restructuring imposed by the IMF and World Bank so long as the country could implement its own, more punishing austerity measures. Thus responsibility for the country's plight was diffused into a general sense of guilt, mystifying the machinations of international capital and displacing blame onto the supposed "excesses" of the nation's citizens—particularly, as always, the excesses of women.[4]

As austerity measures hit Nigeria's universities, students found themselves faced with new fees and cuts in funding for transportation, food, and housing. Whatever its corruptions and contradictions, the civilian government of the Second Republic, forced by widespread working-class demands, had been required to use some of its oil riches to sponsor the mushrooming universities across the country. Remarkably, by the early 1980s, the majority of students at these universities came not from a local ruling elite but from families of small farmers, the poor, and industrial working classes.[5] These accomplishments would not be forfeited lightly. As Ousseina Alidou, Caffentzis, and Federici would later write, "[I]t was seeing our students beaten, tear-gassed, and expelled, that led us, on returning or moving to the U.S., to organize around education in Africa" ("'We'" 63). On May 5, 1985, in clearing the way for a visit of an IMF contingent to the city of Zaria in Northern Nigeria, the University of Ahmadu Bello was attacked by government death squads who would massacre at least thirty peacefully protesting students, an event that might be counted as only the most egregious and visible in a program of sustained terror (Academic). Although most of the murder and torture of student movement activists would remain ignored or mentioned only in passing by the Western media, it would become a primary task of Federici and Caffentzis—working in conjunction with African academics through the Committee for Academic Freedom in Africa, many of whom were forced to immigrate to the United States, including Ousseina Alidou, Alamin Mazrui, and Dennis Brutus—to chronicle and disseminate the history of these student struggles.[6]

The documents reproduced below can represent, of course, only a very fragmentary and contingent view of this history and serve as an entrée into a broader field of works, in various disciplines, related to the trauma and long-term consequences of structural adjustment in sub-Saharan Africa. These are also powerful texts in their own right, many of them originally written as journal entries assessing the situation as Federici gradually came to comprehend it upon her arrival in Nigeria. Necessarily, they involve struggles with her own preconceptions as a young Italian American scholar and activist whose deep involvement with the feminist movement and training in philosophy could not entirely prepare her for the violence of structural adjustment—what she would later call the "new enclosures" round of so-called originary or primitive accumulation—in a third-world context. The influence of Doris Lessing on these writings, whose works Federici read voraciously at the time, will be palpable for those familiar with the author: a fragmentation in viewpoint, diaristic style, and inner monologue that is at once self-deprecating and keenly critical of her interlocutors, particularly when it comes to encounters with "men of the left." However, Federici's prose is distinctive as it moves to indictments of World Bank and IMF discourse or a Marxian feminist analysis of global distributions of labor.

Chosen in consultation with Federici, the following selections begin with an article on the concepts of *development* and *underdevelopment* as she came to consider these highly fraught terms in relation to a village proximate to the major Mobile processing plant in Calabar (see Federici, "Development"). As Dipesh Chakrabarty reminds us, to deploy such terms is to risk reasoning with "stagist and elitist conceptions of history" (14) and must not be folded into any historicist account of the "'real' subsumption" of the laboring subject by capitalist development (49–50). This text of Federici's might be considered, in part, as a variation on this theme. The subsequent transcriptions represent disparate articles and journal entries from 1984 to 1986 developed from conversations with fellow faculty members at the university, her own careful reading of the local press, and observation of the destruction of local trade practices and communal structures. The penultimate document reproduced below is a draft of Federici's attack on the discourse used by the IMF and World Bank to justify its program of "development" in Africa and Latin America. Written circa 1989, it precedes and informs many more polished articles on the subject (see Federici, "Debt" and "From Commoning"). While the later texts should be read for the greater coherency of analysis and careful argument they offer, the virtue of this earlier text is perhaps its rawness, its direct and polemical form. For some perspective on the work, one might keep in mind that the World Bank named its program for structural adjustment in Africa "African Capacity Building," referring by the word *capacity* not to those capacities developed within the humanities and science programs of the higher education systems that were being dismantled by austerity across the continent. Rather, the "capacity" to be developed was a technocratic knowledge appropriate for the tasks of economic liberalization, reinscribing African countries and workforces at the bottom of a hierarchy of nations and knowledges, the consequences of which structure the global distribution of labor and educational infrastructure to this day.

There is a sense in which the fate of Nigeria following independence in 1960 might seem overdetermined. The Second Republic was bequeathed boundaries drawn by the arbitrary if not entirely capricious violence of British colonial planning and an economy with extreme dependency on the vicissitudes of the international oil market, which had come to constitute nearly 80 percent of its revenues and fund massive imports at the expense of local agriculture and production (Falola and Ihonvbere 14). In Wole Soyinka's searing terms, the nation could be counted as the "walking dead," "overqualified for the cemetery of nations" (18), and was to be accepted as a coherent entity only insofar as the concept of a nation might constitute an imperative for repair and reparations: "a duty, that is all," "a responsibility without sentiment" (133). As Caffentzis later wrote, what became modern Nigeria was a nexus for at least three major rounds of so-called primitive or originary accumulation: staging ground for the embarkation of slaves for the plantations of the Americas in the eighteenth century, epicenter of British colonialism in the nineteenth, and subject to the ecological and economic devastation of crude oil extraction and structural adjustment in the postindependence era, with its attendant genocidal assaults on Indigenous communities of the Niger Delta (Caffentzis 228–43, 290–98).

Still, this was a period of tremendous revolts that continue to this day and hold lessons for any encounter with the "structural adjustment programs" of the present. By now, most readers of contemporary (post-)Marxian discourse will be familiar with the essential critiques of Marx's account of the origin story of capitalist accumulation, critiques that have emerged largely from feminist, Black radical, anticolonial, and Indigenous traditions. As translated in the standard English edition of *Capital* by Ben Fowkes (the text used by generations of English-reading students of Marx), the phrase *sogenannte ursprüngliche Akkumulation* is rendered as "so-called primitive accumulation," where the adjective *ursprüngliche* (from the noun *Ursprung*, with its philosophical connotations of absolute metaphysical origin) is rendered as *primitive*, suggesting a progressive-developmental schema with all the baggage of imperialist historiography that the term implies (Marx 873). In calling for a new standard English translation of Marx, Wolfgang Fritz Haug has noted that Fowkes makes something of a complementary error in translating the key concept of *Genesis dieser Geldform* from the first chapters of the book as "origin of the money-form," giving to the German *Genesis* a sense of an absolute origin point more accurately conveyed by *Ursprung* and emptying the term of its imbrication in a genetic, ongoing sequence of transformations without fixed beginning (Haug 64–65). A problem faced by any endeavor to narrativize the phenomenon of so-called primitive accumulation is that any attempt at its representation (including claims to somehow forgo representation itself) must deal with both a specific, irreducible historical trauma and a structural repetition built into the horrific consistency with which "accumulation by dispossession" subjects whole populations to abject vulnerability or death within a program of capitalist (under)development.

Still, stories must be told. This collection of texts might inform an understanding of the background for one of the great accounts/critiques of the concept of "so-called primitive accumulation": Federici's *Caliban and the Witch: Women, the Body, and Primitive Accumulation*, a work that she would continuously write and rewrite throughout her experience of both the 1970s feminist movement and structural adjustment in Africa, finally coming to publish it decades after its original conception.[7] As Federici notes in her introduction to the book, "Not surprisingly, every new revolutionary movement has returned to the 'transition to capitalism,' bringing to it the perspectives of new social subjects and uncovering new grounds of exploitation and resistance" (11).

"Development" and "Underdevelopment" in Nigeria

The text below was written as a journal entry by Federici from Port Harcourt in 1985, shortly after her arrival in Nigeria. It describes a village proximate to the major installation of Mobile Oil. A version of this text was later published by the Midnight Notes Collective in Midnight Notes *11.*

The village sits at the very junction between the Qua River, one of the main water arteries of southeastern Nigeria, and the Atlantic Ocean, on a beach from where, in the past, thousands of slaves, forced onto ships, initiated the

Figure 1
Detail from a draft
essay on debt and
structural adjust-
ment transcribed
in this selection of
fragments.

Source: Silvia Fed-
erici Papers, Femi-
nist Theory Archives
at the Pembroke
Center for Teach-
ing and Research on
Women. Courtesy of
Silvia Federici.

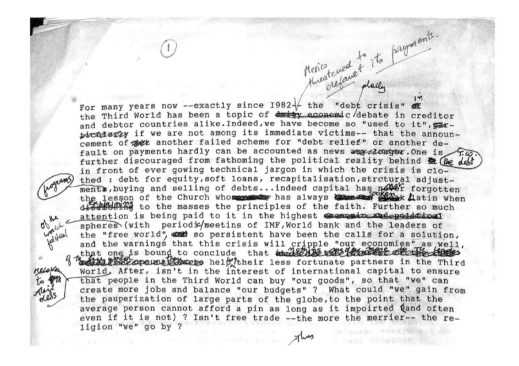

Middle Passage to the Americas. It consists of a few huts of corrugated tin, with mud floors and just enough space for some utensils and beds, which five or six people may share. Children running about, women pounding yams, sorting groundnuts, or squeezing palm kernels into red oil make up the main activities on an average day. No house has running water and few have electricity. Among them is the village "inn," where in the evening men come for drinks and to share, perhaps, the body of the woman who runs it. Here, too, for toilet one goes to the bush; food is a little soup made of palm oil, vegetable leaves, and a couple of pieces of dried fish or meat (for those who can afford them), cigarettes are sold by the stick, while a TV set is the only amenity the place provides.

Yet it would be a mistake to conclude that this area is "underde-veloped." For just one mile down the beach is one of the major oil complexes in the country. It belongs to Mobil Oil, which for fifteen years has been pump-ing oil and wealth out of this seemingly remote corner of the world. The complex is a gigantic, white, round, spaceship-like structure that speaks of millions of dollars and some of the most sophisticated technology the "first world" can provide. At night its rigs cast an eerie flame, which, together with the flare from the burning of natural gas, lights up the sky as if it were northern New Jersey.

Nearby is the airport strip, as the managers prefer to settle in Lagos, from where, every morning, they fly here to supervise the work— despite the protests of the local chiefs, who routinely ask them to contribute to the development of the community. Food in the complex is flown in as well, and so are the various forms of entertainment for the workers, many of whom are foreigners—Americans, Europeans, Lebanese—although at the "lower," manual level one finds Nigerians as well, gathered, by a bus in the morning, from the surrounding localities.

Thus, the Mobil complex, which in February of 1985 celebrated its first one billion barrels, seems an island all of its own. Its life and that of the village are two separate worlds, two time frames, and certainly two incommensurably different standards of living. The only point of contact is the "inn," where in the evening even the *mbakara* (white) men come, trekking down the beach like strange animals looking for some sex or perhaps just a break in the routine. This, however, is not an example of development "coexisting" with underdevelopment. For, as in other oil-producing areas, the company is largely responsible for the pauperized conditions in which people live in the village. It is no accident—with the exception of the road the company needs for its operations—that all the roads in the area are mud paths, which threaten to turn into small rivers in the rainy season. Bad roads keep nosy people out and minimize interaction with the disgruntled surrounding human environment. The same applies to employment practices. Foreign workers are treasured not so much because of their (easily learned) skills, but because they cannot rely on local support networks or give in to their families' demands.

There are even more crucial ways in which "development" here is simultaneously "underdevelopment." Oil extraction and exploration have ruined the environment and deprived many of their traditional forms of sustenance. Because of oil pollution, the villagers can rely less and less on fish for food. Oil spills also affect the cropland and the health of people, who now suffer from the same ailments one finds in parts of New Jersey, but without the resources (limited as they may be) people have in the u.s. to cure themselves. Gas flaring is another example of development turning into planned underdevelopment. Mobil Oil (like all the other companies) has daily flared the natural gas from the beginning of its operations, claiming it has "no economic value," which simply means that it is not sufficiently profitable for them to process. Thus, up in smoke goes (and has gone for years) a potentially incalculable wealth that could provide the villagers with fuel, electricity, and other basic necessities. Meanwhile, people in the u.s. often freeze through the winter because gas prices have gone too high for them to afford adequate heating.

Mobil, here, operates through sea rigs. In other areas oil extraction has implied expropriating farmers from their land, which is usually the most fertile as oil likes to dwell in the moist areas where crops abound. Land expropriation was facilitated by the Land Use Decree passed in 1978 (in the wake of the hike in oil prices), which nationalized all the land in the country. At first the villagers used to receive a pittance for the trees felled and the crops they could not harvest: oil time is very expensive, and the companies, after receiving the green light for their operations, never allowed the farmers to gather their crops. Many farmers, however, are still waiting to get even the little money they were promised, while the government has announced that no more compensations will be forthcoming, for the government now owns the land, and paying people for it can foster bad ideas. The villages of the oil communities have often rebelled and "taken things into their own hands." But this is rare now, for the Anti-Economic Sabotage provision of Decree 20, passed in 1984, makes it a capital offense to engage in any actions that disrupt the operations of the oil companies.

In this context, development for those who had the bad luck of living near oil pools has meant the loss of everything they had, beginning with their land and their sources of food, while all they have gained have been health problems. In the case of Mobil Oil, its only "positive contribution" to the community is the occasional granting of scholarships to "gifted" children; meanwhile, the majority of the village children never see a book, even when they are lucky enough to make it to primary school. When they grow up, most have to leave the area, since with the exception of a few jobs at the company, there is nothing there for them to do. Thus, as their wealth goes up in smoke or finds its way to New York and other capital markets, their only alternative is another forced migration, this time to the urban centers, where the landless of Nigeria congregate, adding to the government's fear of a "population explosion."

On Hawking and Military Government

This journal entry, authored in 1986, describes in detail the destruction of local trade networks around Lagos by the Federal Military Government (FMG) as part of the government plan to control the money supply and extract rents on newly constructed government-run markets.

As in most African countries, hawking, roadside trading, and market vending have traditionally been the main avenue for the circulation of goods in Nigeria. Over the last year, however, the FMG has executed a reorganization of vending practices that has dramatically changed Nigeria's popular markets. The most obvious aspect has been the demolition of millions of "illegal" markets and trading structures nationwide.

The bulldozers appeared on the streets of Lagos, Kaduna, Benin City, and other metropolitan areas in June of 1984, but the destruction of market kiosks and stalls, usually on the fringes of the main market or along roadsides, still goes on. As Governor Mudasiru of Lagos state warned in January 1986,[8] no one should misconstrue this effort as a spontaneous demolition exercise or a "flash-in-the-pan operation." Indeed, Lagos has looked as if an earthquake has hit it for nearly a year. The latest target of the Lagos state bulldozers was the Kalu Road cattle ranch and slaughter area, where hundreds of squatters and traders were given a one-week notice to vacate in June 10 of this year; their stalls and squats were subsequently destroyed.

The rationale usually provided in support of the demolitions is the need to "sanitize the environment," and indeed many urban areas are noticeably cleaner. However, measures adopted by several states indicate that more is at stake. State governments from Bauchi to Cross River have passed laws and decrees against roadside hawking and trading in unauthorized places. Many street vendors (including children) have been arrested and fined or, more commonly, stripped of their wares and given a rough handling by the police.

The legal restrictions on trading zones were later followed by various edicts either banning or regulating market associations. Those associations (largely made up of women) have proven throughout Nigerian history to be powerful autonomous groups capable of resisting government policies, including government attempts to impose price controls. Imo state has banned such associations, claiming that markets in the state should be "free," and has ordered them to surrender all their properties to newly instituted market authorities. In Lagos state the market associations have been forced to register with the government and to give details as to the identity of their officials and their activities. At the same time, market authorities have been set up in the rural areas to ensure that stall fees, rents, and tolls are channeled into the coffers of the local government. Finally, across the country, stall fees, tolls, and rents have been increased sharply (at times by 500 percent). In Lagos state, for example, approved market stalls now require a year's rental in advance—a fee only the richer traders are capable of paying—while the rest must face the increasingly hazardous route of illegal trading.

What does the FMG hope to accomplish by this systematic reform of the markets? The most immediate and obvious goals are to increase tax revenues collected at the market to pay foreign debts as well as to control market activities, thus putting a halt to smuggling and excessive imports of foreign goods. Not accidently, while illegal structures have been demolished and trading zones severely limited, the construction of new "ultra-modern" multimillion-naira supermarkets has been initiated or completed that will operate directly under state or city government control. In Port Harcourt a 9-million-naira market was finished in May; in Calabar, the Cross River state government is funding the construction of a 5-million-naira market. In Kano, 15 million naira have been allocated for completion of a new market, while a new injection of funds has been recently approved for the completion of a new market for Jos that was begun in 1976. These massive investments are particularly noticeable in a period when most capital projects in Nigeria have been abandoned or scaled down. But the hope, of course, is that those investments will pay for themselves, since rents in the new markets are higher and more efficiently collected.

The main reason, however, why the markets are at the center of the Government's attention is that its stated policy objectives—reducing inflation as well as wages, and developing agribusiness—require that the government have the ability to regulate both prices and the money supply of the country. This the FMG has attempted to do since its first days of rule. In the weeks following the coup, soldiers were sent to the markets to force the traders to sell at "fair prices," but the traders went on strike and the FMG had to abandon its efforts. Equally unsuccessful was the attempt to control the money supply by forcing the traders to bring their money to the bank, through the currency exchange of May 1984. This move created havoc in the lives of small vendors and ordinary people. In the meantime, the rich traders managed to remain outside the hawking system, while at the same time draining the new available currency as they were able to either convert the old naira into stockpiles of commodities or to change them piecemeal through various intermediaries.

This is what may have prompted the FMG to adopt stronger measures. Presumably, if speculative practices were eliminated, prices would come down. Thus, the activity of the bulldozers has been accompanied by a campaign fingering the greedy "middle-man" as the cause of the inflationary spiral. So far, however, few market speculators have been caught, while those who have most suffered from the restrictions on trade and the demolition "exercise"—a standard label these days for every unpopular policy—have been the small vendors. These are usually women and teenagers, as they constitute the overwhelming majority of those engaged in trading activities. For them the consequences of the FMG's stringent policies have been devastating. For overnight, thousands have seen their only means of survival destroyed at the very time when retrenchment is in full bloom in every sector, wages are being drastically reduced, and the sale at the kiosk is frequently the only family income.

Far from being contained, moreover, prices have continued to rise at an average annual rate of 30 percent. This is partially due to the steady devaluation of the naira, but undoubtedly the present price hike is also due to the markets' reorganization as traders have passed the increase in the cost of stall fees and rents down to their customers. Thus, so far, the only inarguable result of the market "clean up" has been a reduction in the consumption levels of the bulk of the population, petty traders and customers alike.

Yet, the response to the new measures has rarely been confrontational, as the FMG has made it clear that it is determined to back up its policies with the "necessary force." In a few cities, traders have staged peaceful demonstrations. In some cases, they have also tried to physically resist the demolition crews; but since armed policemen usually accompany the "sanitation men," their resistance has been easily broken. What has taken place instead has been the development of a "night economy" in most Nigerian cities, as many traders, in an effort to elude the eyes of the police and market authorities, now begin their sales at 6:00 p.m. As a fish trader in Lagos said to the press: "Selling at night is safer since government officials do not parade at night."[9] This is still a risky alternative, but for many it is the only option.

Notes on Social Obligations and Funerals

When asked if she would agree to publish these notes on obligation and debt, Federici wished to provide the following introduction: "The transcription below includes two entries from a journal I kept in 1985 and 1986, in the periods when I taught courses at the University of Port Harcourt in Nigeria. Their content was an almost verbatim reconstruction of conversations I had with two colleagues, a man and a woman with whom I shared a house.

The tone of the conversations was ironic and humorous, and yet something very serious was communicated through them about how the spread of the money/capitalist economy was changing social relations and eroding the deeply communitarian ethos that had characterized Nigerian life, especially in rural areas. Thirty-five years have passed since those conversations took place, years in which Nigerian/African societies have been turned upside down by a globalization process that—as I, among others, have argued [see the previous section, "Development" and "Underdevelopment" in Nigeria']—has wreaked havoc on social relations, causing immense impoverishment, displacement, and destruction of local wealth and lives. Yet, revisiting these entries today confirms how, even before the advent of the so-called debt crisis, structural adjustment, and economic liberalization, the extension of capitalist development and monetization was already sowing new divisions and deepening the separation between town and country. This is a process that, in different ways, has been occurring worldwide, which is why I have agreed to the publication of this transcript. A further reason, however, is my admiration for the art of storytelling, in which, it seems to me, Nigerians excel. I thus found myself writing down many of the conversations I had, which introduced me to a world of intense communal and oral relations and the cultivation of skills reserved in the 'developed world' for the theater and other forms of artistic representation. I have withheld the names of my colleagues and housemates, but I have not, in any way, changed their words."

Social obligations, O. mourns, are the curse of Nigerian society. It is very difficult to escape them. Much moral courage is necessary to do so, since all your in-laws, beginning with your mother, will look down on you and feel ashamed unless you fulfill your socially expected duty. Take funerals, for example. According to the traditional way of dealing with death, the relative of the dead person should not be left alone to mourn. Thus, in-laws from everywhere arrive for the funeral and stay for days, weeks after, planning at times to stay with you to distract you from your pain for up to a month. It used to be, in the old days, that, in order to support these friends and relatives coming to visit, everybody in the village contributed some food. Some brought yams, others provided the meat (the young men), and so on. Now these food contributions have been monetized, and they are expected even from distant friends and for months and months after the funeral. If one goes back to the village, even months after somebody has died, one is expected to pay—so that the relatives can have a good time and buy drinks. Of course, when an in-law dies, the matter is much more serious. O. gives the example of his cousin, who went into debt when his wife's father died. He had to provide (there are booklets that specify what is expected of you) a cow, cloth, and, on top of it, pots and pots of rice and stew with different types of sauce, an enormous quantity of beer, and other drinks. He had to borrow 3,000 nairas to cope with it. Few, O. says, have the courage to refuse. They're afraid of public contempt. "Look at this man," they will say, "he has been overseas and does not have money?" Your in-laws will pressure you and your brothers (in Africa all the villagers are brothers and sisters); they will go to your wife and complain, "my brother is making me ashamed . . . people don't believe he's gone overseas." Or, if you don't pay, they believe you have changed and have become selfish. Often the wife protests against all these expenses, since the man, when he goes to the village, spends all the money that should go to her for food for the children. Often they have nothing to eat because they had to give money to the village for drinks. But the protests of the wife are overruled by the fear of the in-laws' contempt and disappointment. Plus, O. reports, there is nothing a Nigerian man fears more than the idea that people may think he is ruled by his wife. "Has your wife married you?" his mother would ask, and this is anathema. Middle-class people ruin themselves because the village that has helped them go to school (at least in Ibo land) has exorbitant expectations of them. They think if you have a degree and have been overseas, your wealth should be endless, and they expect, now that you have become a big person, you to take care of everybody back home. This is possibly why people, under so much pres-sure, become corrupt. Wages aren't enough to satisfy the expectations; one doesn't want to be thought stingy or careless. Besides, being thought rich pays off in terms of prestige, and in any case, appropriating public wealth is not considered a crime. If you have access to public funds, you should of course put your hands on them and distribute the goods to your own people. Such an attitude goes back to colonialism, as robbing the colonial government was approved of. So, you say you don't have money, you point to "so-and-so" and say "yes, he is rich, but he has stolen." "Well," the answer is, "why haven't you"? Your own mother will remind you that "so-and-so," who does not have a certificate and has not gone overseas, has a Mercedes, has built a house, and so on, and what about you?

Funerals are very, very important. People ruin themselves to give their relatives proper funerals. One has the impression, says E., that Nigerians build all their life around their funeral. Most important is the second funeral. The first serves just to dispose of the body and is accomplished with what is at hand, but people prepare months for the second one. The second one is the real one. People prepare for it for months and ruin themselves to do it. Originally, the idea was that a person had to have a second funeral, months after the death, because time is needed to sever the ties with the community. Only after the function and roles a person performed in the community were gradually taken over by others could the person be really considered dead. The second funeral tradition recognized that the moment of physiological death is by no mean the moment when a person disappears; the person is still alive. Death is not a one-minute event, but a process. Nowadays, however, the second funeral is just a display of wealth and status, and people go through incredible ordeals, so much so that one would think Nigerians live and work just for the drama they can display on the occasion of their departure from this world. As most families do not easily gather the money for the second funeral, and since, by tradition, if another person in the meantime dies in the family, this person cannot be buried, then what happens nowadays is that those who die before a relative has been given his/her second funeral are put in a cooler until the family gathers the money. The *Tide* recently complained that thousands of bodies are lying around in Port Harcourt's coolers of people whose relatives are still building up the nairas necessary for the second funeral of the earlier deceased relative, and the poor folks who die in the meantime are put in the back seat. They have to wait their turn. Some people have to wait in the cooler for up to six months, then a house has to be provided for the person to be displayed in. This is considered indispensable, so much so that if a deceased man of any importance hadn't built a house for himself, not only are the families ashamed but the organizations he belonged to have to put out money to build him at least a bungalow. For never would they have the courage to invite other organizations to the funeral and let them know that their brother didn't even have a house. "What is wrong with him?" people would ask. Nigerians are extremely status conscious these days, E. tells me. Particularly if you have an education, not to mention a title, you have to have a proper house, with expensive furniture and status symbols (video equipment, TV, and so on), no matter what it costs. E. says that this applies also to those who have no money. You can go to certain poor neighborhoods in Lagos, where you find squalid houses, houses with one or two rooms and an open sewer passing through the living room so that the visitor sits with legs astride the sewer. But you see women emerging from the houses with their necks full of golden chains, earrings so heavy they almost tear their lobes, arms and rings full of golden trinkets—bracelets, rings—so they look like a lit-up Christmas tree. And of course everybody treats them like gold—"Madame, Madame"—and they walk like they own the world. In the same houses, one would find a lot of video equipment. It doesn't matter that everybody eats *garri* because they have no money and has to sit astride the sewer. The video is status and video must be. So when people come from the village, as they always do, they can spread the news: "My brother is well off, he has equipment." With the funeral, this reaches an apotheosis. Every detail has to reveal the wealth of the family. Not only must a house be built for the man to lie in state, but people are told expressly so: "Brother, where will we put you when you die if you don't have a house where you can lie in state?" And then, of course, there is the orgy of food that is consumed/wasted on the days of the second funeral. Cows and goats are slaughtered. Mountains of meat are piled up, and people, friends, relatives are expected to give money. One goes to the village, finds out so-and-so has died, and is expected to do the rounds: a few nairas here, a few nairas there. E. objects. If the money spent on funerals were given to the deceased before their death, many wouldn't have died. She thinks that it should be abolished and some money should be given only if the relatives are actually in need, but not for drinking. And she objects to mountains of food being provided when people don't have enough to eat during the rest of the time, and there's no refrigeration. Then there is the bed. A special bed where the dead are to be displayed has to be provided. Often it is not just a bed but a special platform covered by yards and yards of fine satin and lace, with matching curtains. By the time the mortuary room is finished, 500–1000 nairas have been spent. Everything conspires for people to appear rich—to put on a display—unless they want to look like fools. The village/extended family is a big *piovra* [octopus]. Wherever you move it doesn't let you go. Nowadays, some people escape to the cities and rarely visit home so as not to have to put up with demands that are impossible to meet. They just don't go home anymore because there is no end to the giving required. The more you give, the more you are expected to give, the assumption being that you would not give unless you had the means. Nobody in the village, O. claims, believes that people would give if they did not have lots of money. This is because the villagers themselves hold on very tightly to whatever money they have. They may cry poverty but have money tucked into their mattresses that they keep for some special occasion and would never touch from year to year. So they don't believe that people are so foolish as to give when they don't have and get very upset when you tell them you have given all you had, I don't have anything more to give. They hate this the most because they think you are fooling them. So the real fools are the newly educated middle classes who have potentially lots of status because they have gone abroad and because they have a university education, but their salaries are not so high—not enough, certainly, to keep a village happy. But they don't want to look stingy, or poor, or careless in the eyes of their in-laws or village brothers (particularly the men who love to play the big shot and are under a lot of pressure anyway). So they starve, go into debt, put up with lots of quarrels with their wives, but they give, with their hearts bleeding because the next step is *garri* for months to eat. All has become corrupt in Nigeria, E. says. It used to be that when you came to the village, people gave you lots of things. You left with your car full of yams and other produce. Now, every time you go to the village, they expect you to dish out money. Everybody now thinks of themselves. Whenever they have to do something, the first question is: "what's in it for me" (my children, my relatives, my clan?—"mine" is the word). No general sense of solidarity, only personal/clan advantage is recognized as worthy of an effort.

E. also speaks of people's relation to sorrow. Wild, disorganized displays of sorrow are not appreciated in Nigeria. People don't like when relatives throw themselves on the floor howling or complaining: "why did you leave me?," "what can I do now?," "don't you know?," and so on and so forth. Sorrow must be displayed, but with dignity. The tradition is to have someone do the crying. Usually the oldest daughter is helped by professional criers who join her in crying the praises of the deceased. It's quite a job, apparently, because she has to learn to cry and recite at the same time. This is done at a quiet moment in the day so that the neighbors, too, can hear. She starts with a recitation of who the dead was, what she/he looked like, his/her physical and moral qualities. Then she goes on to her relation to the deceased and the deceased's position in the community. The professional criers act like a chorus in a Greek tragedy—since the recital has certain ritualistic refrains. She needs the other women, otherwise she would never be able to do the whole job, which is quite a big thing. Men, on the contrary, are not supposed to cry. If one does so at the funeral, it becomes news. "Ah, my brother," one would say, "people were so moved that even so-and-so broke down and cried," and everybody around him would be talking about it. But the crying is very important. Nobody can be buried unless he/she has been properly wept over. The most miserable at the time of the funeral is the wife. In fact, when a man dies, his wife is always in a tough spot. Because she remains a stranger to the in-laws (Africans pay a lot of attention to blood ties: strangers can be killed, but to kill kin is taboo), she is immediately suspected of having killed the man. In the old days, E. tells me, there was an ordeal that women had to go through when their husbands died: the calabar bean proof. Any time a person gets sick and dies, foul play is suspected. No one can accept natural causes. No, it must be some enemy, and of course the wife is close at hand. If a man gets sick and doesn't recover quickly, he goes to the medicine man and the latter tells him, "ah your wife . . . has committed adultery," and if the wife fails to do what the medicine man prescribes, then it's the end. Then there's the split nut proof: the *agbara* is a nut that's kept in the house of the ancestors. It isn't poisonous, but it is believed that if a person is guilty she will die, and women fear the test. She is told to eat it and take an oath that if she is guilty she will die. O. says that it seems to work psychologically, as a form of voodoo, unless a woman has a very strong will. Anyway, the man comes back from the medicine man, and he calls his in-laws and says, "My wife is trying to kill me." So the woman is called and asked to confess. She at first refuses, but then, when she sees that things are getting rough, she may admit: "Oh I forgot to tell you, coming home so-and-so touched my breast." "You forgot," says the husband. "Do you want me dead?"

On the day of the funeral, the women, beginning with the wife, are expected to sit around and cry. "This is the division of labor," says E. Men cannot cry because somebody must be sober to take care of practical business, since the women are expected to do nothing but lament. However, the women are kept on the side by the man's in-laws. The wife cannot go to the cooler. If she does, she is made to wait outside. She cannot wash and dress her husband. The wife is a stranger, says E. In fact, she can be killed. She is also kept out of family meetings, while the sisters of the deceased man, who live far away, are told to come back. O. says that this is because the sisters, in general, know everything concerning the family business—particularly in matters of land, since the fathers generally confide the family business to their daughters. They take their daughters to work with them and tell them, from childhood, about the boundaries of the family property. So, whenever a land dispute arises, the women, the sisters, are those who know, those who are ready to take an oath and swear, "Yes, this land belongs to my family. I remember when my father used to take me there. Yes, we have cultivated this land for many years." O. says he knows nothing about the boundaries of his parents' land, so when he needs some info he has to call his sisters. But E. objects that this is just another proof that the wife is a stranger. She doesn't know what land the husband has. If the man dies, she's in trouble.

Hard Times for Nigerian Women

This article, written by Federici under the pseudonym Iya Agan for the Paris-based journal AfricAsia, *addresses the crackdown on women's "immorality" under the Buhari regime. This is one in a series of articles written under pseudonyms by Federici and Caffentzis for the journal. They recall being paid 200 dollars per article, funds that allowed them to survive when teaching salaries were delayed, unpaid, or rendered inadequate by the devaluation of the naira.*

For months, now, the chastising of women has been yet another exercise in which the Nigerian authorities, well supported by the press, have devoted their efforts. Most prominent has been the attack on women's "greed" and "materialism," to which the capture of a few women smuggling drugs in their "private parts" has given monstrous connotations. Articles featuring "the abuse of womanhood" are becoming a staple of the papers, which rival each other in bemoaning that women nowadays forget their "natural modesty" and are even ready to violate the sanctity of their bodies for the sake of "quick money."

Few news commentators have pointed out that poverty, malnutrition, and hard labor—the realities of life for millions of women—may constitute more serious violations of their bodies than a few grams of cocaine hidden in their "private parts." Instead, the suggestion has been that criminality among women is increasing, and this is taken as a measure of the social problems the country is facing.

Women, we are told, are stepping beyond traditional boundaries and now figure among the industrial saboteurs, forgers, armed robbers, and car thieves. "Not one day passes," the *Nigerian Statesman* concluded in October, "without one woman or another being nabbed for a sordid crime." Women, moreover, are accused of being promiscuous, wearing indecent dresses, neglecting their children, and turning to prostitution in unprecedented numbers. Allegedly, even those who don't make the news contribute to the "demise of womanhood" by their arrogant behavior toward their husbands and their passion for ostentation, for which "they are ready to sacrifice everything, including the family welfare."

No Mercy

The tone of the attacks ranges from the satirical "who wears the trousers in the home?" to the punitive. Some, for example, have argued that, since women are becoming more like men, they shouldn't be granted any mercy with regard to the death penalty. In both cases it's clear that a campaign is underway to remind women of "their place" and mark them as scapegoats for Nigeria's problems.

In a country where statistics are hard to come by, it is difficult to assess whether or not female crime is really on the increase. Reported figures are generally low. While the Kano police reported a doubling of arrests of women in 1984, the total number is still only a modest 842, far from an alarming figure for a city of several million. Even after all the uproar against smugglers, only 12 women have been arrested in 1984 at the international airport for drug or currency trafficking.

Still, it's not too far-fetched to imagine that the growing pauperization the country is experiencing as a result of the government's austerity policies may have forced many women to resort to alternative means of survival, since they are the ones who have been most dramatically affected. Because they make up the majority of hawkers and traders, women have borne the brunt of the nationwide dismantling of their "illegal" stalls. It's also women who have to deal with the skyrocketing price of basic commodities, beginning with the price of milk and other food stuffs for children.

If to these predicaments one adds the retrenchment "exercise" being carried on in the workplaces, one can hardly be surprised that more women are reported abandoning newborn children or that today's prostitute is often yesterday's student or housewife or recently made redundant clerical worker. So little is the security presently provided by marriage that the number of divorces—90 percent of which are filed by women—has been growing at an unusual rate.

"Back to the Land"

As one woman put it to the *Sunday Times* last May:

Take a situation where a tablet of soap costs 2.50 naira and garri becomes 40 naira a tin. House rent is at an all-time high. All this with the husband and wife earning less than 500 naira a month and they may have four or five children as well as extended

families. Add the cost of transportation and education and you
get the picture right. The case of a family where either the husband
or the wife is affected by retrenchment or a purge is even worse.
Then no one should bat an eyelid if a married woman takes to
prostitution to supplement her falling income. Nigerian women,
both married and unmarried, who are taking to prostitution do
so because of the unbearably high cost of living, since they don't
want to take to armed robbery or stealing.

The attack on women is more than a ritual lamentation over a situation
that government policies have helped to create. Rather, it is the *consequence*
of the administration's economic plans whose success largely depends on
women's willingness to lower their social and economic expectations and
those of their families.

The role women are expected to perform in the country's "recovery" becomes clear if one considers the thrust of the "back to the land" program, which is presently advertised as the solution to Nigeria's economic
problems and the road to future development. The back to the land program
entails the establishment of large-scale, mechanized farming, backed by
foreign investment and primarily organized for export purposes. Its stated
aim is to rationalize and increase food production and distribution in the
country, cut dependence on foreign imports, and at the same time, gain
much-needed foreign currency.

Furthermore, by sending many workers "back to the land," the
Buhari government hopes to defuse the explosive situation that the rapid
urbanization of the 1970s has created in most Nigerian cities. For many Nigerians, going to the city represented the promise of a higher standard of living
and more opportunities—all hopes contrasting with the austerity policy the
government has now committed itself to. On both counts—de-urbanization
and the creation of an agri-business economy—reducing the cost of labor is
the openly stated policy of the government. The availability of cheap rural
labor is seen as a *must* if foreign capital is to be encouraged to invest in the
country. Here is where the cooperation of women becomes a sine qua non.

As the Rivers State Commissioner told *Tide* on January 14, "The
future of the nation depends on how badly or how well Nigerian women
perform," for "women have traditionally been the character builders of their
children as well as the most stabilizing element in society."[10] "Character
building" implies that women must teach their children to do with less,

instill in them good work habits, and ask them to compensate with their work for both the fall in family incomes and the diminished amenities available in the countryside. Discipline, self-control, and the ability to live within one's means must become women's watchwords.

As the gatekeepers for most of the food reaching the home, women also have the duty of bringing about a change in the tastes and eating patterns of their families. For example, according to the pro-government press, they must learn to cook all-Nigerian meals, thus reducing the country's reliance on imported food and stretching the vanishing family naira. In order to achieve this goal, however, women have first to discipline themselves, and this is where the call for the "restoration of womanhood" and the complaints of its demise become important.

The government has not confined itself to verbal appeals. Various policies have been proposed or implemented in the last year aimed at curtailing women's economic independence, inducing them to be more parsimonious, and reminding them that their place is in the home. In [the states of] Sokoto and Kano, last spring, the authorities threatened to give unmarried women over thirty years old three months to get married or leave. In Bauchi state, the Zaria area court declared free women personae non gratae and asked them to leave within twenty-four hours. In many cities of the north, landlords have been instructed not to rent property to unattached women. In some states, like Lagos, disciplinary actions have been taken against female students wearing make-up or "indecent dress" and even those curling and coloring their hair. There are reports of uniformed men waging a virtual war against women wearing trousers and, in some cases, tearing them off in the street.

More severe penalties are also being demanded for illegal abortion and the abandonment of children, while last February women were even asked to monitor each other's activities so as to ensure the enforcement of the new sanctions. Finally, the nationwide dismantling of "illegal structures," as well as the increases in fees for market stalls, has already deprived thousands of women and their families of any means of support, thus encouraging the market women to mount the only protest against governmental policies so far. On January 20th of this year more than 3,000 of them in Benin City demonstrated against the increase of the price of stalls from ten to fifty kobo.

The Price of Morality

Whether the Nigerian government will succeed in making women accept their "new economic role" is difficult to predict, though it is hard to imagine that hawking or prostitution can be eliminated when for many women they represent the only remaining access to money. What is certain is that the present trends spell hard times for women and are another example of the Nigerian government's unwillingness, or inability, to face the real problems of the country.

If the back to the land program succeeds in its projected form, the condition of women in particular and of the Nigerian population as a whole will inevitably deteriorate. An export-based agri-business economy will not solve the problems of domestic food supply. Indeed, food will be more expensive for Nigerians when farmers are producing for an international market whose price structure they cannot control. As the history of cash crops and the "green revolution" has shown, large-scale farming and mechanization of agricultural labor always take place at the expense of women, whose low-technology subsistence farming is dramatically devalued.

Contrary to common assumptions, women's farming to this day is still responsible for most food production in Nigeria, and this production would be increased if women had more—and more secure—access to land, subsidies, and infrastructure capable of helping them not only in their work but also in the distribution of their products. In the absence of a real redistribution of land, "back to the village" for women only spells more poverty for themselves and their children, more despair, and more resorting to crime. For crime becomes inevitable when the price of morality is so high as to jeopardize one's ability to survive.

Journal Entries from October 16 and 17, 1984

When Federici arrived in Nigeria, the University at Port Harcourt was already facing the effects of the restructuring set in motion by the fall of the Second Republic and Buhari's military coup. Students had begun to organize against the coming austerity. The faculty found themselves in a rather desperate situation as made clear in the two entries below.

I am slowly discovering a perverse pleasure in my confrontations with the bureaucracy here. George calls his dealings with the state *educational*, but I disagree. As far as the state goes, it is not true that "you know one you know them all." The Nigerian approach would not work in the U.S. because the state bureaucracy there works on different premises. Anyway, my years of unemployment have given me all the expertise I could want in that regard. And I am sure such a system would not work in Italy because people there are much too assured in refusing work to be easily guilt-tripped. So in my case, it is a source of perverse pleasure, at least insofar as I have nothing else to do with the surrounding world but to pester and be pestered. I enjoy the undercurrent of tension masked by my utter politeness. You learn a new use of your body as a persistent presence, like that of a mosquito. Eyes blink, brush you off, think you can be dismissed, and then slowly awaken to the fact that you will not be moved, at which point they pass you on to a different level. You also develop a sixth sense for the crucial moment and the crucial place. There always comes a point in the pursuit of bureaucratic matters, even those of vital importance (for example, getting a salary increase that has to be approved by the registrar, the bursar, payroll, again by the registrar, and then room 9), that this particular person or this particular office becomes the key to everything—not because it is more important, but because consciously or unconsciously, you know that this is the office where everything will come to a halt. It is difficult to know if it was planned this way, but you immediately sense a difference. You know that, short of taking emergency measures, your case will be bogged down forever. This was room 9 for me. I never knew its function in the process, but I know that all previous difficulties seemed smooth once I got there. Room 9 must have been planned as the room of evasion. This is where you are told "all is fine, the case will run its course, you will be informed." You then suddenly realize new techniques are needed. This is where you know the real confrontation begins and if you leave at this point you are lost and nine months from now you'll still be waiting for your money. So you take a deep breath—don't get up: mistake!—readjust more comfortably on the chair, make him feel all the weight of your presence, and change register. "May I ask you when, Mr. O.?" "Mr. O., I hate to insist, but you see these ten nairas (time for a dramatic gesture), this is all I have to take me to my next paycheck. I cannot even make them last to next week. I cannot buy food, I cannot pay for my passport photos . . . so you see why this is urgent for me, why I need to know. . . ." It worked so well, Mr. O. did not even say a word. But suddenly there was a flicker in his eyes as he realized he would not be able to make me vanish, and still without a word, he left the room. When he came back, he informed me I could collect my cash. These may seem petty victories, but in the moment it was immensely pleasurable, a true sense of social accomplishment. Tomorrow it will be a matter of regaining my passport from A. But then I'll have with me P., the best person I have met so far. I could ask C. His problem, however, is that he is convinced I need to be protected and should leave everything in his hands. But he is not a real pusher, and I don't trust the success of his tactics. "See the way I operate?" he asked me a few days ago. "I let a word drop here and there and go back at it." But by the time his few words sow some results, I'll be dead or, more likely, homeless, while I'm sure that if I had kept things in my own hands, the question of my housing would be clarified by now. Once you start on this wild goose chase, you cannot let go. Unless you make yourself (politely, of course) a real nuisance, you don't get anything and spoil all previous efforts. The idea is that they cannot put you out of their minds. They have to be sure that unless you get what you need, they will never have their peace. So, the idea of carefully placed words fruitfully hanging around is an absurdity. Plus, C. is a many-sided person, and while supposedly devoted to getting me a house he's also chasing bags of cement in Enugu. Conclusion: had he left the matter in my hands I would have seen some results. I have already spoiled some golden opportunities, for example, meeting with Chief W., who at the cafeteria asked me about my accommodations and promised to investigate. "Leave it to me," says C., "you have not come here to battle about housing; this is your right. I'll take care of it." And off he goes to Enugu. It's only by a chance meeting with U. that I find out C. has left. I'll be in this house for a while (goodbye private apt), and I'll have a roommate, E. I'm glad about it, but fear they may fill the place to capacity because this house has all the potential for becoming a mass dorm. As a last resort I hope the mouse living in the kitchen will keep out all intruders.

Talking to myself has become a nice habit, particularly since I have nobody to talk to (except for J., who I now meet regularly, sitting in front of his eternal beers while I wait for food at the faculty lounge). The talking is like housework, like cleaning the kitchen: you put it all out, what has been in your mind all day, and then sweep it away and go to sleep. Certainly, looking at my notes there is cause for exhilaration. My intellectual life does not have, at the moment, wings to fly, but this is because I am in an acquisition state and acquisition is no inspiration to the soul.

First, there is the acquisition of food. It is a day-to-day battle, always with new battlefields opening. The food is never enough, and on top of it we're now being fed later every day. By 1:00 p.m. all the new staff members condemned to the guesthouse are moaning and groaning, and there is always one who loudly expresses the collective frustration. But the women working the kitchen hold their ground and are learning new tricks. Today they kept the door closed until 1:00 p.m., and when, after repeated banging they were forced to open it, they closed the window through which the food is passed. Finally, they served us an uncooked okra soup, so sticky and slimy that my first Nigerian meal seemed a precious memory. But this time I ate everything and could have eaten another, because these days I am always hungry.

The acquisition of newspapers, too, is always an iffy proposition since, except for the government press, there are few copies in print, and they disappear immediately. So this is the source of a lot of bargaining, because the man who sells them wants to sell you a bunch so as not to get stuck with the less popular ones. Here, too, I have to use my social abilities, strike up a friendship with the man, convince him I'll be a good customer so he'll set the papers aside as I've seen him do for other people.

Then, matches and oranges, key to my reproduction because they mean cigarettes and drink. By the time I have assembled all the basics for my sustenance, my soul has left, my brain is sleepy, not to mention my legs, and my funguses are thriving.

Draft Book Project: Women of Nigeria

The draft for a book project, below, was designed in collaboration with Pade Badru, a fellow faculty member at the University of Port Harcourt who would later author a history of postindependence Nigeria, Imperialism and Ethnic Politics in Nigeria, 1960–96.

Silvia Federici and Pade Badru, Editors
The aim of the book is to present a comprehensive view of the conditions of women in Nigerian society, their day-to-day lives, their position in the economy, the family, the educational system, their history and their struggles. The book also aims to preserve a precious oral history, which is in danger of being lost.

The book will consist of two parts: a) an introductory section examining the sociocultural transformations Nigeria has undergone in the postindependence period and their effects on women; b) interviews with women from different economic and ethnic backgrounds and age groups. The interviews will focus on the following themes:

Women and Work: A woman's workday in subsistence farming, hawking, trading, and professional occupations. Housework and child

raising. The effects of government policies on women's economic situation (e.g., regulations concerning land and property). Female child labor.
Women's earning abilities. The impact of work on women's health, social
life, and social power.

Women's Position in the Family: The organization of family life
and women's role and power within it. The extended family. The polygamous
family. Women in Purdah. Marriage and divorce. Women's rights according
to present family organization.

Women and Reproduction: Women's attitudes toward childbear-
ing and child-raising practices. The impact of women's struggles on Nigerian
society's preference for male children. Children and social status. The plight
of the "barren" woman. Contraception, abortion, and childcare.

Relations among Women: Women's organizations (community
and market organizations; age groups). Forms of cooperation among women
in market trading, harvesting, and family life. Power relations among
women. The rural woman and the educated urban woman. Women's role in
the socialization process as agent for the transmission of social discipline.
The value women place on their identity as women.

Women, the Education System, and the Media: Women's access
to schooling and educational facilities. The impact of illiteracy on women's
lives. Women's access to information and the media. The impact of education on women's self-perception.

Women's History and Struggles: In Nigeria, some of the main
struggles against colonialism have been conducted by women, and to this
day it is often the (market) women who seem most capable of resisting
government policies. How has this been possible? Women's recollections
of anticolonial struggles. The experience of the Biafran War. The struggles
women conduct on a day-to-day basis to survive, gain better conditions of
living, more mobility, more access to the land, more power with respect to
their husbands and men in general. The impact of urbanization on women's
ability to organize around their needs. Women's involvement in political
organizations.

Women and Religion: The impact of Islamic and Christian reli-
gions on women. The consequences for women of the present revival of
both Islamic and Christian fundamentalism. The meaning and significance
of women's involvement in religious sects and religious organizations in
general.

The purpose of these interviews is to present, in each case,
a specific woman's story and, more generally, to give voice to women's

experiences: how do Nigerian women live and see their lives, what do they think of the world around them (men, children, the government), what do they struggle for, and what changes they want and hope for in the future. The introduction will contextualize these experiences, but the goal of the book is to be a medium for women's voices to be heard.

Requested funds: $15,000
Interpreters and field assistants: $5,000
Traveling and accommodations: $6,000
Secretarial expenses (transcription and typing): $3,000
Field equipment (cameras, recorders) and Xeroxing: $1,000

Notes for an Essay on Debt and Structural Adjustment, Part 1

The two draft fragments below were authored by Federici circa 1989, reflecting on the production of the debt crisis across Africa and Latin America. These themes would be developed in the essay "The Debt Crisis, Africa, and the New Enclosures," published in Midnight Notes *#10 and later updated to address the shifting tactics of debt production in works such as her 2014 article "From Commoning to Debt: Financialization, Microcredit, and the Changing Architecture of Capital Accumulation."*

The debt crisis originated in the aftermath of the oil prices boom of 1974, a turning point in capitalist class relations. It was in that year that, with the strong support of western governments and international, multilateral institutions (the IMF, World Bank, AID, Paris Club), commercial banks, in an unprecedented move, began recycling their petrodollars to countries of the third world. A common view, shared by many on the left, assumes that this move exemplifies the shortsightedness of the commercial banks, who, due to their intercompetition or private greed, began pushing loans onto third world countries regardless of their "creditworthiness" or the use to which these loans would be put. This view also assumes that western governments "went along" because they hoped that by recycling petrodollars they would avert a world recession as the money syphoned to third world nations would allow them to purchase western goods and thus keep western factories in business. But this economistic analysis ignores the political aspect of the crisis of 1974, of the petrodollar recycling, and of the unprecedented role of the banks in this process.

As never before, projects in the third world had been financed by commercial banks. This was the first step—culminating in Reagan's supply-side economics—of international capital's reconversion and recomposition by means of expansion on a world scale. In this context, the banks acted as the shock troopers of international capital. That banks took the lead was part of a long-term strategy centering on the so-called disappearance of the state and the apparent disengagement of the political from economic levels of management. "1974" was a response to the class struggle in Europe and the u.s., the red thread that runs from Detroit to Torino: the threat of Italy exiting from the "civilized world" of industrial capitalism and joining the third world of disaccumulation and underdevelopment; the "British sick-ness" of collapsing productivity; "blue collar blues" in Detroit, where auto workers (see the UAW contract of 1971) were demanding "time out" rather than better wages. In this context, the move by the banks to force loans on an all-too-willing third-world ruling class—cost what they may—was not due to interbank competition or rashness of judgement. Even less was it due to a desire to maintain certain production quotas in Europe and the u.s. If this had been the case, they would have opted for a much simpler solution of reflation policy at home instead of setting up more complex and risky mechanisms of capital export to the four corners of the capitalist world. The last thing international capital wanted was to refuel production at home, given that production no longer guaranteed satisfactory profit rates, though at the time they weren't prepared to shut down the plants at home. The recy-cling of petrodollars to countries such as Mexico, Brazil, and South Korea financed the infrastructure for the industry to come, and first of all for the booming oil industry; and paid for new industrial projects (although many of these would turn out to be a hoax in the long run, a temporary construc-tion bubble). Most importantly, the recycling of petrodollars, through loans to the former colonial world, financed a flight of capital from the danger areas of Europe and the u.s. It also disposed of commodities, beginning with oil itself, that could not be sold off on American or European markets due to rationing. The result was a new, broad expansion of capitalist rela-tions in crucial areas of the third world and their integration into the new international capitalist circuit. Note that the plunging of Poland into debt also dates to this period, an unprecedented move orchestrated by the World Bank to finance oil imports.

Thus it happened that between 1974 and 1976, a huge transfer of capital, approximately 121 billion USD, was transferred to the third world,

Figure 2
Cartoons from *Vanguard*, the Nigerian daily (circa 1986), critical of the austerity measures imposed by the International Monetary Fund.

"Alright say it. I've met all your conditions. Haven't I?"

"The rope first,... then the loan. It's either you CLIMB with it or HANG".

accompanied by a new jargon speaking of "developing countries," of the third world's "developing political clout," and other such inebriating nonsense—pandering to the third world ruling classes. These were the very years when unemployment, soon to become "retrenchment," was growing in the metropoles. But at the time, it was still presented as a temporary downturn and, although a half-hearted token, given the power relations at the time, unemployment benefits were raised to a historical maximum of thirteen months. By 1975, however, the unemployment situation was serious enough to prompt a redefinition of what constituted *unemployment* itself, leading to the attempt to strip large sections of the largely female proletariat from unemployment benefits.

Notes for an Essay on Debt and Structural Adjustment, Part 2

For many years now—at least since 1982—the "debt crisis" of the third world has been a topic of daily debate in creditor and debtor countries alike. Indeed, we have become so used to it that unless we are among its immediate victims, the announcement of another scheme for "debt relief" or another default on payment can hardly be counted as news. One is further discouraged from fathoming the underlying political reality by the ever-growing technical jargon in which the crisis is clothed: debt for equity, soft loans, recapitalization, structural adjustment programs. Capital has not forgotten the lessons of the Catholic Church, which has always spoken Latin when explaining to the masses the principles of the faith.

Further, so much attention is paid to the problem in the highest political spheres, with periodic meetings of the International Monetary Fund, the World Bank, and the leaders of the "free world"; so persistent have been the calls for a solution and the warnings that the crisis could cripple "our economies," that we are bound to conclude that nothing could matter more to politicians in Europe and the u.s. than helping their less fortunate partners in the third world. After all, isn't it in the interests of international capital that people in the third world are able to buy our goods, so that "we" can create more jobs and balance "our" budgets? What could be gained from the pauperization of large parts of the globe to the point that the average person cannot afford a pin if it is imported and often even when it isn't? Isn't free trade the religion that "we" go by?

But, paraphrasing Bertolt Brecht, when the leaders speak of peace, the common folk know to prepare for war. When Citicorp, Bank of America, James Baker, and the World Bank speak of debt relief, we can be sure that all is being done to keep the debts growing. Despite the crocodile tears shed over this "global tragedy" and the "grim realities" facing the third world, the debt crisis is by no means for capital the disaster that politicians à la Bradley would want us to believe, so long, at least, as the people in the debtor countries do not organize to put an end to the systematic plunder of their resources.

That the debt crisis is a bonanza for the "free market world" is by now an irrefutable fact, although each default on interest payments (no country is paying its principal anymore) is bound to cause anxiety on Wall Street, not for the money per se but because of its bad example and potential ripple effect. The only disagreement among economists and politicians is on the extent and timing of the squeeze, with people like Bill Bradley worrying that if the squeeze is too tight or comes too soon, social upheavals will follow before the country in question has put its security forces in order.

Debt or no debt, arms control and riot equipment are being steadily shipped, to the tune of millions, to the debtor nations. In fact, the more the debt owed, the more the repressive gadgets sold to a government. Bradley's position is like that of those ecologists who worry that a too rapid pace of exploitation will kill the goose that lays the golden eggs. Hence their complaints about "selfish," "short-term" interests. But the accounts of the banks speak clearly. The main lenders have been doubling their profits. The fact that the growing debt of third world countries is "good for business" also explains why the combined "intelligence" of the "first world" has not yet been able to solve the problem. Worse yet, year after year, policies are put in place that predictably worsen the debt so that, upon faithfully adopting the prescribed remedies, the debtor countries are poorer, more dependent, and more mired in debt. The problem is "intractable" because it is not meant to be solved, and it is not meant to be solved for the simple reason that *the debt crisis is the long-awaited opportunity for the "free world" to recolonize large parts of the world.*

Why should the so-called free world want to recolonize the ex-colonies? Wasn't the political and economic setup of the postindependence period sufficiently profitable? Hadn't we learned that independence was something of a fraud, with the imperial powers—old and new—still calling the shots? For sure the scenario, for a time, seemed quite promising: subservient third world politicians everywhere satisfied with their apartments in New York and bank accounts in Geneva, raw materials (petroleum, bauxite, copper, cobalt) flowing, as always, to those who "can use them best" in the highest poles of development, fostering the illusion of a prosperity to come while maintaining the mathematics of unequal exchange. As theorists of unequal exchange and dependency, like Gunder Frank, have pointed out, the independence of former colonies was surely not a loss for Paris and London and certainly a big gain for the u.s. We can also hear in the tone of the debates an unmistakable satisfaction. The debt crisis is a great opportunity for the countries of the free world to play the role of austere but benevolent fathers, ready to bite the bullet and impose stiff measures for the good of the undisciplined third world states. We are told that the crisis is forcing third world governments to "see the light," that is, to drop their anti-imperialist stance and, at last, adopt measures they have so far stubbornly resisted: the liberalization of their economies, privatization, and so forth. The debt crisis presumably absolves the free world from the charge that it caused underdevelopment with its imperialist politics extending from slavery to colonialism. Today any shame for the past and all humble tones are gone. Heads are raising again with pride and the word is out: "Didn't we say that you were not mature enough to be left on your own? Let us not hear anymore about the sins of colonialism."

The message is well received, for when a debtor nation is in a pleading position, there is little it can do but to repeat *mea culpa*. Moreover, it is in the interests of the third world ruling class to cultivate the myth that the crisis is the result of the incompetence and corruption of their people. Swallowing its nationalistic pride is a small price to pay for the privilege of continuing to exploit them, now with the assistance of most of the leaders of the rest of the world. For the ruling class of the third world, the debt crisis is a welcome opportunity to change the power relations in their countries and reduce their people's expectations and resistance, while avoiding any blame and appearing to do so under the guns of Washington and Geneva. In fact, if they play their hands skillfully, they can even gain some prestige in the process, through the ballets they perform with creditors and foreign investors: taking a tough posture, refusing to bend to IMF conditions, breaking off negotiations, stopping interest payments (for a while at least—none has yet refused to pay at the end of the day). It is a song and dance that is endlessly repeated, particularly when things in the country get heated. All the while, they impose austerity measures that would make the whole anticolonial struggle worthless, except for the demystification that independence has brought, as it has shown that exploitation and class domination can be color blind.

The U.S., in particular, profits from the debt crisis. It uses a debt it has created to bend elbows, to restructure political alliances, to rearrange the world politically with CityCorp and the World Bank at the helm, and behind them the IMF, running the show of the world. And now that the policy of giving loans has run its course because debtor countries are becoming more and more desperate and threatening to remain insolvent—now that all that could be gotten through loans has been gotten, now that the austerity measures cannot be made more austere short of mass death—they cautiously switch to the "debt for equity" model, making a profit by selling third world loans to each other, bank to bank, bank to private company, and then converting them directly into foreign investment. What this whole obscene story means is that the third world has been enslaved all over again. It is a new financial slavery made of debts, loans, adjustments programs, and restructuring, which means that people go hungry, schools are closed, medicines disappear from hospitals, and people die. The populations affected are counted by the World Bank among the victims of "underdevelopment." It means that the debt will be here to stay because none of these maneuvers are meant to eliminate it.

The problem of third world debt has revealed itself to be so "intractable" because allowing these countries to get out of it was never the goal. On the contrary, the goal was precisely to sink them deeper and deeper into debt so that they could be blackmailed, so that the fruits of the liberation struggles of the '50s and '60s, of the Cubas, of the Angolas and Guinea-Bissaus, would be eroded, so that nobody in the third world would dare to defy the capitalist world any longer and the capitalist world could return to its work as a vulture, to the point of scraping the meat off the carcass as is happening today with rescheduling, refinancing, and finally (the coup de grâce) the "debt-for-equity" swap, which is just a fancy way of saying that the country in question is being sold off piece by piece.

As in the classical demand for a pound of flesh, debt-for-equity, too, is the longed-for revenge triumphing over the postindependence period when governments were forced to show their patriotism by setting certain limits on foreign investment and control. Now the debt-for-equity swaps reset the score right at the point where colonialism was cut off, with even more vengeance because now the whole gang of capitalist agencies (the World Bank, IMF, Paris Club) is working to ensure that none of its members lose its portion of the loot.

University Teachers' Draft Code of Ethics for Global Education in Africa

The brief code below, drafted by Federici with George Caffentzis and Ousseina Alidou, was published by the Committee for Academic Freedom in Africa in their 1995 newsletter and associated with the group's campaign to bar the World Bank from the African Studies Association Conference.

We are university teachers and we publicly declare our adherence to the following principles of academic ethics in our work in Africa:

—we will never, under any circumstance, work (as researchers, with a study abroad program, or in any other capacity) in an African university where students or faculty are on strike or that has been shut down by students' or teachers' strikes and protests against police repression and structural adjustment cutbacks to funding.

—we will never take a position at, take funding from, or cooperate with the World Bank, the IMF, USAID, or any other organization whose policy is to expropriate Africans from the means of the production and distribution of knowledge and to devalue African people's contribution to world culture.

—we will never take advantage of the immiseration to which African colleagues and students have been reduced or appropriate the educational facilities and resources from which African colleagues and students have been de facto excluded because of lack of means. Knowledge acquired under such conditions would be antagonistic to the spirit of multiculturalism and scholarly solidarity.

—we will consult with colleagues and activists in the countries where we carry on research so as to ensure that our research answers the needs of the people it studies and is shaped with the cooperation of people whose lives will be affected by it rather than being dictated by funding agencies' agendas.

Arlen Austin would like to thank all those who have advised on this brief introduction and helped with the preservation of the original texts reproduced here, now housed in the archives of the Pembroke Center for Teaching and Research on Women. He extends his thanks to Silvia Federici and George Caffentzis for offering recollections of their time in Nigeria over the course of many conversations and a formal interview and also to Ousseina Alidou, Alamin Mazrui, Peter Szendy, and the faculty and staff of the Pembroke Center who have helped in the process of collecting and preserving the Federici papers: Suzanne Stewart-Steinberg, Mary Murphy, Denise Davis, Amanda Knox, and Donna Goodnow, among others.

ARLEN AUSTIN is a PhD candidate in the Department of Modern Culture and Media at Brown University where his studies focus on postwar social movements and the economies of mass media.

SILVIA FEDERICI is a feminist activist, scholar, and professor emeritus at Hofstra University. She is the author of *Caliban and the Witch: Women, the Body and Primitive Accumulation* (Autonomedia, 2004). In addition to continued engagements with activist groups globally, Federici is currently working on a collection of essays on the death penalty, as well as a collaborative collection of works related to structural adjustment in Africa and Latin America.

Notes

1   The statistics quoted here are drawn from the World Bank and the Central Bank of Nigeria's statements of accounts collected in Olufemi Fajana's 1993 report, "Nigeria's Debt Crisis," for the United Nations Economic Commission for Africa (Fajana 4, 15, 22). For some perspective on the ballooning of Nigeria's debt, Fajana notes that in 1970 Nigeria was the least indebted of the countries in sub-Saharan Africa. By 1993 it carried the greatest debt burden of the region (3).

2   Among the richest contemporane-
ous analyses of New York's "fiscal
crisis" as a capitalist response to
working-class resistance was a
pamphlet self-published by Donna
Demac and Philip Mattera in June
1976, "Developing and Underdeveloping New York: The 'Fiscal Crisis'
and a Strategy for Fighting Austerity." The piece would be reworked
into an article for *Zerowork 2* and
became a common reference point
for Federici, Caffentzis, and many of
their collaborators.

3   Perhaps the most blistering indict-
ment of the regime of Buhari and
subsequent administrations is in
Wole Soyinka's *The Open Sore of a
Continent.*

4   An analysis of the Nigerian
media's fascination with the
"immorality" of women as a means
of displacing blame for Buhari's
austerity program was written by
Federici under the pseudonym Iya
Agan in 1985 and is reproduced
below. This represents one in a
remarkable series of articles by
Federici and Caffentzis that date
from this period. Unfortunately,
space does not allow us to reproduce more of these works, but the
collection has been preserved in
the Feminist Theory Archives at
the Pembroke Center for Teaching
and Research on Women. Federici
and Caffentzis wrote under the
pseudonyms Iya Agan and John
Ono, respectively, for *AfricAsia*, a
radical journal of political theory
published in Paris. For each
article, the two would be paid
200 u.s. dollars. This money combined with their teaching salaries,
which, when paid at all, came in
the tremendously devalued naira,
allowed them to sustain teaching
work in their respective universities for the years they were able to
remain in Nigeria.

5   One of the more pernicious claims
of the World Bank in seeking to

implement austerity programs that
would defund higher education
across the continent was the contention that African universities
catered only to a local elite and
that funding would be transferred
to a neglected and more "democratic" primary education system.
For a response detailing this claim
of the Bank's and the class composition of the student university
population, see the newsletter of
the Committee for Academic Freedom in Africa (cafa), particularly
cafa no. 10 from the spring of 1996,
which included a detailed chronol-
ogy of student movement struggles
and a collection of reports from
previous issues.

6   The Committee for Academic
Freedom in Africa (cafa) would
publish eighteen newsletters
between 1991 and 2003. Throughout their work, a primary goal
would be to critique prevalent
forms of mainstream media discourse that characterized the
situation in Nigeria as primarily
the product of corruption or ethnic conflict while ignoring the role
of international capitalist investment (see Africa Watch). Among
the immediate goals of cafa was a
campaign to ban the World Bank
from conferences of the African
Studies Association, where the
Bank began to regularly organize panels and present itself as
a champion of academic inquiry
at the Association's conferences
by the early 1990s (see cafa no. 10
from 1996). The main goal of the
group, however, was to publicize
the strikes and protests conducted
by student unions and faculty
at universities in many of the
countries in sub-Saharan Africa.
A selection of writings from the
group was published in Alidou,
Caffentzis, and Federici, eds., *A
Thousand Flowers: Social Struggles against Structural Adjustment in African Universities.*

7   The history of the writing of *Caliban and the Witch* deserves its own serious study. The first iteration, *Il grande Calibano. Storia del corpo sociale ribelle nella prima fase del capitale*, cowritten with Leopoldina Fortunati through the late 1970s and finally published in 1984, should be counted among the classic feminist critiques of Marxian historiography to emerge from the Italian feminist movement steeped in the literature of *operaismo*. Federici would rework drafts of various chapters throughout her time in Nigeria and following her return to the U.S. For an early incarnation of the work in English, see "The Great Witch Hunt," published in the *Maine Scholar* in 1988.

8   Gbolahan Mudasiru (b. 1945, d. September 23, 2003) was an air force officer who held the governorship of Lagos state from January of 1984 through August of 1986 throughout the military regimes of Buhari and Babangida. According to his memorial page on the Lagos government website, he "introduced improved measures to keep the streets clean and orderly."

9   Precise references for this and other quotations reproduced in Federici's journals have been impossible to track down. Newspapers were difficult to obtain, as described below, and what remains in Federici's personal collection are largely articles from *Vanguard* and *The Guardian* both founded in 1983 before the fall of the Second Republic. Both are published in Lagos and remain independent of government control.

10   The *Tide*, a government-run newspaper with headquarters in Port Harcourt, began publishing in 1971. The exact date of this quotation could not be verified. The *Tide*'s archive is digitized to 2006.

Works Cited

Academic Staff Union of Universities. *ASUU and the 1986 Education Crisis in Nigeria*. Ibadan: Academic Staff Union of Universities, 1987.

Africa Watch. *Academic Freedom and Human Rights Abuses in Africa*. New York: Human Rights Watch, 1991.

Agan, Iya (Silvia Federici). "Hard Times for Nigerian Women." *AfricAsia* 16 (April 1985): 8–9.

Alidou, Ousseina, George Caffentzis, and Silvia Federici. "'We No Go Sit Down': CAFA and the Struggle against Structurally Adjusted Education in Africa." *Journal of Higher Education in Africa / Revue de l'enseignement supérieur en Afrique* 6.2–3 (2008): 61–75.

—————, eds. *A Thousand Flowers: Social Struggles Against Structural Adjustment in African Universities*. Trenton and Asmara: Africa World Press, 2000.

Badru, Pade. *Imperialism and Ethnic Politics in Nigeria, 1960–96*. Trenton and Asmara: Africa World Press, 1998.

Caffentzis, George. *No Blood for Oil! Essays on Energy, Class Struggle and War*. Brooklyn: Autonomedia, 2017.

Chakrabarty, Dipesh. *Provincializing Europe. Postcolonial Thought and Historical Difference*. Princeton: Princeton UP, 2000.

Cleaver, Harry. "Background: From Zerowork #1 to Zerowork #2." http://www.zerowork.org/Background-Z1-Z2.html (accessed 3 June 2020).

Committee for Academic Freedom in Africa (CAFA). *Newsletters of the Committee for Academic Freedom in Africa* 1–18 (1991–2003). https://libcom.org/library/newsletters-committee-academic-freedom-africa-1991-2003 (accessed 3 June 2020).

Demac, Donna, and Philip Mattera. "Developing and Underdeveloping New York: The 'Fiscal Crisis' and the Imposition of Austerity." *Zerowork #2* (Fall 1977): 113–39.

Fajana, F. Olufemi. *UNECA Development Research Papers Series No. 5. Nigeria's Debt Crisis.* Addis-Ababa: United Nations Economic Commission for Africa, 1993.

Falola, Toyin, and Julius Ihonvbere. *The Rise and Fall of Nigeria's Second Republic, 1979–84.* London: Zed, 1985.

Federici, Silvia. *Caliban and the Witch: Women, the Body and Primitive Accumulation.* Brooklyn: Autonomedia, 2004.

—————————. "The Debt Crisis, Africa, and the New Enclosures." *Midnight Notes* 10 (1990): 10–18.

—————————. "Development and Underdevelopment in Nigeria." *Work, Energy, War. Midnight Notes* 11 (1993): 87–90.

—————————. "From Commoning to Debt: Financialization, Microcredit, and the Changing Architecture of Capital Accumulation." *South Atlantic Quarterly* 113.2 (2014): 231–44.

—————————. "The Great Witch Hunt." *Maine Scholar* 1.1 (1988): 31–52.

—————————. Introduction. *The New York Wages for Housework Committee 1972–1979: History, Theory, and Documents.* Ed. Silvia Federici and Arlen Austin. New York: Autonomedia, 2018.

Federici, Silvia, and George Caffentzis. Interview. Conducted by Arlen Austin 20 May 2020. Unpubl.

Federici, Silvia, and Leopoldina Fortunati. *Il grande Calibano. Storia del corpo sociale ribelle nella prima fase del capitale.* Milan: Franco Angeli, 1984.

Haug, Wolfgang Fritz. "On the Need for a New English Translation of Marx's *Capital.*" *Socialism and Democracy* 31.1 (2017): 60–86.

Lagos State Government Website. Memorial page for Air Commander Gbolahan Mudasiru. https://governor.lagosstate.gov.ng/2019/04/25/air-cmdr-gbolahan-mudashiru-1984-1986/ (accessed June 3, 2020).

Marx, Karl. *Capital: A Critique of Political Economy.* Vol. 1. Trans. Ben Fowkes. New York: Vintage, 1977.

Soyinka, Wole. *The Open Sore of a Continent: A Personal Narrative of the Nigerian Crisis.* Oxford: Oxford UP, 1996.

Toupin, Louise. *Wages for Housework: The History of an International Feminist Movement, 1972–1977.* London: Pluto, 2018.

The World Bank. *The African Capacity Building Initiative: Toward Improved Policy Analysis and Development Management.* Washington, DC: World Bank, 1991. http://documents.worldbank.org/curated/en/867271468204836253/African-capacity-building-initiative (accessed 3 June 2020).

How Much Is Your African Slave Worth?

I see Menéndez stretched out.
Immobile, tense.
The open lung bubbles.
The chest burns.

His eyes see, are seeing.
The corpse lives.
—Guillén

*T*he title of this essay, "How Much Is Your African Slave Worth?," was generated by two particular readings. The first was my reading of the proceedings of a slave market and the ways in which the slave auction block worked and how the black body was sold. The report states: "The auctioneer brought up Joshua's Molly and family. He announced that Molly insisted she was lame in her left foot [. . .]. She was finally sold for $695. [. . .] And so the Great sale went on for two long days, during which time there were sold 429 men, women and children. [. . .] The total amount of the sale foots up $303,850" ("A Great Slave Auction"). The second reading that led me to this title was a reading of wills. One will is that of a woman called Miss Mary Chapman, who writes the following: "To my beloved son Matthew I give and bequeath my Negro man, Albert, and my Negro girl, Ann, and all my cattle, mules, and hogs."[1]

In these two instances, both the auction and the will, the enslaved black body is not just a body for labor. It is a commodity, monetized, bought and sold on the market (the auction block) and bequeathed as having value to children. Sometimes this body was also mortgaged. Thomas Jefferson,

Volume 31, Number 3 DOI 10.1215/10407391-8744567

who owned 607 slaves during his lifetime, often leased out the enslaved people he owned or used them as mortgage collateral for his plantation. This practice continued after his death when in 1827 his executors sold 130 of the "most valuable slaves" to cover his debts of $107,000. Jefferson often referred to enslaved women as "capital"; he wrote in a letter that "a woman who brings a child every two years" is "more profitable than the best man of the farm" since "what she produces is an addition to capital, while his [the male slave's] labors disappear in mere consumption."

In the social system of racial slavery, a central aspect of domination was that the black enslaved body—sold, used as collateral, or bequeathed—was always under the arbitrary will of the master. The enslaved body was an *objectum*, a thing. But it was a paradoxical thing since, as a human being, the enslaved lived, even if in this life there was death. Eduardo Grüner makes the point that "the slave's 'life' is structurally a substitute *death*" and that to be a slave was "a *suspended death*" (25). The everyday terror of violence on the enslaved body—required to reproduce a slave society in the Americas—made death, or rather the capacity of the master to put the black body to death, constitutive of racial slavery as a social relationship. Death did not just haunt the social, it was a regular practice.

So how does one think through a social system in which regular death does not reside only within the state sovereign's repertoire of power but is also the work of the master? Teasing out some of the elements of this kind of practice creates a ground from which we might think about debt and racial slavery in the Americas.

Debt and Slavery

Historically, one sociological argument about slavery has been that a condition for enslavement was debt or the pursuit of war and conquest (see Graeber).[2] This view about slavery framed John Locke's writings on the subject. In the *Two Treatises of Government*, Locke noted: "This is the perfect condition of *Slavery*, which *is* nothing else but *the State of War continued, between a lawful Conquerour and a Captive*" (284). With regard to debt, the enslaved in such contexts were used as labor in what might be described as indentured servitude, and their body was an embodiment of forms of exchange.

Debt, exchange, war, and Aristotle's conceptions of the "natural slave" were at the heart of the conventional arguments in sixteenth-century Western debates about slavery (see, for example, Vitoria). All these ideas were given a new twist at the historic moment of the Atlantic slave trade. European colonial conquest, racial slavery, and plantation production were critical markers in the emergence of capitalism and the so-called modern world. David Graeber has noted that "almost all elements of financial apparatus that we've come to associate with capitalism—central banks, bond markets, short-selling, brokerage houses, speculative bubbles, securitization annuities—came into being not only before the science of economics [. . .] but also before the rise of factories, and wage labor itself" (345). Central to the emergence of these economic institutions in which debt and credit played pivotal parts was the Atlantic slave trade and racial slavery.[3] Commentators on the Atlantic slave trade have noted how it was a "gigantic network of credit arrangements": "Ship-owners based in Liverpool or Bristol would acquire goods on easy credit terms [. . .] expecting to make good by selling slaves (also on credit) to planters in the Antilles and America" (Graeber 150). This extensive system of credit remained in place for a long time so that when the Manchester mills became known in the nineteenth century as "Cottonopolis," they drew from the credit system put in place by the Atlantic slave trade.[4] Within this extensive system of debt and credit one crucial question would be: how to secure the debt. Perhaps one of the most striking historical instances of how securing the debt worked in a system that the black radical abolitionist Ottobah Cugoano called the "commerce in flesh"[5] is the story of the *Zong*.

In the summer of 1781 a group of Liverpool merchants dispatched a ship to the West Coast of Africa to capture and buy African slaves. Arriving there, the captain of the ship acquired enslaved African people and a new ship named the *Zong*. On this ship were placed 440 enslaved Africans. The ledgers note that, for insurance purposes, the *Zong* was valued at 2,500 pounds and that the value of the enslaved Africans was 13,200 pounds. Baucom notes that both the ship and the enslaved were valued for insurance purposes a total of 15,700 pounds with the insurance sealed by promissory notes. Thus the enslaved African bodies were already considered a collateral for debt. These bodies were already laden with value, and as Baucom astutely notes, this value was "a reversal of the protocols of value creation proper to commodity capital" (17). So let's tarry here for a moment on this point because it is central to the overall argument of the enslaved body as a form of debt and credit.

At the core of the conception of value is labor that is embodied within a commodity, what Marx called "socially necessary" abstract labor (*Capital* 129). Marx also makes the point that the form of labor he is addressing when he is arguing about abstract labor is "free labour," and this is why he insists that "the slave [. . .] is *himself* a commodity, but the labour power is not *his* commodity" ("Wage" 205). Yet there is a problem in this specific formulation by Marx. For in the *Economic and Philosophic Manuscripts of 1844*, in the section on "Estranged Labour," he argues that "labour produces not only commodities; it produces itself and the worker as a *commodity*" (71). Marx misses here the kind of value and labor that the enslaved African represents. It is not simply, in Baucom's words, a value creation that is prior to commodity capital. There is something else that we need to grapple with. The Caribbean theorist Sylvia Wynter, in her unpublished manuscript "Black Metamorphosis," emphasizes that, when being sold to the New World plantation, the African was valued according to a labor power that was quantified. In other words, there was no "abstract labor power" of the slave, since his or her value was already quantifiable through an initial series of equivalences that began with being made captive in Africa and then sold. In the early period of the slave trade, the African slave was sold in the New World as a *pieza*, literally a "piece," which could be equivalent to, say, a bunch of bananas. As one historian noted: "A *pieza de India* ['piece of India'] was not an individual but essentially a measure of potential labor. Thus, younger slaves were counted as fractions of *piezas*" (Postma 228). In the Dutch slave trade, the West India Company created a "price guide" in which "the suggested price apparently alluded to the most common unit," the *pieza de India*, whereas "the price for women *piezas* was [. . .] kept at a lower rate" (Postma 264). Reflecting on the ways in which equivalences functioned in the slave trade, Wynter suggests that the negro-*pieza* as commodity realized exchange value in the exchange that took place when the African was transformed from being a captive into an enslaved body. In other words, value was not only being measured and calculated in terms of labor power but it could not be separated from exchange value. In the period of the African slave trade, the enslaved as "property in person" meant that many of the conventional distinctions around value collapsed. From this perspective we need to find new theoretical space to grapple with this human experience.[6] After this important digression, let's return to the fate of the *Zong*.

In its voyage from the West African coast to Jamaica, the ship ran into trouble, and when it became clear to the crew and the captain that the ship's drinking water supplies would not be sufficient, they decided to throw overboard 130 enslaved Africans. The decision to do this was motivated by the knowledge that if the African enslaved died on land, then the insurers would not pay. During the voyage, over 60 slaves had already perished. Since the ship was running low on water and was over thirteen sailing days away from the town of Black River in Jamaica, the decision was taken to "jettison" the "cargo," thereby allowing for a claim to be made under the category of "general averages," a type of averaging used in insurance for expenses pertaining to the preservation of the ship (Baucom 107–8). The insurance claim by the ship owners was rejected by the insurers and taken to court in London. The Lord Chief of Justice, Lord Mansfield, pointed out that there was "no doubt [. . .] that *the case of the slaves was the same as if horses had been thrown overboard*" (Walvin 153). Although Lord Mansfield ordered a retrial and did not find the insurance company liable, his remarks reinscribed the racial classification system that located Africans as not human. In this regard, John Weskett's study on insurance law, published the same year as the *Zong* massacre, is a document of interest: "The insurer takes upon him the risks of the loss, capture, and death of slaves, or any other unavoidable accident to them: but natural death is always understood to be excepted:—by natural death is meant, not only when it happens by disease or sickness, but also when the captive destroys himself through despair, which often happens: but when slaves are killed, or thrown into the sea in order to quell an insurrection on their part, then the insurers must answer" (Weskett 525; qtd. in Walvin 112). It is now clear why the crew and the captain would have taken the decision to throw the 130 enslaved Africans overboard. If they had died of so-called natural causes triggered by disease, then the voyage would have incurred economic loss for the Liverpool slave merchants and entrepreneurs. How then would they have repaid their credit loan?

My argument here is that the Atlantic slave trade became a commercial system defined in the first instance by its network of debt and credit. Second, it was then defined by the value of the enslaved for which there was a norm calculated around the labor years that the enslaved had to give. As Wynter puts it in "Black Metamorphosis": "The 'negro' was [. . .] now essentially a form of labor power calculated in terms of his exchange value, bought and sold not as a slave, but as a commodity. He was 'labor power' in the economic system, which produced goods for the world market, not on the basis on fulfilling relatively constant needs, but on the basis of maximizing profit, which was limitless" (27). The story of debt, then, is not simply about exchange, value, and the emergence of money; there is another story that begins with the emergence of capitalism and the Atlantic slave trade.

Domination and the Laws of Slavery

We have already noted that in the Atlantic world, the African slave was a "property in person" in perpetuity. As such, he or she was living under a social system of near total domination; however, the enslaved did so as a human being producing commodities: sugar, coffee, cotton, and indigo. Producing commodities and being property in person, the male enslaved experienced a process of *double commodification* within a network of exchange, credit, and debt. On the other hand, the female black enslaved body was triply commodified. At one level she was like the male enslaved African, doubly commodified; however, at another level she was violently used as sexual reproductive labor, giving birth to other enslaved persons.

Within this political and social context of racial domination, the slave body, as Wynter argues, was also "the symbolic object of this lack which is designated as the lack of the human" ("Sambos" 152). It was a disposable body and could be tortured in whatever ways suited the master. C. L. R. James, in some of the most remarkable passages in *The Black Jacobins*, notes how forms of terror were considered pleasurable to the planter class. Specifically, he describes the deployment of dogs that would tear up black enslaved flesh (360). As Saidiya Hartman emphasizes in *Scenes of Subjection*, slavery, a system born in generative violence, reproduced itself by violence.[7] In this social system, the terror in the flesh often obscured the generative violence of the debt and credit systems that became the reproductive mechanisms of the "commerce of the flesh."[8]

The African enslaved represented both labor and capital, then, and these categories were defined by price. This form of representation created by the process of double and triple commodification laid the ground for practices and technologies of *ruling over* that always reached toward forms of total domination. If we argue that racial slavery and colonialism were not incidental or epiphenomenal to the modern world but were embedded within it and shaped its making—not à la Marx, as a specific phase of, say, primitive accumulation, but as one of the critical elements in the growth and consolidation of capitalism—then what we are seeing is the emergence of the modern through the doubly and triply commodified figure of the African enslaved body. Once we mark this, a different archive opens to us, one in which some of the most profound social questions, both historically and in the present, reside.

Modern governmentality, as it emerged from this configuration, created certain technologies of rule over the body of the enslaved that function as credit or debt. These forms of rule based on violence were also methods of saturation.[9] In colonial and racial governmentality, the central repertoire of rule didn't just include discipline, control, or the exercise of *might as right*; it produced subjectivities, like the figure of the Negro and, later, the figure of the Native on the African continent.[10]

In the discussion about racial slavery, the fact that slave laws were the order of the day in the United States is sometimes elided. To put the matter simply, the United States of America, up until 1865, was a *slave* society. So let us pay a bit of attention, for example, to the laws of Virginia around 1600. Let us look at the transition from indentured servitude to slavery. One notes how, after the first African slaves were brought to Virginia in 1619, the laws began to change. In 1662, a statutory provision made it clear that "all children borne in this country shall be held bond or free only according to the condition of the mother" (qtd. in Morris 43). Accordingly, if the mother was enslaved, then the child was a slave, no matter who his or her father was. This is important, because it went against British common law, where it was the father's status that would determine the child's. We are facing here the question of gender in slavery, and the way in which black women's bodies were transformed into breeding wombs for enslaved children. Recall our initial observation that Jefferson called the enslaved woman "capital." This historical fact transformed black women into objects of sexual reproduction for enslaved labor: at the slave market women were specifically advertised and monetized according to their capacity to have children (see Berry; and Morgan).

The other law that I want to mention here is the 1667 law in Virginia declaring that the baptism of slaves did not exempt them from bondage (Morris 393). This is important because one of the practices of racial slavery and colonialism, the construction of the Negro and the making of the Native, circled around who was human and who was not. In this historical period the main marker of being human was to be Christian. Baptism as a ritual of passage that transformed one from being an unbeliever into a follower of Christ was thus critical. The ritual activated one's soul. In Christian theology, once a being had a soul they became a person made in the image and likeness of God. As such, how could they be enslaved? The slave master's answer to this conundrum was to have the colonial slave state and the planters establish a law that made it clear that if a person was baptized, it did not stop them from being in slave bondage. What was at work here was the dominance of the slave system, one in which the soul might be redeemed but the black body was in earthly bondage and therefore could be used as debt or credit, or forced to do slave labor. Moreover, various laws were enacted specifying how and under what conditions slaves could be used as mortgage collateral. What happens if the debtor cannot repay the debt? Can the creditor keep the slaves? What kind of legal mechanisms are required in these matters (see Martin)? Seen within the context of racial slavery, debt is not just about a relationship working through money but is a process of exchange that involves a human body that is enslaved and subjected to violent forms of domination.

Wynter, in the yet unpublished manuscript I have referred to, cites Marx repeatedly. She seems to accept the idea of primitive accumulation, but she also says that, for Marx, those who traded slaves were capitalists themselves. I would therefore argue that within her work there is a tension between an understanding of primitive accumulation as a specific moment in the development of capitalism and an understanding of capitalism as having no prehistoric stage. This does not mean that capitalism was the only system of human society, that there were not currents, economic and social, that then congealed into capitalism. Rather, it means that there is another history in which the Atlantic slave trade, the plantation, racial slavery, and colonialism were not just elements in but were critical to the congealing of capitalism and the making of the modern world. It points to a different history of the so-called modern.

In this regard, I would point to the Dutch merchant bankers of the period. In the early 1600s, they had established companies like the East India Company and the West India Company, which were essentially joint stock companies functioning through debt and credit.[11] Not only was the West India Company involved in the slave trade but they often acted as bankers to the planters in the Dutch Caribbean. The point I want to make is this: when one thinks about the African enslaved body as debt and credit, one also has to think about the business of the plantation itself as a certain site, a node within the network of debt and credit. Wynter in her unpublished manuscript insists that the secret of capitalism is to be found "not in the factory but in the plantation" (582). The consequences of this for critical and radical thought is indeed far reaching.

The black African enslaved person was essentially a form of labor, calculated in terms of his or her exchange value, bought and sold not just as a slave but as a commodity. At the point of exchange in Africa, he or she was a commodity monetized as a captive. Insured on the slave ship, the black body was of value not as an abstract form of labor but as value already wrought through exchange. That body then produced goods for the world market as labor power. Such a social system rested on violence in myriad forms that tended toward total domination.

Now, if one operates from this historical ground, then how does one think about debt today? Much contemporary thinking around debt focuses on the writings of the Italian theorist Maurizio Lazzarato, who considers the financialization of the future from the point of view of debtors and questions the right of creditors to be repaid. From my historical perspective, the question I ask is: how does debt in the form of a human body trouble the matter of repayment? What are we to make of the enslaved African who was used as collateral for a mortgage, who was always marked, in Shakespeare's phrase, as a price for "a pound of flesh"? How are we to think of power working through this price of flesh? And not just flesh with the brutal markings of the body of the enslaved but flesh as part of an exchange process in which debt is key?

With these questions in mind I want to make my closing remarks. The way I think about history and its relationship to theory is that history travels in sediments and deposits that carry forward things and structures not as repetition but as adaptation and rearrangement. If critical theory is not only emancipated thought and critique but also entails grappling with the social world and constructing what I have called elsewhere a "hermeneutic of the world" (Bogues, *Humanities*), then critical theory grapples with history because it is *in* history that we make the social world. The motion of history as it adapts and rearranges creates what Stuart Hall calls a "conjuncture." We live in a specific conjuncture of late capitalism, namely neoliberalism, an ideological force on which a great deal of theoretical work has been done, notably by Hall himself in "The Neo-Liberal Revolution," an essay he wrote just before he died. Constructed around the human qua *homo economicus*, neoliberalism as a form of power has a drive toward totality. And in this drive and for the work of saturation, debt is central. To have credit means you have to be in debt, and indebtedness today creates a particular subjectivity.

When debt becomes the engine of contemporary economy, it begins to appear and work as a certain technology of rule in which power seems to act freely, because we who are indebted seem to choose that. Yet if we examine this enactment of debt, isn't our so-called choice produced by a point of saturation, by the way in which we have been saturated?

Within such a context, aspects of governmentality might no longer operate in the flesh, or through various forms of discipline, but through desire. My point here is that capitalism itself operates not only through forms of exploitation and domination but also by always creating forms of life, practices of life and of living, what I like to call *modes of being human*. If in racial slavery the black body could be deployed and exchanged as debt, as credit, as commodity, it seems to me that in this contemporary drive of capital to make us all indebted humans, then the drive to create a saturated commodified body draws from the practices that instituted racial slavery. Castoriadis makes the point: "Society is always the self-institution of the social-historical" (372). In this process, I would suggest that commodification has a longer historical moment, one, I would argue, that opened up with the colonial slave trade and racial slavery.

ANTHONY BOGUES is the Asa Messer Professor of Humanities and Critical Theory and the inaugural director of the Center for the Study of Slavery and Justice at Brown University. He is also a visiting professor and curator at the University of Johannesburg. The author/editor of nine books in the fields of intellectual history, political theory, and art, he has curated exhibitions in the u.s., the Caribbean, and South Africa. He is currently working on a book titled "Black Critique" and editing with Bedour Alagraa a volume on Sylvia Wynter's work. He is the co-convener of two major exhibition projects, one titled *Slavery, Colonialism, and the Making of the Modern World*, with the National African American Museum of History and Culture; and the other an African and African diasporic contemporary art project/platform on Black lives today, titled *The Imagined New*.

Notes

1   For a discussion of wills and American racial slavery, see Brophy and Thie.

2   On Locke's support of the African slave trade and African enslavement in the New World, see Bernasconi and Mann.

3   A robust debate about slavery and racial capitalism was ignited by the work of the late Cedric Robinson and his seminal *Black Marxism* (1983). Numerous texts are being written today that define the capitalism that emerged in this historical period as racial capitalism. See, for example, Baptist; Johnson; and the *Boston Review*'s 2017 forum titled *Race Capitalism Justice* (Johnson and Kelley).

4   For a good discussion of cotton and slavery, see Beckert.

5   On Cugoano's political thought, see Bogues, *Black Heretics* 25–46.

6   For extensive discussion of the slave as "property in person," see Bogues, *Empire* 30–31. The phrase is that of the Caribbean historian Elsa Goveia.

7   In the African American literary tradition, this violence has become signified by Aunt Hester's scream, described in the *Narrative of the Life of Frederick Douglass*. Fred Moten, in his recent *Black and Blur*, pays attention to this scream (viii–xiii).

8   I owe this point about the generative violence of the business practices of the Atlantic slave trade to discussions with Africana graduate student Malcolm Thompson, who is working for the Global Curatorial Project on an exhibition about slavery, colonialism, and the making of the modern world. This is a project that involves several international museums and is co-convened by the Center

for the Study of Slavery and Justice (Brown University) and the National African American Museum of History and Culture at the Smithsonian.

9   In deploying the term *saturation*, I want to suggest that this is a form of rule in which interpellation occurs that seeks to shape desire and imagination. If, according to one of Foucault's paradigms, the exercise of the "pastoral" form of power has as one of its conditions the ability to direct the individual, then saturation is a technology of rule that seeks to create forms of subjectivization that operate through desire, forms and practices of naturalized common sense. In the system of racial slavery, the discursive practices of creating the so-called Negro were crucial to saturation. For further elaboration, see Bogues, *Black Critique.*

10   For an extensive discussion of the Native, see Bogues, *Black Heretic.* In *Empire of Liberty* (73–74), I have argued against the idea, posited by both Hannah Arendt and Michel Foucault, that violence is the opposite of power. Instead, I suggest that a serious examination of racial slavery illustrates that power operates in this context as "power in the flesh."

11   For a discussion of the Dutch state and its relationship to these companies, see Brandon.

Works Cited

Baptist, Edward E. *The Half Has Never Been Told: Slavery and the Making of American Capitalism.* New York: Basic, 2014.

Baucom, Ian. *Specters of the Atlantic: Finance Capital, Slavery, and the Philosophy of History.* Durham: Duke UP, 2005.

Beckert, Sven. *Empire of Cotton: A Global History.* New York: Vintage, 2014.

Bernasconi, Robert, and Anika Maaza Mann. "The Contradictions of Racism: Locke, Slavery, and the *Two Treatises.*" *Race and Racism in Modern Philosophy.* Ed. Andrew Valls. Ithaca: Cornell UP, 2005. 89–107.

Berry, Daina Ramey. *The Price for Their Pound of Flesh: The Value of the Enslaved, from Womb to Grave, in the Building of a Nation.* Boston: Beacon, 2017.

Bogues, Anthony. *Black Critique: Towards an Alternative Genealogy of Critical Thought.* London, Pluto (forthcoming).

——————. *Black Heretics, Black Prophets: Radical Political Intellectuals.* New York: Routledge, 2003.

——————. *Empire of Liberty: Power, Desire, and Freedom.* Hanover: Dartmouth College P, 2010.

——————. *The Humanities and the Social Sciences: Knowledge, Change, and The Human Today.* Providence: Brown University Publication, 2013.

Brandon, Pepijn. *War, Capital, and the Dutch State (1588–1795).* Leiden: Brill, 2015.

Brophy, Alfred, and Douglas Thie. "Land, Slaves, and Bonds: Trust and Probate in the Pre-Civil War Shenandoah Valley." *West Virginia Law Review* 119.1 (2016): 345–97.

Castoriadis, Cornelius. *The Imaginary Institution of Society.* Cambridge, MA: MIT P, 1998.

Douglass, Frederick. *Narrative of the Life of Frederick Douglass, an American Slave.* New York: Penguin, 2014.

Foucault, Michel. *Power: The Essential Works of Foucault.* Vol 3. Ed. James Faubion. New York: New Press, 1994.

Graeber, David. *Debt: The First 5,000 Years.* London: Melville, 2011.

"A Great Slave Auction." *New York Daily Tribune* 9 Mar. 1859. https://chroniclingamerica.loc.gov/lccn/sn83030213/1859-03-09/ed-1/seq-5/.

Grüner, Eduardo. *The Haitian Revolution: Capitalism, Slavery, and Counter-Modernity.* Trans. Ramsey McGlazer. Cambridge: Polity, 2020.

Guillén, Nicolás. "I Came on a Slaveship." *Man-Making Words: Selected Poems of Nicolás Guillén.* Amherst: U of Massachusetts P, 1972. 185–86.

Hall, Stuart. "The Neo-Liberal Revolution." *Cultural Studies* 25.6 (2011): 705–28.

Hartman, Saidiya V. *Scenes of Subjection: Terror, Slavery, and Self-Making in Nineteenth-Century America.* Oxford: Oxford UP, 1997.

James, C. L. R. *The Black Jacobins: Toussaint L'Ouverture and the San Domingo Revolution.* New York: Vintage, 1989.

Jefferson, Thomas. Letter to John Wayles Eppes. 30 June 1820. https://founders.archives.gov/documents/Jefferson/98-01-02-1352.

Johnson, Walter. *River of Dark Dreams: Slavery and Empire in the Cotton Kingdom.* Cambridge, MA: Harvard UP, 2013.

Johnson, Walter, and Robin D. G. Kelley, eds. *Race Capitalism Justice.* Forum 1. Spec. issue of *Boston Review* (Winter 2017). http://bostonreview.net/forum-i-winter-2017.

Lazzarato, Maurizio. *The Making of the Indebted Man: An Essay on the Liberal Condition.* Los Angeles: Semiotext(e), 2012.

Locke, John. *Two Treatises of Government.* Ed. Peter Laslett. Cambridge: Cambridge UP, 1988.

Martin, Bonnie. "Slavery's Invisible Engine: Mortgaging Human Property." *Journal of Southern History* 76.4 (2010): 817–66.

Marx, Karl. *Capital: A Critique of Political Economy.* Trans. Ben Fowkes. Vol. 1. London: Penguin, 1976.

——————. *Economic and Philosophic Manuscripts of 1844.* Marx and Engels 66–125.

——————. "Wage Labour and Capital." Marx and Engels 203–17.

Marx, Karl, and Friedrich Engels. *The Marx-Engels Reader.* Ed. Robert C. Tucker. New York: Norton, 1978.

Morgan, Jennifer. *Labouring Women: Reproduction and Gender in New World Slavery.* Philadelphia: U of Pennsylvania P, 2004.

Morris, Thomas D. *Southern Slavery and the Law, 1619–1860.* Chapel Hill: U of North Carolina P, 1996.

Moten, Fred. *Black and Blur*. Durham: Duke UP, 2017.

Postma, Johannes Menne. *The Dutch in the Atlantic Slave Trade, 1600–1815*. Cambridge: Cambridge UP, 1990.

Robinson, Cedric J. *Black Marxism: The Making of the Black Radical Tradition*. London: Zed, 1983.

Shakespeare, William. *The Merchant of Venice*. New York: Applause, 2001.

Vitoria, Francisco de. *Political Writings*. Ed. Anthony Pagden and Jeremy Lawrance. Cambridge: Cambridge UP, 1991.

Walvin, James. *The Zong: A Massacre, the Law, and the End of Slavery*. New Haven: Yale UP, 2011.

Weskett, John. *A Complete Digest of the Theory, Laws, and Practice of Insurance*. London: Frys, Couchman, and Collier, 1781.

Wynter, Sylvia. "Black Metamorphosis: New Natives in a New World." Unpubl. ms., n.d. Schomburg Center for Research in Black Culture, New York.

———. "Sambos and Minstrels." *Social Text* 1 (1979): 149–56.

Narrative and Strategy in Sovereign Debt

*O*ne of the first classes generally taken by entering American law school students often bears the title "Lawyering," "Legal Research and Writing," "Legal Skills," or something similar. And one of the exercises frequently undertaken in this course involves the construction of compelling narratives in the service of an imaginary client—an artful selection and presentation of facts applied to carefully framed legal rules, often with a moral overlay, and ultimately connected to the desired legal outcome. This exercise necessarily entails the recognition of the centrality of narration in legal disputes but also, implicitly, the plasticity of narrative itself.

Unsurprisingly, the significance of narrative for much legal practice is widely acknowledged: a well-crafted account, carefully shaped within the discursive parameters of legal rules and expectations, can further an attorney's argument. Still, acceptance of the ways in which narrative not only works within the law but also shapes law's contours and possibilities has not uniformly permeated every area of legal study. Although critical legal studies, law and literature, legal feminism, and critical race studies have changed the nature of legal study and scholarship, certain issues—in particular international finance and debt—have received less attention than they might from those interested in narrative.

As such, in this essay I argue that issues of sovereign state debt repayment and collection—too often assumed to be free of the contingency and elasticity of narrative—are deeply shaped by historically grounded discourses of sovereignty that delineate boundaries between the public and the private arena. Gilles Deleuze and Félix Guattari famously noted that money and its circulation "is the means for rendering the debt infinite" (215). And anthropologist David Graeber highlights that money further has the "capacity to turn morality into a matter of impersonal arithmetic," arguing that "[t]he difference between a 'debt' and a mere moral obligation [. . .] is simply that a creditor has the means to specify, numerically, exactly how much the debtor owes" (14). This simultaneously infinite and numerically definite nature of monetary debt holds significant power in international finance. But, at least in the sovereign state context, its infinitude and mathematical certainty do not in and of themselves address the questions of *who* should repay that debt and *whose assets* should be collected in the event of nonpayment. For answers to these inquiries, the narrative of debt needs to be understood as embedded within narratives of sovereignty, which construct and shape who holds ultimate authority within a given territory.[1]

Although mainstream legal argument and practice in sovereign debt tend not to attend to this narrative dimension, I draw from my prior research to argue that in fact these narratives enable, construct, and limit the possibilities in debt repayment and collection. They suggest an often overlooked degree of conceptual flexibility in international financial practice and in its key enforcement mechanism of reputation, which requires a narratively steeped ideological consensus for its functioning. As part of this, I consider the potential of counternarrative as a critical strategy and suggest that, although sovereign debt practices are not written in stone, the historically specific material and ideational structures out of which these narratives emerge caution against too sanguine an understanding. In particular, thinking strategically about narrative and debt necessitates a layered approach—involving attention both to how narrative works in a particular case or context and to how it emerges from and reinforces these broader structures.

Narratives of Sovereignty in Debt Repayment

Even if we acknowledge that creditors have lent money to a country and a debt of sorts has been created, there remains an open question as to which entity actually borrowed the money. On the one hand, "the sovereign state" has obviously borrowed the money—and most global economic actors would leave it at that. But what or *who* constitutes the sovereign state is one of the most complicated and controversial questions in political theory, international law, and international relations. And, as I have pointed out in previous writing, the answer to this controversial question has significant consequences for when we should expect debt to be repaid.[2]

By *sovereignty*, I mean very broadly the ultimate authority within a given territory. Historically, a "sovereign" may have referred not only to a state or governmental form but also to an individual—a king, empress, tsar, or sultan—who embodied and ruled that state, with the individual and the polity inextricably intertwined.[3] Recently, sovereignty has been more commonly associated with the governmental institutions and officials that represent a territorially bound collectivity, or perhaps even with the underlying population itself. Ultimately, these different narratives of sovereignty construct what appears reasonable and possible in the arena of sovereign finance. Without adopting and participating in one of these approaches, the idea of "sovereign debt" and related concepts such as "sovereign asset," "sovereign wealth," and "sovereign reputation" lose their meaning. This is true regardless of whether the narrative is adopted explicitly or, as is more often the case in international finance today, implicitly.

Usually the question of who is the sovereign in sovereign financing—of who borrowed the money and therefore who should repay the debt—remains in the background of international debt practices. But the centrality of sovereignty narratives for ongoing debt repayment emerges clearly when we consider hypotheticals around potential changes of rulership under different approaches to sovereignty. To begin with, imagine a setting in which "sovereigns" are not ongoing political collectivities but rather individuals who battle each other for control over territory and people. In the event that one individual gains control over territory, that person would constitute the sovereign ruler in that space, at least while they and perhaps their descendants lived. Imagine now that a bitter rival successfully ousts this first ruler or ruling family, destroying monuments and vowing to eliminate the family from the territory's memory. In this scenario, would creditors of the overthrown ruler expect to approach the victorious new sovereign for payment of the ousted rival's debts? They could certainly try—but should perhaps think carefully about the potential risk to their safety.

Although this situation is merely a hypothetical, such personalistic forms of rule have of course existed at various moments in history. Persian chronicler and Mongol bureaucrat Ata-Malik Juvaini describes the election of Mengü (grandson of Genghis) to the status of Great Khan in 1251 and in particular notes the subsequent despair felt by creditors of his predecessor and first cousin Güyük. These creditors did not feel *owed* by Mengü or his polity, even after an orderly succession among family members to control the same territory according to established custom (Weatherford 175). Juvaini notes that all relevant commentators agreed that in this instance "there was no obligation to pay the amount due [. . .] and that no mortal would have cause to object" to the nonpayment. After all, the commentary continues, "from what book of history has it been read or heard from reciters that a king paid the debt of another king? And no mortal ever discharged the obligation of his enemies." Ultimately Mengü did choose to make Güyük's creditors whole, which was considered evidence not of the creditors' rights but rather of Mengü's unusual generosity and nobility (Juvaini 602–4; qtd. in Lienau, *Rethinking* 35).

Even beyond this colorful historical anecdote, situations of regime change generally shed light on the centrality of our narratives of sovereignty for expectations around sovereign debt. This is particularly the case if the new regime aims to radically alter the polity's political and economic structures as part of an explicit rejection of its predecessor. Should a new revolutionary communist regime be responsible to the creditors of a preexisting absolute monarchy—contrary to the thirteenth-century Mongol bureaucracy's view that one should not be expected to discharge the debts of one's enemies? Or imagine that a corrupt dictatorship has been overthrown by a new liberal democracy, which then argues that it is the first manifestation of the territory's true sovereign, the underlying people who have heretofore been unable to exercise their power. Is the new democratic republic merely a continuation of the previous autocratic regime and therefore responsible for its debts despite receiving no benefit from the borrowed funds? Is there some underlying connection of language or culture that justifies an ongoing insistence on debt payments even in the absence of any other legitimating structure, and is that enough? Or, alternatively, do we instead see in each of these instances the emergence of an entirely new sovereign, though it exists on the same territory as the previous polity?

Asking these questions throws into high relief the degree to which sovereign debt practices inherently rest on an "imagined community" of the nation-state, to use Benedict Anderson's famous phrase. These narratives of nationhood and sovereignty construct modern statehood and thus shape, justify, and are reinforced by myriad international financial practices involving those states. Depending on the theory of sovereignty implicitly or explicitly adopted, the practices of sovereign debt can be expected to diverge significantly. An approach that considers the content of and changes in a state's internal structure, interests, and popular support irrelevant to its sovereign status—a theory of sovereignty that I call *statist*—could easily embrace uninterrupted debt payment.[4] After all, democratic voice and popular benefit are immaterial to this narrative of sovereignty. Conversely, if a nonstatist conception of sovereignty privileging popular control, rule of law, or public benefit is accepted, then a debt contract signed by a non-democratic government—particularly a contract that did not aim to (or actually) benefit the underlying population or hew to the regime's own written rules—should not be presumptively enforceable against successive regimes. Without an implicit narrative of sovereignty, there would be no grounds on which creditors could insist on the repayment of debt beyond the lifetime of an individual ruler. Political discourse is the essential link converting the promise made by an individual or set of elites into an obligation that can indefinitely bind an entire collectivity.

Any practices or norms that underpin sovereign debt are likewise dependent on this underlying narrative. In particular, an implicit adoption of one or another discourse of sovereignty is embedded in any reputational or creditworthiness assessment of a sovereign borrower, especially any assessment of whether additional loans should be extended if a regime declines to pay a predecessor's debt. A creditor or other international actor who conceived of sovereignty as merely control of the same territory and its population would consider any controlling regime—whether it be violently autocratic, democratic, or anything in between—to be a continuation of the same sovereign state. Through this statist lens, the creditor might argue that the polity, though now under different rulership, had not repaid its own debt and therefore could not be trusted with additional funds. However, if a creditor or other international actor accepted nonstatist arguments that legitimate sovereign statehood and action necessitates a stronger, nonexploitative connection to the underlying population, it might make a different creditworthiness assessment. In particular, it could reasonably understand that the willingness of a new regime to repay a loan depends on the degree to which its population benefited from or authorized the loan. If the previous debt was used to oppress the population or was entered into in order to facilitate corruption, then a subsequent regime's unwillingness to repay this obligation may not have much bearing on its readiness to pay "legitimately" contracted or publicly beneficial loans in the future.[5] Thus, even if we accept that creditworthiness plays a central role in international finance, that acceptance in and of itself is indeterminate of reputational outcomes without selecting among the different narratives of sovereignty that might underpin reputation.

So what has been the actual narrative of sovereignty sustaining global sovereign debt practices? Has it leaned in a democratic direction, preferred a deference toward basic constitutionalism and the rule of law, or adopted a statist indifference toward absolutism? For all the talk of commitment to democratic sovereignty, good governance, and popular benefit, particularly since the end of the Cold War, these nonstatist discourses do not seem to have translated significantly into the sovereign debt arena. The general background rule has been to expect continuous debt repayment, even in the face of regime change, with any deviations few and far between. Even postapartheid South Africa, which succeeded a regime that explicitly denied full rights to the majority of its population, was expected to pay (and did indeed acknowledge) the debts of the apartheid regime.[6] Of course, this is not at all to say that actual debt *payment* has been absolute. As the financial pages of any major newspaper make clear, states commonly default on their debt and seek to restructure their payments.[7] But the expectation has been that states will either repay or suffer the consequences of nonpayment.

Unsurprisingly given the large sums owed and the difficult austerity measures pressed on debtor states, the background norms of ongoing repayment have met with significant criticism. Periodically, legal scholars and activists have called for the adoption of something like a doctrine of "odious debt," according to which a predecessor regime's debts should not be paid unless they either were authorized by the underlying population or benefited that population.[8] Many have also called more generally for debt cancellation and the easing of debt payments, pointing out both the structural and historical inequities underlying the international financial system and also the counterproductive nature of debt payments and austerity measures in the absence of sustainable economic growth.[9] And the disconnect between sovereignty narratives in different arenas of global relations and international law surely underpins some of this anger, given that it exhibits at least a degree of hypocrisy. Indeed, by the turn of the twenty-first century we could imagine the international community prosecuting leaders of a fallen regime for crimes against a state's population while simultaneously asking that same population to repay the fallen regime's debts. On the one hand, international criminal law denies the validity of absolutist forms of sovereignty, contending instead that ruling regimes must have some relation of benefit and respect for a territory's population. And yet, on the other hand, international financial law adopts an entirely different approach, insisting on debt payments even when loans support the self-serving elites of arguably criminal regimes.

While this disconnect provides the basis for legitimate condemnation, it also points to the contingency and potential changeability of these practices. To the extent that the sovereign debt arena depends on and reinforces narratives of sovereignty, and these narratives are themselves variable, then debt practices are at least potentially variable as well. Indeed, as I have written about elsewhere and touch on below, this theoretical flexibility has in fact been joined by a degree of historical variability over twentieth- and early twenty-first-century practice. Although the rule or expectation of continuous debt repayment has been dominant, and deeply embedded in contemporary conceptions of the reputational underpinnings of capital markets, it has not been absolute. In particular, in the early part of the twentieth century, several cases suggested the possibility of alternative narratives in sovereign debt. For example, in 1918 the new Soviet Union annulled the foreign loans contracted by the tsarist regime, arguing effectively that they constituted personal debts of the tsar and not legitimate debts of the new Soviet Republic and its people. Although this alienated creditors of the fallen government, several banks newer to international lending actually attempted to facilitate the issuance of Soviet bonds, in practice accepting the alternative sovereignty narrative presented by the new regime in making their own creditworthiness assessments.[10] The virtual disappearance of this type of counterdiscourse in the middle part of the twentieth century resulted from the shock of the Great Depression and particularly the institutional, economic, and geopolitical exigencies of the post–World War II era. As I discuss extensively elsewhere, creditor structures moving into the late twentieth century, along with a degree of discursive path dependency, solidified a dominant statist approach until a potential reopening in the post–Cold War era.[11]

In short, despite its seeming strength, the expectation of continuous debt payment should not be mistaken for an inevitable element of the financial world. Far from being a neutral and unchanging feature of economic practice, this expectation is deeply dependent on sovereignty narratives with clear historical trajectories and political valences. This invites investigation into not only how they develop and strengthen but also, to the extent that they result in problematic distributional outcomes, how they might be weakened.

Debt Collection and the Public/Private Divide

Just as narratives of sovereignty necessarily underpin expectations of debt repayment, they similarly shape the assumptions underlying debt collection—the practice of *whom* sovereign debt should be collected from in the event that payments are not forthcoming. This again implicates and depends on how we conceive of sovereignty and especially of the possible unity or distinction between a state entity and the individuals that control it. In particular, if a ruling official signs a debt contract in a sovereign capacity, when might creditors be able to turn to that ruling official's own assets to collect on unpaid debt?

Returning again to a historical counterpoint can help throw the centrality of different sovereignty narratives into relief. Although it may seem obvious today that a sovereign state's wealth, and a creditor's claim to it, remains separate from the personal wealth of an individual ruler or head of state, this was not always the case. For example, at the dawn of the Hundred Years' War, King Edward III of England arrived in Flanders with insufficient funds to support his military ambitions. He turned to private creditors on the European continent for financing, and as a special inducement offered as collateral all of his jewels, those of his wife, their golden chalice and lesser crowns, his war horse, and even his grandfather Edward I's Great Crown.[12] Dissatisfied with his inability to pay, the creditors seized the Great Crown in 1339, along with several of his family members who had personally guaranteed the loans. One cousin, the Earl of Derby, was held hostage for several months, and the Great Crown itself was not returned until 1345 (Fryde 1155, 1166). While hardly widespread, this pattern of a ruler pledging his or her personal property for sovereign borrowing seems to have been an accepted practice. Charles IV and Maximilian I of the Holy Roman Empire also secured loans with a crown, coronation robe, and personal jewels (Hoeflich 40).

Of course, such a practice is again not entirely surprising in eras of personalistic rule in which the sovereign is at once a state and an earthly individual, with the mechanisms and benefits of control and final personal responsibility all ultimately resting with a single person or family.

Even without a pledge of collateral, creditors would presumably have felt entitled to seize even the most personal of property from a ruler's family if not for the nuisance of castle walls and defending armies. And such seizure would have seemed very reasonable: An individual or family might enrich itself by virtue of sovereign control of a given territory through taxation or through loans implicitly or explicitly backed by the treasure of the land. As such, the personal benefits and individually enjoyed luxuries resulting from that control should also be at risk if things go awry.

How have things looked more recently? As in the case of sovereign debt payment, practices of debt collection have shifted across time and place, at least in part enabled by changing narratives of sovereignty and the norms surrounding public/private distinctions in international finance. As noted above, it has become the norm for creditors to lend to and then insist on repayment from "sovereign states" without any attentiveness to the nature of the link between ruling officials and the underlying population. Through this practice, they implicitly adopt and reinforce a statist narrative of sovereignty that assumes the existence of continuous sovereign statehood across individuals or entities that control a given territory, even when faced with significant regime change. Such a narrative thus remains indifferent to the connection or lack thereof between individual rulers and a territorially defined "state," whether that state is constructed in terms of popular sovereignty, cultural nationhood, or control by pure force.

This statist conceptual approach has meant that, generally speaking, debt collection efforts in recent memory have focused on the assets of the entity conceived of as *the sovereign*, and not the wealth or assets of the individual officials who might have signed the loan contract and perhaps siphoned away some of the proceeds. This narrative, which declines to peer behind elite contentions that the state's identity and assets should be understood as separate from their own, has been supported by the norms of private banking and private wealth management. As I detail in a recent legal article, financial houses focused on wealth management have taken the utmost care to protect the boundaries of the private and the personal ("Sovereign").[13] Historically, the fact that a private banking client might have held high public office or had significant access to public money in some other way was not considered relevant. Once funds had been deposited, the rules and norms of this privacy regime effectively reified the designation of such property as "personal" rather than "sovereign."

Although the secrecy norms of twentieth-century private banking meant that information on the provenance of this personal wealth was not publicly available, of course the financial institutions themselves may have had some idea. Still, their discretion (or complicity) was normatively protected by the indifference inherent in a statist sovereignty narrative: ruling officials were accepted as separate and private individuals, distinct from indefinitely and independently existing sovereign states characterized by control of a territorially grounded population through any available means. In his 1966 description of Swiss banks, historian and commentator T. R. Fehrenbach contended that "no Swiss bank will knowingly accept stolen money," but tellingly noted that funds deposited by tyrannical public actors

> *cannot legally be described as stolen money. In the days when they secured it, Colonel Perón, President Batista and Premier Tshombe were the law in their respective countries. The fact that most dictators [. . .] used shotguns, armed thugs, military force and nauseating tortures on many of their subjects to raise it, does not change the fact. In point of law, [such] money is as "legal" as the royal allowance paid by the Socialist government of Great Britain to Elizabeth II. (127)*

Whether or not such money was in fact obtained "legally" is a complicated matter, given that the actual written rules of these autocrats' countries may well have prohibited their specific methods or their siphoning of funds. Of course, the law on the books does not necessarily track the law in practice.[14] And it is certainly the case that the dominant statist sovereignty narrative underpinning these global practices remained fairly unmoved by any such laws, given that it does not consider sovereign statehood to be constituted or constrained by any domestic set of rules.

As in the debt repayment context, this discursive state of affairs has supported the development of arguably perverse distributional consequences. In particular, ruling officials of these states have for some time been able to have their cake and eat it too. In their external interactions—with financiers as well as private wealth management firms involved in sovereign lending—they have benefited from territorially grounded notions of sovereignty indifferent to internal relations. This enabled them to borrow money on behalf of the separate entity of the sovereign state—even if that money was used to oppress rather than benefit the underlying population—and trust that creditors would expect repayment from that state rather than the officials, even in the event of a major political revolution. And this also meant that, even if the state proved unable to pay, they could generally expect their personal wealth (including wealth of questionable provenance) to be protected from collection. Thus a particular narrative of sovereignty, married to discourses of the public/private divide and the primacy of private property, has underpinned problematic international financial practices.[15] It has meant that those in control of sovereign states have in some cases managed to personally enjoy a level of luxury and power that would be unavailable to them absent the backing (or plundering) of a political territory's treasure, while fully expecting that their personal lifestyles and access to funds should not be interrupted should things go wrong for the state itself. In a strange way, this puts more recent autocrats in a better position than the explicitly personalistic monarchs of old, whose wealth was more openly tied into that of the sovereign state and thus at greater risk in the event of debt collection.

Furthermore, these officials are not the only entities to have profited from this narrative structure. Certain members of the international banking establishment may also have benefited twice over. Although we often think of financial institutions as primarily engaged in credit or lending activities, they have in some cases been involved on both sides of the sovereign debt/private wealth equation. Due to banking secrecy provisions and the increasing use of shell corporations, it is exceedingly difficult to find data on whether government officials of sovereign borrower states have also partaken in the wealth management services of major private financial institutions. Still, it is noteworthy that private lending to sovereign states in the post–World War II era, at least through the early 1990s, was generally organized through major international banks along the lines of Chase Manhattan, Citibank (in its various iterations), and BNP Paribas. And many of the largest and most internationally involved financial institutions had and continue to have both sovereign lending departments and private client services. One would expect the most important of these international banks to have established long-term relationships with not only sovereign state clients but also their ruling elites. The relationship with the ruling elites would be inevitable given the need to interact with some range of actually existing natural persons who (ostensibly) act on behalf of, and enter into debt and other contracts for, the underlying state. But these banks may have developed relationships with the same individuals through their private client or wealth management departments as well. As such, these banks had access to two income streams: those associated with both sovereign lending and private wealth management.[16] Just as importantly, the dominant sovereignty narratives allowed these two income streams not to interfere with each other. A statist understanding of sovereignty enabled the dominance of lending and payment expectations divorced from requirements of internal public authorization or benefit. And, in conjunction with a strict (and perhaps simplistic) conceptual distinction between public and private property, it allowed banks to accept funds from powerful officials and then circumscribe those funds as "personal" without serious inquiry into how the officials themselves might blend the lines between private and public assets in their own states.

Still, as with the repayment example discussed above, this narrative structure has not been entirely uniform in the arena of debt collection. Recently, certain entities, in particular so-called vulture funds, have challenged the separation between sovereign state assets and the ostensibly private assets controlled by a state's officials. Vulture funds work by purchasing "distressed debt" from other creditors at a deep discount, when countries are in trouble and the initial creditors are trying to offload the debt. Then, instead of participating in the debt restructuring and accepting discounted payments like most investors, they hold out for a better deal, usually suing for the debt's full face value and then collecting assets wherever they can find them or eventually pressuring countries into a favorable settlement—an outcome that could significantly hamper a country's capacity to provide basic services and pull out of an economic downturn. These funds have used infamously aggressive tactics, including seizing navy ships, claiming foreign aid funds, and holding payments to cooperative creditors hostage (see Raymond). But what stands out for my purposes is a debt collection substrategy that explicitly targets the depersonalized statist sovereignty narrative that has permeated much of international finance. Instead of disregarding an official's internal relations with a state's population, on several occasions these funds have looked inside the boundaries of the state to argue that the lines between "sovereign" and "private" wealth have not been respected by the country's officials. They have contended that certain sovereign assets have been improperly siphoned into personal accounts or shell entities controlled by those officials or their close associates and that therefore these ostensibly private assets should be understood as public money—and, consequently, collectible by creditors of the sovereign state.

The use of this strategy in the relatively recent case of Congo-Brazzaville is illustrative.[17] The Republic of Congo, with its capital at Brazzaville, is among the poorer and more troubled countries in the world despite its natural wealth and, like many other states, Congo weathered a crisis during the 1980s in which it defaulted on its debt. Eventually a vulture fund called Kensington International purchased the debt on the secondary market, presumably at a deep discount. Starting in the 1990s, during the

Congolese civil war, Kensington started requesting payment on the debt, eventually suing and receiving a favorable judgment in English courts in the early 2000s. When Congo nonetheless failed to pay, Kensington began attempting to seize Congolese assets.

As part of this effort, it uncovered a series of shell companies that had a potentially dual purpose. These shell corporations, which seemed to lack any meaningful independent business, allegedly obscured the flow of Congolese oil assets from aggressive creditors like Kensington but also provided a mechanism by which funds could be diverted with little notice. In attempting to seize these companies' assets, Kensington alleged "a conspiracy to misappropriate [Congolese] resources [. . .] for the private use of allegedly corrupt public officials and to facilitate and conceal that misappropriation, all at the expense of the Congolese people and of legitimate creditors like Kensington" (*Kensington*). The recovery efforts eventually took an unusually personal turn, with Kensington discovering and helping to publicize records of how related shell companies paid for the extravagant personal expenditures of high officials and presidential family members (who were often one and the same) ("Congo"). The optics were even worse for Congo-Brazzaville given that, around the time of these revelations, the country was arguing in favor of debt relief at the United Nations. Indeed, Kensington enthusiastically participated in the public embarrassment of Congo's leaders, with a senior portfolio manager associated with the fund pointing out their profligacy in the face of the country's poverty and highlighting that the presidential New York hotel suite cost "more per day than the average Congolese makes in a decade" (Allen-Mills). Ultimately, perhaps encouraged by these efforts, Congo-Brazzaville chose to settle with Kensington.

The Congo example thus highlights how alternative sovereignty narratives open up, and perhaps are reinforced by, different debt collection strategies in the international context. It also points more generally to the way in which narrative is central to legal strategy not only at the relatively microlevel of a trial. Particular narrative choices also work through broader or macro strategies, which can involve numerous interconnected legal and public relations efforts across multiple jurisdictions. Kensington's goal was not to win at trial per se, but rather to collect assets or reach a favorable financial outcome either through court or a settlement. This goal involved formulating arguments and atmospherics that adopted and reinforced nonstatist sovereignty narratives, which insisted—in a deeply self-serving fashion—that a link of responsibility and trust should exist between political officials and the territory and population they administer. Although this is hardly the same sovereignty narrative that underpinned the personalistic debt collection of earlier rulers such as Edward III—indeed, it is quite far from traditionalist monarchy—it did echo that earlier approach in rejecting an *indifference* as to the individuals actually in charge of a state.

In doing so, this vulture fund strategy also reinjected an element of risk for officials who might treat the contemporary dividing lines between public and private wealth as loose recommendations rather than rules worthy of strict observance. Of course, the populations of these states get nothing from this reintroduction of risk. Indeed, they are immiserated twice over: first by their ruling elites and then by vulture funds who use the language of public good to extract debt settlements and assets from countries already undergoing significant economic suffering.[18]

Critical Counternarrative and Its Limitations

At one level, the vulture fund effort demonstrates what activists have known and practiced in the service of the greater good for years: namely, that counternarratives generally, and even alternative approaches to sovereignty in particular, can ground a critical take on prevailing norms. But we too often miss that these critical narratives are not remotely the first introduction of moral discourse or normative language into the realm of international finance. Rather, sovereignty narratives are already and always inherently constitutive of the sovereign debt arena, and particularly the practices of debt repayment and collection. Without some narrative of sovereignty, sovereign debt practices would lack all meaning. As such, any critical counternarrative, in international finance as much as any other social field, should highlight the central and constitutive nature of narrative itself, along with the political and distributional ramifications that might result from particular narrative structures. Given that those who work in international finance tend to eschew, sometimes self-consciously, "theological discussions"[19] of sovereignty or morality, it is important to emphasize how their standard approach to sovereign debt is itself "theological" through and through.

There is reason to target the international financial arena in particular for narrative critique. A key feature of international financial law and indeed much international economic practice is that rules and norms are enforced largely through reputational sanction, as hinted at in the discussion of debt repayment above. This points to the importance of relative agreement among those who make reputational judgments in maintaining the strength of a rule or expectation: As Beth Simmons and Zachary Elkins have noted, "the reputational payoffs associated with policy choice" can be altered by the presence or lack of ideological consensus (173). Therefore, working to break down the ideological accord that underpins reputational assessments and sanctions in a given area has the potential to weaken or undermine a problematic practice. Indeed, in the sovereign debt restructuring discussions after the 2003 fall of Saddam Hussein in Iraq, the background arguments around odious debt ideas and the illegitimacy of Hussein's regime—a nonstatist sovereignty narrative that countered the expectation of continuous debt repayment—may have had some indirect impact. According to Iraq's lead debt restructuring attorney, even though these arguments were not formally brought to the negotiating table, "the issue was definitely present—the atmospherics are unavoidable [. . .]. If we have reached a point where we could legitimately make a claim on odious debt, then they're already softened up."[20] This making available of legitimate counterarguments, grounded in alternative discursive structures, is precisely how critical narratives might be able to impact the expectations and reputational impact surrounding more heterodox international financial choices.

That said, determined action and counternarrative alone will hardly change global financial practices, including those of sovereign debt payment and collection. Although these practices are theoretically and historically contingent, and therefore potentially changeable, they are also deeply embedded in the broader material and ideational structures of particular historical moments. While we should not assume that the interests and narrative approaches of creditors and other international actors will always be uniform—indeed, creditors can be threatened as much by each other as by sovereign debtors—under certain market and ideological conditions they may be more or less open to alternative approaches. For example, the fact that creditor structures were fairly competitive in the 1920s may have made certain banks more open to the nonstatist sovereign debt narratives presented in the Soviet debt repudiation (see Lienau, *Rethinking* 78–91). And it is no coincidence that the vulture fund debt collection strategy arose in an early twenty-first-century moment of disaggregated creditor interactions and was built on nonstatist sovereignty narratives that were already well received in other international legal arenas. Both the debt repayment and debt collection examples demonstrate not only the potential flexibility of narrative but also its historicity and embeddedness in broader social worlds.

This is hardly to say that the work of narrative formulation and critique should be abandoned. Rather, it needs to be pursued with an attentiveness to the material and ideational structures in which it is grounded, perhaps in conjunction with political strategies to weaken any of those structures that might be more problematic. This is not an easy conceptual task, particularly given that the multiple and sometimes conflicting narratives at the heart of sovereign debt practices often stay hidden in the background, covered over by the quotidian hum of global market functioning. But, to the extent that sovereignty narratives do real work in the financial world, anyone with a concern for the consequences of that world should seek to understand how these narratives function and how they can be put to strategic use.

I would like to thank Peter Szendy and Emmanuel Bouju for inviting me to reflect on the role of narrative in my work for this special issue of differences *and Denise Davis for excellent editorial insight. I am also grateful to Brown University's Cogut Institute for the Humanities for hosting the Narratives of Debt conference in April 2019, from which this special issue is drawn and at which I received valuable feedback.*

ODETTE LIENAU is a professor of law and a member of the Graduate Field of Government at Cornell University. She is the author of *Rethinking Sovereign Debt: Politics, Reputation, and Legitimacy in Modern Finance* (Harvard University Press, 2014), which won a book award from the American Society of International Law, and a number of articles at the intersection of international economic law, debtor-creditor relations, and legal and political theory. She has served in an expert capacity for the IMF and UNCTAD and practiced at a major New York City law firm prior to entering academia.

Notes

1   Of course the well-known quote from Deleuze and Guattari is itself contextually embedded in a discussion of state power and the close link between state power, money, debt, and taxation. I focus here on a different vector of narratives of sovereign statehood.

2   See, in particular, Lienau, *Rethinking* 4–5, 34–52 and "Who Is" 63–69.

3   For a classic presentation of this dual feature of sovereignty, see Kantorowicz.

4   I define and discuss alternative schools of sovereignty and think through their ramifications for debt payment continuity in *Rethinking Sovereign Debt* 5–6, 34–52.

5   For a more extensive discussion of sovereignty and reputation, see Lienau, *Rethinking* 26–29.

6   For an excellent overview of the financial decisions made by the new South African government—including its decision to adopt an austere fiscal program in order to gain credibility with international investors—see Hamilton and Viegi.

7   For a more scholarly macrolevel consideration, see Reinhart and Rogoff.

8   The most thorough and successful restatement of odious debt recently is Jeff King's *The Doctrine of Odious Debt in International Law.* See also, for example, Buchheit, Gulati, and Thompson; and Jayachandran

and Kremer. These scholars are reviving a 1927 formulation of the doctrine by Alexander N. Sack (157).

9   In addition to a range of scholars focused on sovereign debt, nongovernmental organizations focused on economic justice and debt have been at the forefront of making these arguments.

10   Ultimately, these underwriters and investors were unable to issue the bonds due to resistance from officials within their own government. For more on my reinterpretation of the meaning of the Soviet repudiation for understanding sovereign debt and the role of reputation, see Lienau, *Rethinking* 57–99.

11   This historical argument of the development of the debt repayment norm makes up the bulk of my *Rethinking Sovereign Debt.*

12   See Fryde 1142, 1144, 1154–55, 1158, 1165–66, 1176. See also Hoeflich 39–40.

13   Of course, I speak here of financial matters. In making the public-private distinction, I do not mean to engage directly (though perhaps there is still an indirect connection) with the characterization of the private as the sphere of the body or the domestic, as distinct from a more communal, communicative, and cerebral public (as in Arendt or Habermas). Instead, I intend *private* here to connote more specifically the sphere of an individual's (and perhaps his or her family's) own personal use and enjoyment, including the exclusion of others from that sphere. As such, I use the term in a way that mimics more closely the colloquial understanding of private property, with its suggestion of exclusive use and protection from exogenous claims or even from external view and judgment.

14   This insight is central to the larger tradition of law and society scholarship, which emphasizes the importance of studying and understanding law in its social, political, and economic context. I argue elsewhere that market principles in particular, such as the principle or expectation of continuous sovereign debt repayment discussed above, deserve greater attention as a type of historically shaped and contextually grounded law. See Lienau, "Law in Hiding."

15   I argue elsewhere that the norms and legal practices of global finance in the arenas of sovereign debt and private wealth have led to a significant market failure, in particular the oversupply of sovereign borrowing and a related misallocation of global capital away from its most productive uses. See Lienau, "Sovereign" 299.

16   It is also possible that the banks themselves were held back from more aggressive debt collection by this internal conflict of interest. For more on the structure of credit markets and banks and how this might have an impact, see Lienau, "Sovereign" 316–22.

17   I discuss the Congo case and the case of Argentina at length in "Sovereign Debt, Private Wealth, and Market Failure" 326–43.

18   Although the vulture fund strategy arguably provides some good in uncovering mechanisms of corruption, this does not outweigh the serious damage they do in international finance. For more on the problematic aspects of vulture funds in the international financial architecture, see Lienau, "Sovereign" 344–51. It is also worth pointing out that their use of a nonstatist sovereignty narrative is hardly complete. Indeed, their strategy writ large is somewhat logically incoherent, given that it

uses a statist approach to insist on debt repayment and a nonstatist approach in attempting to collect that debt (350–51).

19   The *Financial Times* used this term in suggesting that odious debt discussions after the 2003 fall

of Saddam Hussein in Iraq should be put aside in favor of a more "pragmatic" approach ("Iraq's").

20   Author's interview with Lee C. Buchheit, quoted in *Rethinking Sovereign Debt* 214.

Works Cited

Allen-Mills, Tony. "Congo Leader's £169,000 Hotel Bill." *Sunday Times* 12 Feb. 2006. https://www.thetimes.co.uk/article/congo-leaders-pound169000-hotel-bill-z7k8hwdk9lb.

Anderson, Benedict. *Imagined Communities: Reflections on the Origin and Spread of Nationalism.* London: Verso, 1983.

Buchheit, Lee, Mitu Gulati, and Robert B. Thompson. "The Dilemma of Odious Debts." *Duke Law Journal* 56.5 (2007): 1201–62.

"Congo Leader Son Fails in Gag Bid." *BBC News* 15 Aug. 2007. http://news.bbc.co.uk/2/hi/africa/6948281.stm.

Deleuze, Gilles, and Félix Guattari. *Anti-Oedipus: Capitalism and Schizophrenia.* Trans. Robert Hurley, Mark Seem, and Helen R. Lane. Minneapolis: U of Minnesota P, 1983.

Fehrenbach, T. R. *The Gnomes of Zurich: The Inside Story of the Swiss Banks.* London: L. Frewin, 1966.

Fryde, E. B. "Financial Resources of Edward III in the Netherlands, 1337–40 (Part 2)." *Revue belge de philologie et d'histoire* 45.4 (1967): 1142–1216.

Graeber, David. *Debt: The First 5,000 Years.* London: Melville, 2011.

Hamilton, Lawrence, and Nicola Viegi. "Debt, Democracy, and Representation in South Africa." *Representation* 45.2 (2009): 193–212.

Hoeflich, Michael H. "Through a Glass Darkly: Reflections upon the History of the International Law of Public Debt in Connection with State Succession." *University of Illinois Law Review* (1982): 39–70.

"Iraq's Debt." *Financial Times* 16 June 2003: 20.

Jayachandran, Seema, and Michael Kremer. "Odious Debt." *American Economic Review* 96.1 (2006): 82–92.

Juvaini, Ata-Malik. *Genghis Khan: The History of the World Conqueror.* Trans. J. A. Boyle. Manchester: Manchester UP, 1997.

Kantorowicz, Ernst. *The King's Two Bodies: A Study in Medieval Political Theology.* Princeton: Princeton UP, 1957.

Kensington Int'l Ltd. v. Société Nationale des Pétroles du Congo. United States District Court, Southern District of New York. *West Law* 2006 846351 (31 Mar. 2006): 1–11.

King, Jeff. *The Doctrine of Odious Debt in International Law: A Restatement.* Cambridge: Cambridge UP, 2016.

Lienau, Odette. "Law in Hiding: Market Principles in the Global Legal Order." *Hastings Law Journal* 68.3 (2017): 541–607.

——————. *Rethinking Sovereign Debt: Politics, Reputation, and Legitimacy in Modern Finance.* Cambridge, MA: Harvard UP, 2014.

——————. "Sovereign Debt, Private Wealth, and Market Failure." *Virginia Journal of International Law* 60.2 (2020): 299–362.

——————. "Who Is the Sovereign in Sovereign Debt: Reinterpreting a Rule-of-Law Framework from the Early Twentieth Century." *Yale Journal of International Law* 33.1 (2008): 63–69.

Raymond, Nate. "Argentina Faces Creditor Lawsuit over U.S. Satellite Contract." *Reuters* 25 Mar. 2014. https://www.reuters.com/article/usa-court-argentina/argentina-faces-creditor-lawsuit-over-u-s-satellite-contract-idUSL1N0MM28U20140326.

Reinhart, Carmen M., and Kenneth S. Rogoff. *This Time Is Different: Eight Centuries of Financial Folly.* Princeton: Princeton UP, 2011.

Sack, Alexander N. *Les effets des transformations des états sur leurs dettes publiques et autres obligations financières.* Paris: Sirey, 1927.

Simmons, Beth A., and Zachary Elkins. "The Globalization of Liberalization: Policy Diffusion in the International Political Economy." *American Political Science Review* 98.1 (2004): 171–89.

Weatherford, Jack. *Genghis Khan and the Making of the Modern World.* New York: Crown, 2004.

New from
prize-winning
biographer and
social activist
MARTIN DUBERMAN

THE DEFINITIVE STORY
OF THE RADICAL FEMINIST
AND CONTROVERSIAL
ANTI-PORNOGRAPHY
CRUSADER, BASED ON
EXCLUSIVE ACCESS TO
HER ARCHIVES

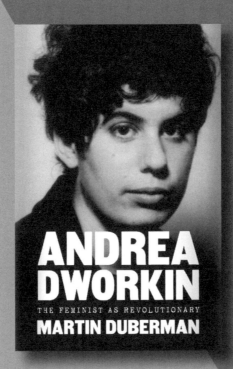

"Thanks to this landmark biography by Martin Duberman,
you will now be able to meet one of the greatest thinkers, writers,
and activists of our time." –GLORIA STEINEM

"A sympathetic, clear-eyed portrait that gives Dworkin
her due without smoothing over her rough edges."
–*Kirkus Reviews* (starred review)

"Duberman masterfully navigates the swift current of
Dworkin's ahead-of-her-time insights ... This compelling portrait
comprises an essential chapter in the history of feminism
and human rights." –*Booklist*

THE
NEW
PRESS
www.thenewpress.com

Keep up to date on new scholarship

Issue alerts are a great way to stay current on all the cutting-edge scholarship from your favorite Duke University Press journals. This free service delivers tables of contents directly to your inbox, informing you of the latest groundbreaking work as soon as it is published.

To sign up for issue alerts:

1. Visit **dukeu.press/register** and register for an account. You do not need to provide a customer number.

2. After registering, visit **dukeu.press/alerts**.

3. Go to "Latest Issue Alerts" and click on "Add Alerts."

4. Select as many publications as you would like from the pop-up window and click "Add Alerts."

read.dukeupress.edu/journals

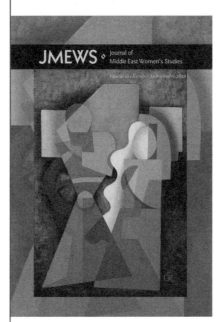